OFF THE BEATEN PATH® SERIES

EIGHTH EDITION

OFF THE BEATEN PATH®
VERMONT →

A GUIDE TO UNIQUE PLACES

Revised and Updated by

ROBERT F. WILSON

gpp®
travel

Guilford, Connecticut

The prices and rates in this guidebook were confirmed at press time. We recommend, however, that you call establishments before traveling to obtain current information.

Interior design: Linda R. Loiewski
Layout: Joanna Beyer
Maps: Equator Graphics © Morris Book Publishing, LLC

ISSN 1533-8037
ISBN 978-0-7627-4880-8

Printed in the United States of America
10 9 8 7 6 5 4 3 2 1

Contents

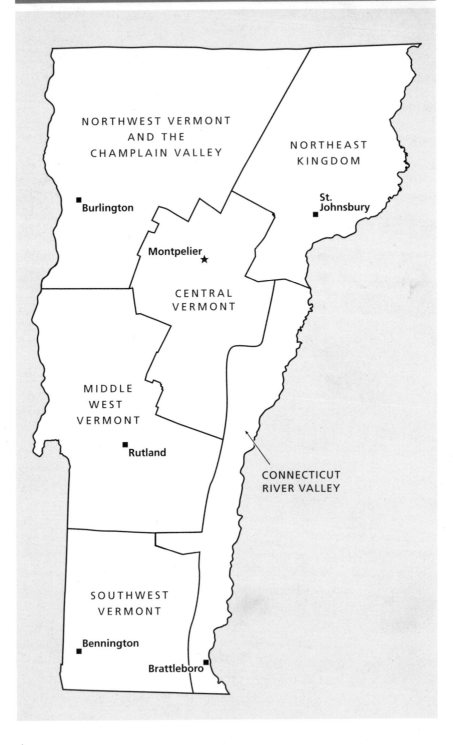

NORTHWEST VERMONT
AND THE
CHAMPLAIN VALLEY

NORTHEAST
KINGDOM

■ Burlington

St.
Johnsbury ■

Montpelier ★

CENTRAL
VERMONT

MIDDLE
WEST
VERMONT

■ Rutland

CONNECTICUT
RIVER VALLEY

SOUTHWEST
VERMONT

■ Bennington

Brattleboro ■

Introduction

Vermont is as much a state of mind as it is a place. To the rest of the country, the Green Mountain State signifies a back-to-basics attitude that is becoming an all-too-rare commodity in America today. To the people who live in Vermont, this attitude is held on to fiercely because they are well aware that it is one of the last bastions of peaceful rural life, of our roots. That's why tourism is a leading industry in the state.

This attitude is at the bottom of one of the hottest debates to embroil the state in years: to zone or not to zone. Those Vermonters who are in favor of limiting development and establishing specific criteria about what residents can and can't do with their land want the pastoral Vermont landscape to stay the same for future generations. Those Vermonters who oppose zoning tend to have great pride in their ancestors, that they were able to create this state from nothing more than rocks, thin soil, and sweat. They say, "My family fought for it, I own it, and it's mine to do with as I wish. Don't you trust me, an eighth-generation Vermonter, to know what's best for the state?"

What these actions have in common is a desire to hold on to the old way of life, but with two very different views of the best way to make it happen.

Just about everything that can be said about Vermont has been said— then quoted ad infinitum. No other state has been so discussed, directed, observed, recorded, and sentimentalized. The myth that hangs over Vermont is far larger than the state itself, but all the words written and spoken reflect the inescapable fact that Vermont is unlike any other place. There is a lot here to see, to absorb, and to think about, and if it is the kind of place some visitors would like to think of as home, that makes the myth more understandable.

Many people have wanted a part of the state. Before it became a republic in 1777 and was granted statehood fifteen years later, everyone from New Hampshire to Massachusetts to New York fought over the land that even then possessed a special but hard-to-define aura.

Because Vermont relies so heavily on tourism these days, even in some isolated pockets of the state it's difficult to find attractions that are specifically geared toward locals, unless you count feed and grain stores.

It used to be true that you weren't considered a native until your family had lived here for eight generations. Given the great exodus from the state during several periods in its history, those eighth-generationers are not easy to find. Many of Vermont's hill towns lost half their populations during the great westward expansion. Even now, some Vermont towns have smaller populations than they did in 1840. In 1850, 154 towns in the state had more than 1,000 people. By 1960, that figure had fallen to 94; but by 2000, the number had climbed back to 106.

Basic Travel Information

Visitors come to Vermont throughout the year; however, some months and seasons are more beautiful—and thus more crowded—than others. Foliage season—usually the last two weeks of September and the first two weeks of October—is Vermont at its best and most crowded. Rooms at inns and hotels, despite sharply increased "foliage rates," typically fill up six months in advance, so it's best to make reservations early.

The last two weeks of October in Vermont are generally just as gorgeous. And while many places and shops will have closed up for the season, there are still lots of attractions to explore. You'll find less traffic; unhurried, friendly service; and some of the maples and oak trees still radiant with their color. Best of all, the weather is perfect: sunny, warm, Indian summer days interspersed with cool, crisp nights accompanied by the smell of wood smoke.

In summer Vermont is lush, green, and fragrant. During the winter, the Presidents' Day holiday usually finds the ski areas throughout the state at their busiest; try visiting a week or two later instead. Some of the roads that

Reservations at State Parks

Reservations for camping can be made up to eleven months in advance. (A camping site for the entire month of July, for example, can be reserved in August of the previous year. To make a reservation 14 days or less in advance, call individual parks directly (see listings at www.vtstateparks.com). For reservations 15 days or more in advance, reserve online or call (888) 409-7579. To reserve camping sites online, the Parks Department requests that those interested complete a six-page online tutorial before reserving. Our recommendation: Try phoning first.

Some Vermont parks are open year-round. Others open in late April, still others in late May. Closing dates for those parks vary from mid-September until mid-October, depending on area climates. A four-day minimum-stay policy is waived for campers on a first-come, first-served basis; as well as for hikers, bicyclists, and paddlers.

A season-pass car sticker costs $80, good for frequent park visitors, and allowing up to eight people to use facilities on each visit. See the Vermont State Parks Web site list above for details.

Restful Wi-Fi

All Vermont visitor centers at highway rest stops now offer Wi-Fi access, so anyone with a laptop and wireless capabilities can use the Internet from anywhere on the premises. It's not free, but you can buy in various time periods, even by the year, a plan designed for business travelers. Now you can get a map, ask directions, browse the brochure racks, walk the dog, take the kids to the bathroom, and check your e-mail all in one stop. What's next? Hey, a neck massage would be nice!

are closed in winter and spring are marked on good road maps, and others are closed temporarily if they're simply impassable. In spring, many tourist-oriented businesses shut down from March through mid-April, during the notorious "mud season" and before the first buds appear on the trees. During the spring thaw, high water can close many of the smaller bridges.

Vermonters are Yankee to the core, and they simply can't see any reason to waste all those condo and hotel rooms, restaurants, shops, and recreation facilities at the foot of their ski slopes after the snow melts. Nearly all ski areas have become year-round recreation resorts, with guests paddling happily during the summer in ponds that provide snowmaking water six months later; or riding the lifts for mountaintop views in August where cross-country skiers glide in January. Everyone wins, especially visitors looking for a base that includes activities for days when they don't feel like touring the countryside. Just as in winter, these resort complexes offer package deals that may include golf, guided hikes, nature programs, meals, day camp, and water sports.

Seasonal attractions in small towns throughout Vermont include sugar-on-snow festivals in spring and Fourth of July celebrations and parades in summer. Winter features ski races and Christmas fairs and bazaars.

Tourist Information

Ask for a copy of the Vermont Traveler's Guidebook and the Vermont Winter Guide, as well as a state highway map, available free from the Vermont Chamber of Commerce, P.O. Box 37, Montpelier, VT 05601; (802) 223-3443; www.vtchamber.com. For more information, contact the Vermont Department of Tourism and Marketing, 6 Baldwin Street, Montpelier, VT 05633; (802) 254-4593. The Web site is www.vermontvacation.com, and the toll-free number is 1–800–VERMONT. Welcome centers are located on interstate highways 91 (Massachusetts border), 89 (Canadian border), 93 (New Hampshire border), and on Vermont 4-A at the New York border. A complete selection of brochures is available at each welcome center.

The Vermont Crafts Council, P.O. Box 938, Montpelier, VT 05601; (802) 223–3380; www.vermontcrafts.com, has a Vermont studio tour guide listing crafts shops, events, and "open studio" tours. Ski information is available from the state tourist office and from Vermont Ski Areas Association, P.O. Box 368, Montpelier, VT 05601; (802) 223–2439; www.skivermont.com. Nordic and alpine skiers in Vermont have their own snow conditions Web site to check for conditions: www.xcountryski-vermont.com.

NORTHWEST VERMONT AND THE CHAMPLAIN VALLEY

Proximity to Lake Champlain has had a huge effect on the development of the northwest corner of the Green Mountain State. It all started with the French explorer who named the lake, Samuel de Champlain. Thanks to his colonizing efforts—he founded the city of Quebec in 1608—Champlain was named the "Father of New France." Access to the major thoroughfare and trade route of **Lake Champlain** allowed settlement to occur relatively early in the state's history. Burlington, for instance, was chartered in 1763, and **Swanton,** northernmost town on the lake and historic site of the Abenaki Indian village of Missisquoi, was chartered the same year. Settlement of a town by families from Connecticut or Massachusetts could take longer, but towns and villages on Vermont's northwestern shore were populated about the same time as those on the state's southwestern border.

After the Revolutionary War, settlements began to flourish along much of the 120-mile length of Lake Champlain, as did subsequent trade north to Canada. During the nineteenth century, both commercial and passenger steamboats—and later, railroads and the automobile—generated an efficient transportation network. Together with the nearby fertile fields

NORTHWEST VERMONT AND THE CHAMPLAIN VALLEY

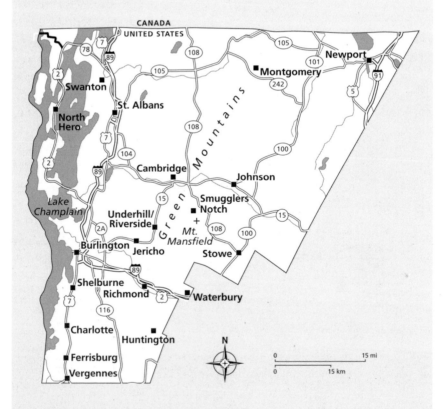

CANADA
UNITED STATES

Newport

Montgomery

Swanton

St. Albans

North Hero

Green Mountains

Cambridge

Johnson

Lake Champlain

Underhill/Riverside

Smugglers Notch

Mt. Mansfield

Burlington

Jericho

Stowe

Shelburne

Richmond

Waterbury

Charlotte

Huntington

Ferrisburg

Vergennes

N

0   15 mi

0   15 km

and plentiful forests, this fortuitous combination of diverse assets has led to rapid growth—and built the dynamic Northwest Vermont and Champlain Valley region that exists today.

Burlington

Burlington is about as cosmopolitan as Vermont gets; so much so, in fact, that people in other parts of the state sometimes say that Burlington is not part of Vermont. With five area colleges and frontage on Lake Champlain—not to mention a population of close to 40,000—Burlington is where many rural Vermonters in search of a dose of urban activity go before they head back to the countryside.

Burlington is a great city to walk around in. It's small enough for slow walkers to manage, yet offers plenty of sights, shops and eateries, so that the adventurous need not be bored. From the waterfront, walk a few blocks up the hill on Main Street and visit **Mirabelle's,** a bright, airy cafe with chintz tablecloths and seat covers, and food and drink to match, a la afternoon tea. At least ten different kinds of teas are available, and they come in pots both large and small. Sandwiches, scones, pastries, croissants, and miniature walnut pastries called "ruggies"—after the pastry rugelach—are there to go with the tea.

Mirabelle's has an unusual drink, at least for Vermont: hot white cocoa. White cocoa powder stirred into steamed milk tastes like a white chocolate Easter bunny. Choose from a great selection of rich cakes and tarts, chocolate truffle cake, and create-your-own deli sandwiches on sourdough or rye bread or a baguette. Mirabelle's also offers its version of panini, including croquet monsieur, portobello mushroom with fresh mozzarella, and black bean with smoked chiles, cheddar cheese, and guacamole. Full breakfast is available every day except Sunday.

Mirabelle's, 198 Main Street, Burlington, (802) 658–3074, is open from 7:00 a.m. to 5:00 p.m. Monday through Friday and from 8:00 a.m. to 5:00 p.m. on Saturday; 8:00 a.m. to 2:30 p.m. on Sunday.

AUTHOR'S TOP HIGHLIGHTS

Lake Champlain Maritime Museum	Sterling Falls Gorge
Montgomery County's covered bridges	Smugglers Notch

Chocoholics may want to skip lunch entirely and visit **Lake Champlain Chocolates,** where more than one hundred varieties of chocolate truffles await them. Lake Champlain Chocolates, 750 Pine Street, Burlington; (802) 864–1808 or (800) 465–5909, www.lakechamplainchocolates.com, is open Monday through Saturday from 9:00 a.m. to 6:00 p.m. and Sunday from noon until 5:00 p.m. Cheese lovers will want to head for **Cheese Outlet Fresh Market** for the wide variety of cheese, much of which is made in Vermont. In fact, this is a good place to get picnic supplies, drawing from the good selection of wines, over eighty beers, several kinds of olives, pâtés, fruit, and deli items. It's open Monday through Friday from 8:00 a.m. to 7:00 p.m.; Saturday from 9:00 a.m. to 6:00 p.m.; and Sunday from 10:00 a.m. to 5:00 p.m.; 400 Pine Street, Burlington; (802) 863–3968 or (800) 447–1205; www.cheeseoutlet.com.

The Flynn Center in Burlington is a cultural institution that brings arts of all kinds to Vermonters. All forms of performance art—ballet, musicals, top vocal performers—come to the Flynn, which averages at least three major performances a month. Flynn performances have included jazz and Latin bands and productions by national touring companies of Broadway musicals. Call the box office at (802) 86–FLYNN for a schedule of upcoming acts. The Flynn Center is at 153 Main Street, Burlington; (802) 863–5966; http://flynncenter.org.

On Church Street (near Bank Street) is **Frog Hollow,** one of two Vermont State Craft Center galleries featuring the work of more than 250 juried Vermont artisans. Both exhibit a unique collection of fine traditional and contemporary Vermont craft, including hand-blown art glass, ceramics, fine pottery, furniture, jewelry, paintings, and photography. Both are centrally located repositories for the work of master craftspeople who live in rural areas that might not otherwise be viewed or sold. The Burlington Frog Hollow is a contemporary gallery in a pedestrian-friendly area with street musicians and entertainers, and near excellent restaurants and shops.

Frog Hollow began in 1971 as an after-school clay program for local young people. Since then it has expanded by offering courses to students of all ages in different media—among them glass, painting, photography, fiber, metal, and wood. Frog Hollow is open Tuesday through Thursday from 11:00 a.m. to 6:00 p.m., Friday 11:00 a.m. to 7:00 p.m., Saturday 11:00 a.m. to 5:00 p.m., and Sunday 11:00 a.m. to 4:00 p.m. Closed Monday. 85 Church Street; (802) 863–6458, www.froghollow.org. Vermont's other Frog Hollow gallery is in Middlebury.

India House is an attractive restaurant on a busy corner near the University of Vermont Medical Center, about a fifteen-minute walk up Main Street from downtown. Appetizers include the vegetable dumplings called samosas with two sauces; coconut and mulligatawny soup; and a vegetarian platter—all

ANNUAL EVENTS IN NORTHWEST VERMONT AND THE CHAMPLAIN VALLEY

Early March: Smugglers Notch Area Winter Carnival
Nordic ski races, snow sculptures, community breakfasts, snowshoe hikes, and social events; (802) 644–8851.

May: Noon Music in May
Each Wednesday at the Stowe Community Church might be anything from a piano duet or operatic selections to Polish dance music or chamber jazz. Concerts are free, but a donation is appreciated; (802) 253–7257.

May through October: Stowe Farmers Market
Mountain Road, next to the Red Barn, each Sunday 11:00 a.m. to 3:00 p.m. From fresh-baked breads and goat cheese to country sausage and maple creams, the market features locally grown and produced foods and plants; (800) 24–STOWE.

Late June or early July: Stowe Flower Festival
Features thirty-plus events, crafts, and garden tours; (800) 24–STOWE; www.gostowe.com.

Late June through August: Meadow Concerts, Trapp Family Lodge, Stowe
Bring a picnic on scheduled evenings and enjoy the sunset to music; (800) 24–STOWE.

Mid-July: Annual Flynn Garden Tour
Benefits the Flynn Center, with nine outstanding Vergennes gardens open for the day and an elegant afternoon tea; (802) 863–5966.

Late July: Vermont Mozart Festival
Trapp Family Meadow, Stowe; (802) 24–STOWE.

Late July: Stowe Tango Fest
Held at Landgrove Inn in Stowe, in late May; includes not only professional dancers but workshops and classes; (802) 253–8511; www.stowetangofest.com.

Mid-August: Shelburne Craft Fair,
At the Shelburne Museum, with more than 200 exhibitors; (802) 985–3648.

Late September: Annual Quilt Show
Williston Armory, Williston; (802) 985–2783.
For up-to-date information on other attractions, lodgings, and dining, visit the following Web sites: Lake Champlain Chamber of Commerce, www.vermont .org; Franklin County Chamber of Commerce, www.stalbanschamber.com.

accompanied by puffed bread and rice with four different sauces: yogurt and cucumber, chickpea, lentil, and pea.

At India House you learn the many varieties that curry can take, with eight different lamb curry dishes, twelve chicken curries, fourteen vegetable curries, and eight seafood curries. India House mixes the spices for its curries fresh every day, combines them in different ways for each dish, and also varies them to different degrees of mild, medium, hot, and extra hot. In fact, this personal attention toward the exact amount of spice for each dish wakes up the taste buds without overpowering them. India House is at 207 Colchester Avenue, Burlington; (802) 862–7800. Open Tuesday through Sunday from 11:30 a.m. to 2:30 p.m. for lunch, and from 5:30 to 9:30 p.m. for dinner, until 10:00 p.m. on Friday and Saturday. The Sunday brunch at India House, from noon to from 11:30 a.m. to 2:30 p.m., is famous in Burlington.

Lest you think the only choices for dinner are Asian, we should mention **Trattoria Delia,** an almost subterranean enclave of Mediterranean dining. Skip lunch if you plan to order both a *primi* and a *secondi,* since the pasta course is far from scanty. You'll find choices you don't see elsewhere: *oricchiette* with *fricone*—an Apulian fried tomato sauce with plenty of garlic—or *tagliatelle* with braised wild boar, porcini mushrooms, red wine, sage, rosemary, and cream. *Secondi,* priced from $19.50, may include a wood-grilled fish of the day, with a marinata of olive oil, garlic, lemon, parsley, and black pepper; or *osso buco* (braised veal shanks) over saffron risotto. Breads and pastas are made in-house, and the menu changes seasonally. Two days in advance is not too early to call for reservations here on weekends, but if you can't get a table, they also offer a take-out menu. Trattoria Delia, open every day from 5:00 to 10:00 p.m., is at 152 St. Paul Street (just off City Hall Park), Burlington; (802) 864–5253; www.trattoriadelia.com.

For an authentic churrascaria, where meats are served direct from the grill, take a good appetite to **Souza's Brazilian Restaurant.** Picture a buffet where the food choices are brought to your table, instead of your going

WORTH SEEING

Shelburne Museum,
Route 7, Shelburne, is unlike any other, with its almost endless collections of early New Englandiana, from quilts and toleware to entire homes and a steamship; (802) 985–3346; www.shelburnemuseum.org.

Lake Champlain ferries leave from Burlington, Grand Isle, and Charlotte to cross the lake into New York. They carry cars, and also make a great passenger excursion, at $3.75 one way per passenger; $9.50 one way with car. (802) 864–9804; www.ferries.com.

Ben & Jerry's Ice Cream Factory,
Route 100, Waterbury; half-hour tours cost $3.00, children under twelve free. Open daily, but ice cream is made Tuesday through Friday only; (802) 882–1240; (800) BJ–TOURS; www.benjerry.com.

Cold Hollow Cider Mill, Route 100, Waterbury Center; (802) 244–8771 or (800) 327–7537.

to them. Various meats—spicy sausages, bacon-encased turkey breasts, lightly seasoned beef and pork—arrive on long skewers, still sizzling on the outside, moist and juicy inside. You choose which and how much you want of these and the side dishes of beans, rice, and pasta. Souza's is a good choice for families with children because it is informal, friendly, and there's more action than in most restaurants, which keeps them from getting bored. Look for Souza's at 55 Main Street, Burlington, 5:00 to 10:00 p.m., Tuesdays thru Sundays; (802) 864–2433.

Upstairs at the corner of Cherry and Winooski Streets, **Penny Cluse Cafe** serves breakfast and lunch daily, with dinners on weekends. Pancakes are always on the menu, along with other favorites to start the day, often with a southwestern touch to the side dishes. The cafe is at 169 Cherry Street, Burlington, open weekdays, 6:45 a.m. to 3:00 p.m.; weekends, 8:00 a.m. to 3:00 p.m.; (802) 651–8834; www.pennycluse.com.

To see more of Lake Champlain, take a cruise on the **Ethan Allen II,** perhaps combining it with lunch or dinner. Every day in the summer, cruises leave at 10:00 a.m., noon, and 2:00 and 4:00 p.m., lasting about an hour and a half. A deli service and cash bar are available. Prices are $14.99 for adults, and less for children. Every evening a two-and-a-half-hour sunset dinner cruise is offered for about $48.00 for adults (less for children), and each night a special theme cruise is offered. Fridays are Lobstah-on-the-Lake clambake days, which include lobster, chowder, steamers, and corn on the cob. Thursday is the Murder Mystery night, and on Friday and Saturday night, you can join the Captain's Dinner Dance Cruise for about $44. The *Ethan Allen II* leaves from the Burlington Boathouse on College Street. Reservations are essential; (802) 862–8300; www.soea.com.

On the lakefront at the end of College Street, look for Vermont's only **All-America Display Garden,** where you'll find the brightest and the best of the new flowering ornamental plant varieties, blooming in profusion all summer.

Shelburne, the next town south of South Burlington, was chartered and settled early. The town charter was granted in 1763, and Shelburne was settled five years later by two German men who had been loggers in Canada. Reportedly, they were killed by soldiers sent from Montreal, supposedly to protect them from Indian attacks, but this story has never been substantiated. Five years after this initial settlement, two of Shelburne's earliest residents were killed by Indians and Tories, acting together to cut down the fledgling village. The entire settlement would have been destroyed, except that some of the settlers put out the fires in the burning dwellings with a stash of home-brewed beer.

At **Vermont Teddy Bear Company,** you can pick out your own teddy bear, stuff it just the way you want it, and someone will sew it up for you. There are bears with just about every personality and theme. The showrooms, open daily from 9:00 a.m. to 6:00 p.m. in summer, from 9:00 a.m. to 5:00 p.m. in winter, are on Route 7 in Shelburne; (802) 985–3001 or (800) 829–BEAR; www.vermontteddybear.com.

Shed Sales is like a huge household sale running through a half-dozen rooms. The owners buy the contents of entire houses and bring them here for sale, the ultimate recycling. This home of miscellany is 3 miles south of Burlington on Route 7 at 3614 Shelburne Road, Shelburne. It's usually open Monday to Friday from 10:00 a.m. to 4:00 p.m. in the summer and 11:00 a.m. to 3:00 p.m. in the winter. Saturdays and Sundays are "catch us if you can," so before you make a special trip, call (802) 985–8511 to be sure it's open.

The next town south on Route 7 is Charlotte, pronounced with the accent on the second syllable. Charlotte is a quiet town that belies its close proximity to the bustling urban center of Burlington, a fifteen-minute drive away.

Take a right off Route 7 onto Ferry Road to reach downtown Charlotte. About a mile and a half down Ferry Road is the **Church & Maple Glass Studio** of creative glass blowers, dedicated to designing and manufacturing art glass and sculpture. It's a fascinating place to visit but is open intermittently so call ahead. Ferry Road, 1.5 miles from Route 7, Charlotte. (802) 578–0166 or 0168; www.churchandmaple.com.

It's worth your while to find your way to **Authentica African Imports** in Charlotte. Follow the signs to the New York State ferry and turn right at the country store in Charlotte. Lydia Clemmons's unusual shop is ¾ mile up on the left. As you drive to her shop, keep looking west; the view of New York State is breathtaking.

Lydia has been operating Authentica African Imports for many years, and every week she receives new pieces of art, clothing, and jewelry from all over Africa. Check out the five-pound ankle bracelets from Zanzibar. Drums, tapestries, pottery, and handwoven scarves from Ghana are crammed into two rooms of Lydia's old Vermont farmhouse, while a woodstove keeps the rooms warm. The mixture of African items and old-style New England decor works well. Some of the more exotic items include Masai spears and a Yoruba ceremonial drum. Lydia also offers for sale unusual figurines that tell about daily life in Owo and are carved from 2- to 4-inch thorns that grow on egun and ata trees.

For information and a catalog, write to Lydia Clemmons, Authentica African Imports, Greenbush Road, Charlotte, VT 05445; (802) 425–3137. Several times a year Lydia goes on buying trips to Africa, so be sure to call ahead. Open 2:00 to 6:00 p.m. Thursday to Saturday, by appointment Sunday to Tuesday.

Ferrisburg, on Route 7, is home to **Dakin Farm,** a farmstead that was settled in 1792. Sam Cutting, president of Dakin Farm, marvels that his own family has assumed the heritage of the farm for nearly forty years, with the third generation of Cuttings learning what it's like to grow up on a farm.

Not everyone is so lucky, of course, so if you make a stop at Dakin Farm, you can at least get a taste of what farm life is like. You can watch the family and employees smoking meats, sugaring in March, and waxing cheese to mail it to people all over the country.

Even though Dakin Farm has a large mail-order operation, as well as a retail store in the Champlain Mill farther north in Winooski, it still remains truly a family business. Dakin Farm, 5797 Route 7, Ferrisburg; (802) 425–3971 or (800) 99–DAKIN; www.dakinfarm.com.

While you're in Ferrisburg, look for the **Rokeby Homestead** on your left. Rokeby holds twin distinctions: It served as the home of Vermont's most illustrious writer from the nineteenth century, Rowland Robinson, and it was a major stop on the Underground Railroad. Robinson was an accomplished writer and artist who conveyed the Vermont of the 1800s through his writing and pictures.

Many nineteenth-century houses in Vermont are frequently described as having been Underground Railroad stations—most often by zealous real estate agents who perceive every root cellar or hidden basement cubby space as having special historical significance. Usually these claims cannot be proved, since very little written evidence was kept by the owners of such homes for fear of prosecution.

Rokeby, though, is one house where ample evidence was kept; after all, a writer lived there. The house, which dates from before 1784, contains eight rooms of clothing, furniture, and other artifacts from Robinson's family.

The homestead is open to the public Thursday to Sunday from May through October; tours are conducted at 11:00 a.m., 12:30 p.m., and 2:00 p.m. Thursday through Sunday; admission is $6.00 for adults, $4.00 for seniors and students, and $2.00 for children under twelve. Their hiking trails are open year-round. The Rokeby Homestead, Route 7, Ferrisburg; (802) 877–3406; www.rokeby.org.

The city of Vergennes, one of only nine municipalities so designated in the state, is the third-oldest city in the nation and, at 1,152 acres, the smallest. Its boundaries form a perfect square. Vergennes is also a nautical city. The Otter Creek bisects it, flowing northwest into Lake Champlain.

One of the most striking displays at the **Lake Champlain Maritime Museum** in Vergennes is an exact working replica of the 54-foot, square-rigged gunboat *Philadelphia,* which is so real it seems to have transcended two and a half centuries and come straight from the Revolutionary War.

Other exhibits that position Lake Champlain's impact on the area's history are housed in six buildings in a spacious setting on the lake's shore, including a number of boats that were recovered from its waters. There's a 16-foot rowboat from the mid-1800s, a 1929 speedboat, and the logging boat used in filming the movie *Where the Rivers Flow North.* Blacksmiths and shipbuilders demonstrate their skills, and exhibits show in detail the shipwrecks that ended the activities of many vessels in the lake's early days.

Those days are re-created in pageants re-enacted by museum hosts representing the French, English, and Native Americans who lived and traded around the lake in those times. A Kids' Maritime Festival in mid-June includes model-boat building and a chance to paddle a kayak. You can rent small boats—sailboats, rowboats, canoes, and kayaks—by the hour or by the day.

In its Burlington location ("Burlington Shipyard"), the museum has undertaken the construction of an authentic 1862-class canal schooner. For several years the museum has sent divers to the bottom of Lake Champlain to take

Make Way for the Champ

Samuel de Champlain, discoverer of the lake named for him, was a down-to-earth man who reported things in his diary in a straightforward way. In July 1609 he reported a serpentine creature about 20 feet long, with a horse-like head and about as big around as a barrel. As settlers began to establish farms around the lake, occasional other sightings were reported—one in 1819 in the *Plattsburg Republican* noted that several settlers were frightened by the appearance of a large creature close to Port Henry, New York—and other newspaper accounts have echoed similar descriptions. The largest group ever to report seeing "Champ," as followers of the phenomenon have named it, were on a sightseeing excursion boat when the creature surfaced.

The similarities to Nessie, the legendary monster of Scotland's Loch Ness, are remarkable, which has led interested scientists to note the similarities in the bodies of water: each large, deep, and cut off from a former connection to the sea. The chances of your seeing this shy beast, if indeed it exists, are pretty slim (unless you've brought along a lot of Long Trail Ale on your lakeside picnic), but you can bone up on the history, scientific investigation, and sightings at the nature center at Button Bay State Park, or in the Lake Champlain Maritime Museum.

measurements of the long-sunken **General Butler** and has re-created it as closely as possible. A new ship launched in 2004, the **Lois McClure,** is located on the Burlington waterfront, where visitors can board her and see firsthand an example of this popular nineteenth-century means of transportation. The ship is open May through October at the King Street Ferry Dock, (802) 864–9512.

Admission to the museum is $10.00 for adults, $9.00 for seniors, and $5.00 for children ages five through seventeen, and is good for two consecutive days. AAA members get a $1.00 discount. The museum is open from early May through mid-October, daily from 10:00 a.m. to 5:00 p.m. Follow Basin Harbor Road from the center of town, just south of the bridge. Lake Champlain Maritime Museum, 4472 Basin Harbor Road, Vergennes; (802) 475–2022; www .lcmm.org.

After exploring the museum, you'll be ready for lunch or dinner, and you're in the right place. South of town on Route 7 is *Roland's Place* (802–453–6309), which you can learn more about on page 182 in the Middle West Vermont chapter. It's a little nearer to Middlebury but is such a good restaurant and so close to Vergennes, you need at least to know its name here.

Shortly past the turnoff to Basin Harbor on Route 22A, you'll see the elegant *Strong House Inn* on the right. The completely restored Federal mansion is the home of Mary Bargiel and her husband, Hugh, who live there and who greet each guest. It's their personal approach and involvement that puts the capital H in Hospitality here, as well as their knack for creating beautiful rooms filled with the little details that make a stay memorable—thick robes matching the towels in each of the private baths, for example. Each room is different—in size, shape, and style—ranging from frilly Victorian to the Vermont Room, bright, spacious, and overlooking the Adirondacks and furnished in pale pine and shades of blue. Their popular weekend seminars include fly fishing, quilting, landscape design, scrapbooking, and even a psychic weekend with lectures to help you develop your own psychic powers.

The property is planted in gardens that you can enjoy from the gazebo or tables on the terrace. Cross-country, snowshoe, and walking trails begin from the backyard, and for winter fun a sledding hill (including sleds) is on the property, along with a skating rink. If you don't feel like going out to dinner after a day's skiing, Mary can order an elegant basket dinner for you from Roland's Place, and you can enjoy it in your room on fine china and linens. Rooms and suites range from $110 to $300. Strong House Inn, 94 West Main Street, Vergennes; (802) 877–3337; www.stronghouseinn.com. Check the Web site for current activities.

Vermont Bicycle Tours (VBT) pedals clients all over the globe, so it's not surprising to find a trip right at home in Vermont. Their trips are typically

Other Cycling Options

VBT offers a trip along the Connecticut River Valley from Woodstock to Windsor, Chester, Grafton, and Saxtons River, then back up through Springfield, with a side trip across the river into New Hampshire to the home of sculptor Augustus Saint-Gaudens (from $975 to $1,075). Yet another biking option is the Mad River tour, which starts in Waitsfield and wanders south along the Mad River, then south to Ludlow, before heading north through Woodstock, Bethel, Strafford, Tunbridge, Randolph, and Roxbury. The Woodstock-Windsor trip is rated easy to moderate (daily rides from 25 to 40 miles, with options), and the Mad River trip is rated moderate (daily mileage from 25). Contact VBT at P.O. Box 711, Bristol, VT 05443-0711; (800) 245-3868; www.vbt.com.

six-day, five-night tours. An example is one called "Vermont and New York's Lake Champlain Valley tour." It begins and ends in Burlington, touching Lake Champlain at Basin Harbor, Vergennes, and Fort Ticonderoga on the New York side. Along the way, clients pass through beautiful rolling farmland on the western side of the Appalachians, stopping at a Morgan-horse farm. In addition to biking, there is an opportunity to kayak on Lake Champlain in an area where Revolutionary War–era gunboats fought it out. The rates (which are about $1,545) include lodging, five breakfasts, three dinners, and two lunches, as well as use of a VBT bike, helmets, maps, trip leaders, and a support vehicle for those who wither along the way. The terrain is rated moderate to easy, with expected mileage from 20 to 30 miles per day; optional routes available for longer mileage. For more information: 614 Monkton Road, Bristol, VT 05443; (800) 245–3868; www.vbt.com.

The Eastern "Suburbs"

The best way to drive east from Burlington is on U.S. Route 2 (also Williston Road), which runs parallel to I–89 between the University of Vermont campus, where it's called Main Street, to Taft Corners on Essex Road, 3 miles south of Essex Junction. It passes through South Burlington, which is slightly south—but mostly east—of Burlington.

About halfway to Taft Corners (Essex Road) on Williston Road (Rte. 2), you'll see a sculpture on your right that seems a bit incongruous for Vermont. **Reverence** (more often called the **Whales' Tails**), is a sculpture of polished black South African granite that celebrates Vermont's commitment to environmental harmony. The statue is of two graceful, 13-foot whales' tails diving into a sea of grass, atop a slight rise in the land.

Artist Jim Sardonis created the work, which was sponsored by the Environmental Law Foundation in Montpelier and dedicated in 1990. Ten years later it was moved to its current location from Randolph, 60 miles to the south, where it had been commissioned by a British metals trader whose financing fell through. To see the sculpture up close, take Williston Road to Kennedy Drive (about 1.5 miles from I-89 exit 14). Turn right to Kimball Avenue, about 200 yards. Turn left to Community Drive, about a half mile. On the right you'll see Technology Sculpture Park. Drive halfway around the circular drive. Walk across the field toward Route I-89. The sculpture is on the highest point of surrounding land.

Near the Essex Road-Williston Road intersection you will find three excuses to stop, all within sight of one another.

Fine cheese is expensive, but you can find the good stuff and skip the high prices at **Cheese Traders.** You never know what specials you'll find here, from Kenya AA coffee at half the regular price to creamy chocolate truffles, but you can depend on fine cheeses at prices you won't see elsewhere.

Shelves are stocked with a number of Vermont-made products, along with imports, many at serious discounts. Hot-sauce aficionados should look for the bright-red shelf in the middle of the store, where dozens of brands, including the locally made "Vermont Hots," stand row on row. Steve, the owner, says there are more than 30,000 producers of hot sauce in the United States—a figure that makes even his impressive collection seem small. Cheese Traders is open Monday through Saturday from 10:00 a.m. to 7:00 p.m. It's at 1186 Williston Road, South Burlington; (802) 863–0143; www .cheesetraders.com.

Almost next door to Cheese Traders is a salesroom for **Snowflake Chocolates,** whose "factory" is in nearby **Jericho,** home of Snowflake Bentley. While you can't watch chocolates being made here, the selection is good and they are just as delicious as they are in Jericho. The shop is at 1174 Williston Road, South Burlington; (802) 863–8306; www.snowflakechocolate.com.

Food snobs can skip this, but those who long for really good fries, and maybe a corn dog or hamburger, should head a few yards east to the shiny diner facade of **Al's French Frys.** Lines are long at lunchtime, especially on weekends, and you may have trouble finding a spot in the parking lot, so Al's is clearly not undiscovered. A pint of fries will set you back less than $2.00, and you can take them out or munch them at one of the red upholstered booths. Al's is at 1251 Williston Road, South Burlington; (802) 862–9203; www .alsfrenchfrys.com. Hours are 10:30 a.m. to 11:00 p.m. Monday through Thursday, and until midnight on Friday and Saturday. On Sunday Al's is open 11:00 a.m. to 11:00 p.m.

The *Inn at Essex* has all the warmth of a vintage country inn, without the squeaky floorboards and thin walls. Rooms are spacious and elegantly decorated, with quality furniture and nice touches, such as a woven lap robe on the rocking chair. Suites have fully equipped kitchens (complete with an apron), dining areas, and comfortable sitting rooms. Whirlpool tubs are roomy enough to share. The bakery provides excellent scones, croissants, and occasionally pain au chocolat for breakfast. The inn practices recycling and other earth-friendly and environmentally aware programs. A well-stocked library off the lobby provides travelers with books to curl up with, and the lobby bake shop is ready with cookies, tarts, or chocolate truffles. The inn is at 70 Essex Way, Essex Junction, off Route 15 east of Burlington; (802) 878–1100; www.innatessex.com.

It is rare that you can stay at an inn where there are more chefs than guests, but that's the case at the Inn at Essex, which is also the Burlington campus of the New England Culinary Institute (NECI). Along with the bakery goods sold in the shop, the students and their instructor chefs create all the dishes for both the *Tavern Restaurant,* a casual upscale pub, and the inn's more formal *Butler's.*

The Tavern menu features lighter foods to accompany the wide choice of local brews, as well as sturdier dinner entrees. We have never tasted a better seafood soup—really a stew—than the bouillabaisse-like bowlful set before us there. Each type of fish and shellfish—silken scallops, tender juicy shrimp, plump mussels, and delicate whitefish and salmon fillets among them—was added to the savory saffron-and-leek broth at exactly the right moment to cook each to its point of perfection.

Guests enter Butler's by walking past the evening's dessert selections, a mouthwatering start to a meal. Locally grown and produced ingredients are the hallmark of Butler's, and we especially liked finding less-common vegetables on the menu, such as fennel. Whatever you choose for an entree, begin with the pâté and rillettes sampler plate. Forget, for a moment, both your waistline and your cholesterol level to savor these delicately flavored morsels. Hope that someone at your table orders the quail stuffed with wild mushrooms, served with an onion tarte tatin, so you can sample that, too.

Each course gets full attention, even the salads, which often include one pairing green and red apples with curly endive and Vermont blue cheese. Entrees, like the appetizers, change every day, but you are likely to find a duck specialty, perhaps pan-seared with pistachios, coconut, and currants. Butler's is open daily for three meals, with dinner beginning at 6:00 p.m. Both restaurants are in the central building of the inn; reserve for Butler's at (802) 764–1413, the Tavern at (802) 764–1489. For a preview of current menus or to make online reservations at either, visit www.necidining.com.

If the architecture in the downtown district of Richmond (east of Burlington on Route 2) seems newer than that in the rest of Vermont, it's for good reason: In 1908 a fire raged out of control and burned down the entire business section of the town.

While we were sad to see Our Daily Bread bakery close, we heartily welcome its replacement, **Toscano Café and Bistro,** in the rustic storefront at 27 Bridge Street in Richmond, where John and Lucy Faith now welcome guests in their bright and attractive dining room. A longtime musician in Vermont clubs, John changed careers and trained at New England Culinary Institute before working in several Vermont restaurants and finally opening his own.

The Mediterranean-inspired menu is rich in Italian influences that make the most of the fresh local ingredients and produce he insists on. For lunch we tried his grilled flatbread Genovese with pesto, Vermont chèvre, sun-dried tomato, and roasted garlic, a bright red, white, and green delight full of the flavor of garlic, as this peasant dish should be. The seafood piccata special was linguine with a fresh tomato sauce and chunks of blackened mahi-mahi, salmon, and crab. It was both piquant and fresh.

Dinner at Toscano offers wild-mushroom ravioli sauced with Gorgonzola and roasted garlic cream with walnuts, or a veal saltimbocca with prosciutto di Parma and crimini mushrooms. Not only is the food worth a trip, but it is served at prices that make this restaurant one of Vermont's best bargains. Pasta courses start from $9.95 to $10.50 and other entrees from $13.95. Open for lunch and dinner Tuesday through Sunday, Toscano also serves a Sunday brunch from 9:30 to 2:30. Find them at 27 Bridge Street in Richmond; (802) 434–3148.

Within an easy walk of Toscano, on Route 2, **Richmond Victorian Inn** sits grandly on a hillside. Innkeeper Frank Stewart is a genuine Scot, with a rich burr accent to prove it. Guest rooms in his restored and turreted home are fresh and appealing, each different and nicely furnished. All have private baths. The tower room is particularly sunny, with large windows, pink walls, plum floor, and white wicker furniture set off by a gleaming brass bed. The beds all have pieced quilts and all rooms have comfortable bathrobes. Room rates are $119 to $165. In February, the Chocolate Lover's Special with a two-night minimum stay includes Lake Champlain chocolates and sparkling cider, perfect for Valentine's Day retreats.

A full country-inn breakfast (including Vermont's famed Harrington bacon and sausage) is included in the rates, and during the fall and winter seasons guests are invited to join local people and other visitors to town for a Victorian tea, served in the front parlor. Full tea with sandwiches, homemade scones, and dessert is $15.95, while a simple tea with scone is $8.95. Ploughman's Plate is $8.95. Reservations for tea are suggested. While the inn does not accept pets, they will arrange pet boarding close by. The inn is on Route 2, 191 East Main Street, Richmond; (888) 242–3362 or (802) 434–4410; www.richmond victorianinn.com.

Richmond is also home to the **Old Round Church,** one of the most unusual buildings in the state. It's not exactly round—it has sixteen sides—but it holds the distinction of being the first community church in the country, since its construction in 1813 was the joint effort of five separate denominations: Methodist, Congregationalist, Universalist, Baptist, and Christian. In fact, it's rumored that sixteen men each built one side of the church, and the seventeenth built the belfry.

The congregations initially held joint services at the church, but they eventually broke away, and the church became the town hall. Henry Ford once tried to buy the Old Round Church so that he could bring it back to Dearborn with him, but the town gave him a thumbs down.

Today the church is a historical site, and regular tours are offered in summer and during foliage season. For more information, write to the Old Round Church, Bridge Street, Richmond, VT 05477, or call (802) 434–2556.

South of Richmond is the village of Huntington. Huntington abuts a parcel of land called **Buels Gore,** most of which is taken up by Camel's Hump State Forest. Gores are odd-shaped parcels of unincorporated land, usually rocky or otherwise worthless. They are not part of any town and are often uninhabited. Buels Gore was named for Major Elias Buel, who back in 1780 wanted to start his own town of Montzoar in the gore, which totals 3,520 acres. He purchased all the existing land titles to the gore but neglected to have them recorded or to pay the taxes on them. To pay the taxes, the lands were subsequently sold for a grand total of $11.02.

Continue down the main road that runs through Huntington and turn west onto Sherman Hollow Road to reach the **Green Mountain Audubon Nature Center.** The center has an extensive trail system that is equally accessible to walkers and cross-country skiers. The small, slanting shack alongside the barn has trail maps inside.

Inside the main house is a nature museum occupying several rooms of the house. The Nature Discovery Room has a board with dates of recent sightings of common and not-so-common Vermont-based birds. Live turtles and garter snakes, a cubbyhole filled with fifteen different birds' nests—the center calls them avian architecture—and matching games are in this room.

One of the upstairs rooms serves as a teacher's resource center and library. Steel yourself before you pull out the drawers of actual preserved bird species, from blue jays to pine grosbeaks and owls and swans. If you're at all squeamish, head out to the barn, which is filled with more exhibits and examples of taxidermy that are a bit easier to take.

The center is open year-round from 8:00 a.m. to 4:00 p.m. daily. Green Mountain Audubon Nature Center, 225 Sherman Hollow Road, Huntington, (802) 434–3068; www.audubon.org (click on Vermont).

Route 2 from Richmond to Waterbury pretty much parallels Interstate 89, crisscrossing from one side to the other. About halfway between the two, at the town of Bolton, Route 2 crosses under the highway to the north side and immediately after the bridge is a road to Bolton Valley. For miles the road climbs upward until you reach **Bolton Valley Resort** at the end of the road.

This ski resort is family oriented, without the glitz of larger ski meccas to the south, but with all the amenities. In winter the resort is among the first to open and last to close because of the altitude and the way that the mountain catches snow. Each year 300 inches of natural snow falls here, ensuring the best conditions on their sixty trails. Grooming is expert, the staff taking to the trails as soon as skiers have left for the day. The trails all face northwest, preserving the snow and giving skiers a wonderful view of Vermont's signature mountain, **Camel's Hump.** Be sure to save time to ski the Cobrass trail from the top of the Vista chair as the sun goes down—it's inspirational. But you don't have to stop skiing at sunset: They have night skiing as well, Wednesday through Saturday, the only ski area in Vermont to offer it.

But alpine is not all the skiing that goes on here. The resort also has an excellent cross-country program with more than 40 miles of groomed trails.

Bolton has a respectable vertical drop of 1,704 feet and spreads out over three peaks, most all of the trails ending up back in to base area. Of the total 65 trails 27 percent are labeled for novices, 47 percent are intermediate, and

Another Presidential Scandal?

Although President Chester A. Arthur is known to have been born in 1829, no one is quite sure where. Fairfield, Vermont, claims the honor, and a replica of his boyhood home was erected there in 1953. The town of Waterville, however, based on a memoir of a friend of his mother, has staked a claim that he was actually born in that town and taken to Fairfield when he was five days old. But wait, there's more. His mother came from across the border in Dunham Flats, Quebec, and they claim that she went there for the delivery. If that's true, then he was not born in the United States and shouldn't have acceded to the job of president in September 1881, after the assassination of President James Garfield. But no one in either Vermont town has much truck with that claim, and it's a little late to quibble about the validity of Arthur's presidency.

26 percent are expert, making this a good place for family and recreational skiing. Six lifts serve the trails, including two quads, three doubles, and a new top-to-bottom quad. Boarders will also like the 1,500-foot fully groomed terrain park.

Bolton Mountain Resort has both hotel and condo lodgings available and offers some nice packages. For example, ski-and-stay packages priced from $79 to $139 per person per night include lodging, continental breakfast, lift ticket, and access to the sports center. Lift tickets start at $49 for adults. Restaurants and other facilities, including a child-care center that can handle up to thirty children, are also available. Bolton Valley Resort, 4302 Bolton Access Road, Bolton; (877) 926–5866 or (802) 434–3444, snow conditions (802) 434–7669; www.boltonvalley.com.

On the access road to the ski resort is *The Black Bear Inn,* a rustic Alpine inn that reminds us of the cozy places where skiers used to stay before the days of condos and destination resorts. The roaring fire in the big fireplace in the ample lobby/guest lounge makes this a warm place in both senses of the word, and the innkeepers are most accommodating. Black Bear Inn is pet-friendly; call for details. A ski lift connects to Bolton Valley's trails and slopes, and the inn has a dining room. Rates run from $89 to $330, depending on the season. Contact the inn at 4010 Bolton Access Road, Bolton Valley, 05477; (802) 434–2126 or (800) 395–6335; www.blkbearinn.com.

While every traveler bound for Burlington on I–89 passes the Waterbury exit, and those bound for Stowe or Ben & Jerry's Ice Cream Factory join Route 100 there, not very many people go into the charming old town itself. They're missing a lot, since *Waterbury* has some very fine Victorian buildings (one house has a large horseshoe window overlooking Route 2), a charming little museum, and one of our favorite inns.

What is there about a checkered past that makes an inn irresistible—especially when it's been carefully restored and nicely furnished with unusual antiques and handmade furniture, and its innkeepers have a sense of humor? The *Old Stagecoach Inn* began as a coaching stop and town meetinghouse in 1826, and its Victorian facade with porches was added late in the century. Local opinion is divided from that point on, but most agree that the meetings that began to take place here were not of a civic (and certainly not public) nature, and a photograph the innkeepers have does seem to show a lot of women posed alluringly on the porches. Other local residents remember that the house was haunted, and the inn staff admits to some unusual encounters in Room 2, the one with the magnificent carved four-poster bed.

Today the guest rooms vary in size and shape, reflecting the architectural history of the house itself, a colonial-style building with significant Queen

Anne overlays. Room rates are $75 to $180. The innkeepers love to cook, and guests are the beneficiaries, enjoying fresh, home-baked croissants for breakfast as well as their choice of hot entree as part of the full country breakfast included in the rates. If the weather's nice, the porch overlooking the garden is the place to eat. The Old Stagecoach Inn is at 18 North Main Street (Route 2), Waterbury; (802) 244–5056 or (800) 262–2206; www.oldstagecoach.com.

A walking trail leaves from the inn's backyard, winding through a cemetery with stones from the 1700s and along the river. Just up the street is the town library, and upstairs is the ***Historical Society Museum,*** a classic mélange of local history, curiosities, and treasures brought back by intrepid travelers. It has some excellent examples of miniature Berlin work, beading, and handmade lace; an interesting rocking butter churn, and an armadillo shell. Be sure to look at the album of photos of the 1927 freshet, a flood that washed out much of Vermont's road and bridge system. The library and museum are located at 28 North Main Street, Waterbury; (802) 244–7036, and are open Monday through Wednesday 10:00 a.m. to 8:00 p.m., Thursday through Friday 10:00 a.m. to 5:00 p.m., Saturday 9:00 a.m. to 2:00 p.m.

Free musical programs are presented at 6:30 p.m. on Thursday evenings in summer in ***Rusty Parker Memorial Park*** near the train depot. (Waterbury is one of the rare Vermont towns with regular train service.) Programs may include the Vermont Jazz Ensemble, a banjo concert, bluegrass, or big-band sounds. Bring your own blanket or chairs to sit on. Program schedules are available after May; call Tami Bass at (802) 244–5308 or go to www.virtual vermont.com or www.waterburyvt.com.

Green Mountain Coffee Roasters, whose brews you'll see mentioned by name on the menus of Vermont restaurants and cafes, has a factory outlet store in Waterbury, the only place where all the full-bean coffee collection is assembled in one place. You'll also find overstock items, mostly coffee-related, such as espresso cups and grinders. The outlet store, just off Main Street, 33 Coffee Lane, is open from 7:30 a.m. to 9:00 p.m. Monday through Friday and from 9:00 a.m. to 6:00 p.m. Saturday; (800) 223–6768; www.greenmountain coffee.com.

South of Waterbury, on Route 100, watch for signs to ***Grunberg Haus,*** a three-story, hand-built chalet, where each of the ten guest rooms on the second floor has its own balcony. Although Grunberg Haus is off the beaten path, it is very close to many of northern Vermont's more mainstream attractions, such as Ben & Jerry's Ice Cream Factory in Waterbury, Cold Hollow Cider Mill, and Stowe. Be warned: Grunberg Haus is so pleasant a hideaway that you may have to consciously drag yourself out into the world, away from the queen-size beds with downy comforters. One of the guest rooms even has a tiny built-in alcove that houses a bed big enough for an eight-year-old, or maybe a couple of cats, or you, if you really want to get away from it all. Breakfast is accompanied by piano music.

Call Chris Sellers at (802) 244–7726 or (800) 800–7760 to reserve a room at Grunberg Haus, 94 Pine Street, Route 100 South Waterbury; www.grunberg haus.com.

Stowe's reputation as a top ski area undoubtedly owes much to Mount Mansfield's location in Vermont's snowbelt. The first recorded descent of the mountain on skis was made in 1900 on barrel staves, but things moved slowly until the Great Depression years, when Stowe got its start as a major ski area. In 1932 the first skiers from New York City arrived in Waterbury to get to the top of Mount Mansfield—where Stowe's ski area is located—via an electric railway from Waterbury. Although it took the rest of the decade to cut trails and hook up rope tows, by 1940 Stowe could boast the first chairlift in the country. The town hasn't been the same since.

A quiet place to escape the crowds is the **Helen Day Art Center** in Stowe, which exhibits the work of internationally and nationally-recognized artists, as well as Vermont-based artists. The building itself was previously the town high school.

A variety of special events and discussions are also held every few weeks at the center, in conjunction with the current displays. In its special exhibits you may find hooked rugs, food labels, paintings, drawings, and other works of art covering the walls of the gallery. The gallery is open Tuesday through Saturday, 12:00 p.m. to 5:00 p.m.

For a list of current exhibits, contact the Helen Day Art Center, School Street, P.O. Box 411, Stowe, VT 05672; (802) 253–8358; www.helenday.com.

Although Stowe is not exactly off the beaten path, we'd be cheating you if we didn't mention a few of its attractions. Despite the numbers of tourists year-round, Stowe still manages to remain a real town, and one of its most appealing inns overlooks its main street. Rooms in the **Green Mountain Inn** are all different, at least those in the original building, often with quirky charming shapes. All are approached along corridors with an occasional up or down step. But there are no rough edges—look for carpeted corridors, original artwork throughout, canopy beds, whirlpool baths, fluffy towels, terry-cloth robes, premium bath amenities, electric fireplaces, and a host of other details of fine innkeeping. In the afternoon everyone gathers for cider and fresh-baked cookies, which you can take to a porch rocker to watch the comings and goings on Main Street. A pleasant dining room overlooks the street, and breakfasts are interesting and varied, including crepes filled with whole pistachios and ricotta.

Rates begin at $129 for standard rooms, and include all the facilities of the health club and pool. Main Street, P.O. Box 60, Stowe, VT 05672; (802) 253–7301 or (800) 253–7302; www.greenmountaininn.com.

The *Blue Moon Café,* located in an older home near Main Street, offers superb dining. The menu changes weekly, with an emphasis on local produce, lamb and beef, fresh fish, and bread baked in a wood-fired oven. Appetizers, beginning at $6.75, include sweet potato and frisee salad with oranges and toasted pecans; or crispy bok choy–wrapped tuna, with seaweed salad. The entrees, starting at $18.00, feature creative offerings such as grilled lamb chops with Greek spinach pie and roasted tomato coulis. There is an award-winning wine list and simple but excellent desserts. The Blue Moon is located at 35 School Street, and is open from 6:00 until 9:00 p.m. Sunday through Thursday and 6:00 until 9:30 p.m. Friday and Saturday. Phone (802) 253–7006. Reservations recommended. www.bluemoonstow.com.

On Main Street, behind Stowe Hardware Store, is the beginning of the 5.3-mile *Stowe Recreation Path,* a paved multi-use corridor that follows the river through meadows and woodlands, roughly parallel with Mountain Road. Walkers, cyclists, in-line skaters, and cross-country skiers share the path, which leads past lodgings, dining establishments, gardens, a farmers' market, and endless views. If you want to take advantage of this beautiful path on wheels, stop at Mountain Sports, where bikes are available for rent. The price is about $11 for two hours, $16 for four hours. They are at 580 Mountain Road, at the intersection with Weeks Hill Road and right on the path; (802) 253–7919.

Mountain Road is itself about as beaten as a path can get, lined with restaurants and lodgings of every stripe announced by a succession of signs lined up like street touts.

At 1457 Mountain Road is *The Gables,* a warm and welcoming family-owned inn without the pretensions of many of its neighbors, and loaded with just as many pampering comforts, including fireplaces, whirlpool tubs, and candlelight dining. Breakfast here is legendary and lasts most people through a full day's skiing. The Gables is a particularly good place for people traveling or skiing alone, since the hosts make everyone feel like they're visiting relatives and will make sure skiers have a ride to the slopes and arrive safely home. Rates are $90 or up to $250 for suites in high season. 1457 Mountain Road, Stowe; (802) 253–7730 or (800) GABLES–1; www.gablesinn.com.

Leaving Mountain Road on nearly any side road, you'll find quiet lanes and mountain views. To the east of Mountain Road (Route 108), on West Hill Road.

If you continue past what was formerly a sheep farm and go left on Sterling Valley Road, you'll come to *Sterling Falls Gorge.* This series of three waterfalls, six cascades, and eight pools is within a short distance of the road. A walking path parallels them; from its dizzying height you can see how the stream carved its way through the schist, forming irregular potholes and swirly rock surfaces. Do be careful here, especially if the trail is wet, and don't lean over to take pictures (photographing the falls is nearly impossible, unless you're a bird). Don't look for the falls on any map—even some Stowe residents looked at us blankly when we asked about it.

Off the west side of Mountain Road is the *Trapp Family Lodge,* which overlooks rolling meadows, a valley, and the Green Mountains. The air is distinctly Austrian, and very von Trapp, but it's never overwhelmingly *The Sound of Music* (the score of which was unknown to the actual Von Trapp Family singers, who but rarely sang in English). Music is often in the air, however, with Sunday morning jazz and coffee, evening sing-alongs, and a harpist in the dining room each evening. Rooms are beautifully decorated, and all overlook the valley views. A full schedule of activities keeps guests busy year-round. In the winter you can enjoy cross-country skiing (the trails are open to the public and known as some of the finest in New England), snowshoeing, sleigh rides, and maple sugaring. Summer programs for families and for children of various ages include fishing, birding, hiking, nature walks, swimming, and llama treks.

Rooms begin at $245 in the summer; $225 in the winter (except for Presidents' weekend; and $195 from March 30 to July 2 (except for Memorial Day weekend. The dining room, serving European specialties such as Wiener schnitzel along with game, is open to the public, but reservations are essential. 700 Trapp Hill Road, Stowe; (802) 253–8511 or (800) 826–7000; www.trapp family.com.

Not far off Route 100 south of Stowe is *Gregg Hill Gardens,* where a natural rock outcrop is the setting for herb, perennial, and annual gardens and a unique PYO cut flower farm. Giant peonies, poppies, dianthus, phlox, irises, daisies—name a color and they can find you a bouquet to match. The gardens are open Tuesday through Saturday May through September. In the late summer and fall, you'll find dried flowers, and the owner does gardening workshops and specializes in wedding arrangements as well. For a schedule, contact Gregg Hill Gardens, 3463 Gregg Hill Road, Waterbury Center, Stowe, VT 05672; (802) 244–7361; www.gregghillgardens.com.

You could easily miss the intersection where you turn to Gregg Hill Gardens because your attention will be drawn to the other side of Route 100 and the *Spinning Wheel.* The entire yard of this shop is a sculpture gallery filled with life-size (and larger) woodcarvings of moose, fiddlehead ferns, bear cubs, and a larger-than-life Mountie in his red coat.

Between Stowe and Jeffersonville, to the north, lies **Smugglers Notch,** crossed by Route 108. The road through the notch is so narrow at the top that it is impossible to get plows through to keep it cleared of snow, so it closes until spring melts it clear. When it's open, however, the steep, winding road is one of the most interesting in the state, especially at the top, where it weaves among giant boulders. Stop there (there are pull-outs for a few cars) and climb a short distance to see views to Canada and the Adirondacks in New York. Trailers and large RVs are not allowed over it. (For more information on how this unusual notch was formed, see the book *Natural Wonders of Vermont,* by Barbara and Stillman Rogers.)

politicsispolitics andbusinessis business

From the time of the Jefferson embargo of 1808 through the War of 1812, Vermonters defied federal agents and continued to do business with Canada, their natural trading partner. The route through the notch was an important one for farmers seeking to sell their beef to the British in Canada, even while other Vermonters fought to keep British troops at bay— which is how it came to be named Smugglers Notch.

There's an old upcountry Yankee story that has since become an all-purpose bromide about the Flatlander who stopped to ask directions of a farmer, who replied, "You can't get there from here." He might well have been talking about **Smugglers Notch Ski Resort** in the winter. Getting there from Stowe in summer is a simple matter of driving straight uphill on Route 108 through the narrow rock-bordered passage, then dropping down the other side. When this unplowable road is closed in winter, you have to continue north on Route 100 to Morrisville, take Route 15 west through Johnson and Jeffersonville, and drive back along Route 108. If you are a skier, it's well worth the trip, however you manage it, and it certainly is off the beaten path.

Skiing is available on three separate mountains, and all of it is superb— with state-of-the-art grooming. We've arrived at midnight in a blizzard that dropped more than a foot of snow and awakened to perfectly groomed trails the next morning. The ski school is also tops—instructors tailor the lessons to your skills and weaknesses after watching you ski, even in group lessons. A special program is designed for adults who want to learn snowboarding. It's a family resort with all manner of accommodations for kids, including a day-care center toddlers won't want to leave. Not surprisingly, since the ski resort is designed especially for families, the children's learning program gets high priority. Unlike many areas, where the preschoolers' day includes mostly indoor play time with an hour's on-slope instruction twice a day, the practice at Smugglers Notch is to put children as young as four or five on the slopes for at least two hours, morning and afternoon. Imagine a five-year-old's pride at ending a weekend there proficient on the chairlift and able to ski down the mountain on real trails. Put them in the ski camp for a week, and they'll be leaving you behind in a cloud of fresh powder by Thursday.

The entire Smugglers Notch complex is self-contained, with a shuttle bus between two base lodges and all lodgings. Slope-side condo units are huge, with full kitchens, fireplaces, stereos, VCRs, and whirlpool tubs. You can't ski right out your door and onto the slopes from the new North Hill lodgings, but they have their own activities center with a pool, hot tubs, and other facilities. Condos here have four-season sunrooms, multiple fireplaces, and a lot of extras: quality kitchen appliances, oversized whirlpool tubs, and a washer/dryer in each unit. Shuttle buses take skiers to the slopes from all the mountain lodgings. Package plans include lifts, lessons, lodging, and such extras as access to the pool, teen center, theater, cross-country trails, guided winter walks, and other activities. These package inclusions bring the cost of Christmas and New Year's stays down to regular rates. There's plenty to do here in the summer, too, with hiking, climbing, kayaking, nature programs, tennis, kids' camp, and more. Its secluded location and relaxed air make it seem like another world. Smugglers Notch Resort, 4323 Vermont Route 108 South, Smugglers Notch; (802) 644–8851 or (800) 451–8752; www.smuggs.com.

Smugglers Notch Resort, long an environmental leader, has gone one step further. If you're in the neighborhood, stop in to see the **Living Machine Wastewater Treatment Plant.** The plant incorporates a three-stage process that includes use of a large greenhouse full of tropical and subtropical plants to purify wastewater from the resort. Odor-free, the greenhouse has a deck around it with signs that explain the treatment process. It is included on the several different property tours of the resort.

Farther along Route 108 you'll come to Cambridge and the **Boyden Valley Winery,** not exactly what you expect to find this far north, set on a fourth-generation dairy farm in the Lamoille River valley. The owners of the winery use their own grapes, local berries, and apples along with maple syrup to make wines, cordials, and hard ciders. You can tour the 1878 carriage barn to see the process and taste the results from June through December, seven days a week from 10:00 a.m. to 5:00 p.m., and January through May, Friday through Sunday. The winery is at the junction of Routes 15 and 104, 70 Route 104, Cambridge; (802) 644–8151; www.boydenvalley.com.

While on Route 15, continue east past Jeffersonville and just a tad farther you'll come to Johnson, and in its center, **Johnson Woolen Mills.** The company goes back a century and a half ago, when local farmers brought

Fun in the Snow: No Skis Required

While most people think of coming to Vermont in the winter only for skiing, an increasing number are discovering the joys of this active winter vacation land for its many other diversions. Non-skiing companions of skiers have long known this secret: While everyone is on the slopes, all the après-ski recreation facilities are nearly empty. To learn about other indoor and outdoor diversions, check out the book *New England Snow Country: 701 Ways to Enjoy Winter Whether You Ski or Not*. In its Vermont section you will find opportunities for snowshoeing, sleigh rides, skating parties, igloo building, dogsledding, ice fishing, winter carnivals, and activities for those who prefer the warmer pursuits of shopping, museums, art galleries, and fine dining. The book is available in bookstores or from Herbitage Farm Bookshelf, Box 232, Swanzey, NH 03446. The price is $14.95 (plus $3.50 shipping).

their wool to the mill to have it spun and woven into cloth. In the late 1800s Johnson began making warm woolen trousers from the cloth. Meeting with the rousing approval of people who had to do farm chores in the dead of winter, a decade or so later the company added jackets, shirts, and vests. That's what it still makes, along with blankets, mittens, and hats, all of which are sold in a shop located in the original mill building. You'll find first quality at factory-store prices and seconds at unbelievable bargains. You also can buy wool yard goods for sewing or rug braiding. The store is open all year from 9:00 a.m. to 5:00 p.m. Monday through Saturday, and on Sunday from 10:00 a.m. to 4:00 p.m. Main Street, P.O. Box 612, Johnson, 05656; (877) 635–WOOL; www.johnsonwoolenmills.com.

If you return to Burlington on scenic Route 15 or the unnumbered, almost parallel route through Pleasant Valley, you'll travel through **Underhill,** which snuggles up against the western slopes of Mount Mansfield. If you happen along on Saturday evening in the last weekend in June, you'll find one of the last of the old-fashioned **Strawberry Socials** that used to fill the all-too-brief season when fields of strawberries ripen. Jericho-Underhill Lions Club members start picking just after sunrise on Saturday morning. By 10:00 a.m. they're back at the United Church of Underhill, washing, hulling, slicing, and baking the biscuits. Real shortcake isn't made with sponge cake baked in little molds, or with pound cake; it uses "short" biscuits, and that's exactly what these are. From 5:00 to 8:00 p.m. the Lions hide these biscuits under juicy fresh berries and freshly whipped real cream and serve about 350 people, who stay until they've eaten their fill. No one asks how many bowls you've eaten, only if you'd like another—or a refill on the coffee, tea, or milk that goes with it. Adults pay $4.50, seniors and kids $3.50; if you have a lot of kids, pay $20.00

He Certainly Picked the Right Place to Be From

Wilson Bentley of Jericho, known locally as Snowflake Bentley, had by the age of twenty-one developed a photographic microscope that was able to record the intricate patterns of individual snow crystals. The process was not a simple one, requiring a cold working area, great patience, and Bentley's ability to hold his breath for a full minute.

He discovered, after photographing thousands of snowflakes, that no two were alike, that they were all six-sided, and that each flake developed from a tiny nucleus into a hexagonal pattern. Today, more than a century later, much of what we know about snow is based on his research, and Bentley's photographs are among the prized collections of several museums, including the Fairbanks Museum in St. Johnsbury and the Peabody at Harvard. Although he never attended high school, Bentley was elected a fellow of the American Academy for the Advancement of Science.

for the whole family. It's easy to see why the only advertising is the sign out on the village green.

Just down the street from the green is **Sinclair House Inn,** a striking Victorian with one of the loveliest gardens in the valley. When you follow the path from the front porch, you see only a part of the succession of flower beds that flow down the slope to the flat circle of lawn that just begs to have a bride and groom exchanging vows against a backdrop of Vermont farms and hillsides. The owners have lavished the same attention on the house itself, restoring its paneled interior and decorating its rooms in Victorian antiques and country furniture. We like the bright front rooms—one with a lattice window, the other with stained glass. Rates are $95 to $130 in winter and $130 to $150 in summer, and guests can buy lift tickets, rentals, and lessons at Smugglers Notch, 18 miles away. One room is wheelchair accessible, even to the wheel-in shower and low closet hooks. The Sinclair Inn Bed & Breakfast, 389 Vermont Route 15, Jericho; (802) 899–2234 or (800) 433–4658; www.sinclairinnbb.com.

North of Burlington

The stretches of the Champlain Valley north of Burlington offer a flatter, more fertile landscape than many other parts of the state. This rich farmland played an important role in the early development of northwest Vermont.

As you head north on Route 7 out of Burlington and into Winooski just north of the Champlain Mill, the VFW hall on the left has a *World War II–vintage army tank* perched on its lawn. Route 7 is a pretty stretch of highway as you wind your way into Milton, named after the poet John Milton. Just north of the town is a gorgeous body of water, the dammed-up *Arrowhead Mountain Lake.* In summer there's a lot of traffic on the lake.

In St. Albans the *Vermont Maple Festival* is an annual bash in mid-April that signifies the official end of winter. Sugar-on-snow, arts-and-crafts displays, relay races, and other town activities serve to wake up the towns-people in an area of the state where winter hangs on for a good five months of the year. For the dates of the festival, call the St. Albans Chamber of Commerce at (802) 524–2444 or write to the Vermont Maple Festival, 132 North Main Street, St. Albans, 05478. The Franklin County Regional Chamber of Commerce Web site (www.fcrccvt .com) is an excellent resource for visitors to this area.

itwaswar, y'all

St. Albans was the site of the northernmost battle—more accurately, "event"—of the Civil War, when, on October 19, 1864, a group of Confederate soldiers took over the town, robbed all the banks, blew up the Sheldon Bridge, and escaped to Canada. They were apprehended but were acquitted of any crimes because the jury felt they were acting on the basis of "legitimate warfare."

On the main drag of *St. Albans,* which is actually quite a bustling city for these parts, is *Jeff's Maine Seafood,* a gourmet-food and seafood shop and restaurant. The take-out section offers fish both uncooked and prepared, along with a large selection of ready-to-eat dishes like pesto lasagna, smoked bluefish, salads, sandwiches, and specials like chicken burritos and spanakopita, a savory Greek pastry made with paper-thin phyllo sheets. Gourmet desserts are available both to eat in and to take out and include Toll House pie and chocolate hazelnut torte. Jeff's also carries a large selection of French, California, and Italian wines.

There's also a sight rarely seen in any part of Vermont: a live-lobster tank. A fish tank sits atop the deli showcase containing two well-fed goldfish. They must feel nervous about overlooking their relatives below, who enter the store from Maine on Tuesday, Wednesday, and Friday.

If you'd rather eat here, the lobster dinner comes with a cup of seafood chowder, coleslaw, French bread, and a tossed salad, all at a reasonable market price.

Jeff's retail and wine store is open from 10:00 a.m. to 6:00 p.m. Tuesday through Saturday. The restaurant is open Monday through Saturday 11:30

Fine Crop of Rocks This Year

The small stones in the fields actually grow there. Ask any farmer, who will tell you that even though a field is clear of stones in the fall, a new crop has grown there when plowed in the spring. It's the truth: As the ground freezes and thaws in the winter and spring, it heaves up rocks from below in a never-ending process. The original settlers, after they'd cleared the land of trees, moved the larger rocks to the edges and used them to build *stone walls,* which were more to contain livestock than to mark boundaries (although they served both purposes). As each winter turned up more rocks, the settlers would add them to the walls. In some of these fields, rocks are about the only thing that *will* grow.

a.m. until 3:00 p.m. and Tuesday through Sunday for dinner from 4:30 to 9:00 p.m. Jeff's Maine Seafood, 65 North Main Street, St. Albans; (802) 524–6135.

Swanton on Route 7 is home to the largest number of Abenaki Indians in the state, who have lived in Vermont since 800 BC. The Missisquoi Abenaki village was established in 1682, and the first white settlement in Swanton occurred in 1740, when the French sailed through what is today Missisquoi Bay into the headwaters of Lake Champlain.

An enjoyable stop in this area is **West Swanton Orchards, Cider Mill and Farm Market,** open from June through October. Apple varieties are McIntosh, Cortland, and Red Delicious, which you can buy at the stand or pick yourself. As the name implies, the stand carries the trilogy of other Vermont products: honey, maple goodies, and cider, in addition to pies and baked goods and Vermont gift items. The farm is on Route 78 West, about 4 miles from Swanton at 32 Church Road and 752 North River Street, Swanton; (802) 868–7851. East of Swanton is **Highgate Center.** This part of the state looks noticeably different from the rest. Route 78 parallels the Missisquoi River, a very wide, 86-mile-long rocky river that begins in the town of Lowell, heads north into Canada, and then swings back into Vermont by way of Lake Champlain.

Here, and elsewhere in Vermont, you'll see boulders and rocks in the fields, and you may wonder where they came from. The big ones came from nearby mountains, often quite some distance away. As the great glaciers of the last ice age moved over the mountains, they pulled off pieces of mountaintop and carried them along, dropping the rocks as they melted. These boulders are called "glacial erratics," and local settlers sometimes cut them up to use as building stones; more often they just plowed around them.

Once you reach Enosburg Falls, take Route 108 north a couple of miles until you reach **Berkson Farms Inn** on the left. This working dairy farm on 600 acres is open year-round and offers guests the opportunity to stay for a night or two or for an entire week, participating in standard farm chores, from milking cows to bringing in sap buckets in the spring to helping to drive a fence post into the ground.

The inn, unlike many, does accept families with children. The nineteenth-century farmhouse has four rooms for guests, and these rooms are furnished with handsome Victorian furniture, quilts, and large, comfortable beds. One room has a private bath, and all rooms come with a country breakfast. The most popular breakfast is French toast with sausage and home fries. The kitchen and dining room are huge and welcoming and feature lots of antique furniture. One of the living rooms has an old pump organ and a Victrola.

If a couple of nights aren't enough for you, they will accommodate you for a full week with a room, three meals a day, and a barbecue, plus other activities; the rates are upwards of $330 per adult and $180 per child. The rates for a room by the night—including breakfast—are $75 for the room with a private bath for two adults and $65 for the other three rooms. In addition to a herd of milking cattle, the inn is home to an assortment of sheep, swans, geese, chickens, and rams, as well as a friendly housecat named Sleepy. The Berkson gives you a good idea of what it's like to live on a farm. Berkson Farms Inn, Enosburg Falls; (802) 933–2522; www.berksonfarms.com.

East of Enosburg, the town of **Montgomery** has two villages, 2 miles apart, and is known as the **Covered Bridge Capital** of Vermont. There are seven bridges here, most still in daily use. Most are also within sight of a main road, or very close to one, making them easy to tour. Three of them span gorges with waterfalls, although these are usually difficult to see, because the banks are steep and wooded.

As you drive east on Route 118, just before the sign that welcomes you to Montgomery, is the Longley Covered Bridge, built in 1863 by the Jewett brothers, as were the next two.

The second covered bridge is the Comstock, built in 1883 as a lattice-type bridge. The third covered bridge, which was built in 1890, is the Fuller Bridge, located just off the green past the post office.

Two more stand just to the west of Route 118 as it heads south from Montgomery Center. The first, on Hutchins Mill Road, sits astride a falls and gorge that you can actually get a pretty good look at. The other is on the old Gibou Road. A new bridge now bypasses the old one, situated almost over the falls, but you can see the unused bridge right beside the new road.

Breakfasts at the ***Phineas Swann Bed & Breakfast*** are not just a meal, they're an event, with home-baked breads and jams made from the berries grown in the backyard. The whole place is welcoming (to both you and your pet), with well-decorated rooms and big-band music in the background at afternoon tea. But it's not a bit fussy, and you'll be perfectly at home here in your hiking boots or ski clothes. The owners are long on sense of humor and short on pretensions, although their inn ranks right up there with the best. Rates start at $99 in the main inn, while the suites in the carriage house overlooking the river, with whirlpool baths and fireplaces, are as high as $295. Rates include a full gourmet breakfast and afternoon tea. Cooking is what co-owner John Perkins loves most, so ask ahead if they will serve dinner while you're there. The inn is right on Main Street, P.O. Box 43, Montgomery Center, 05471; (802) 326–4306; www.phineasswann.com.

Down the street is ***Trout River Traders,*** in a classic old Vermont country-store building. It's a handy place to stop for lunch or pick up a picnic. The owners search Vermont for the best products—breads, coffee, meat—and much of the food is made on site. Pick up an espresso or cappuccino and sit and watch the Trout River flow by. The store also carries a nice line of Vermont products, including maple syrup, of course, as well as pottery, Vermont books, kitchenware, penny candy, candles, and antiques. You will also want to look at their gallery of art by local artists.

Besides the unusual collection of items for sale, one of the attractions is the soda fountain, built in 1929. The fountain countertop is a solid slab of Vermont green marble. The back of the store overlooks Trout River, which can be pretty exciting in the spring. You can savor your homemade chili at a table on the back porch.

The original store was built in 1876 and served as a post office, general store, and town clerk's office at various points in history.

Call them at (802) 326–3058. The store is open for breakfast, lunch, and dinner from 8:00 a.m. to 10:00 p.m. Wednesday through Sunday, www .troutrivertraders.com.

Jay Peak, the state's northernmost ski area, is north of Montgomery along Route 242. Here, the snow falls deeper than in other parts of the state and the skiing is among the best in Vermont. But it is not only for skiers; it is a year-round resort in the northern Vermont wilderness.

In summer the aerial tramway brings hikers and walkers to the top of the mountain. The resort has a self-guided tour called the ***Mountain Ecology Nature Trail;*** pick up the small guide to the nature trail at the resort welcome center. The trail winds down the mountain and takes about an hour and a half for the average hiker. At the upper end it passes through conifers and by an alpine pond, where the delicate ecosystem is explained. At lower levels the Forest Loop Trail travels past typical north woods trees and plants. Look for the trees hollowed by woodpeckers, the tracks and droppings of moose and deer, and the headwaters of the Jay Branch. The upper end of the famed ***Vermont Long Trail*** passes through the area.

Winter at Jay brings some of the best skiing in Vermont, on seventy-six trails. Covering two peaks, the alpine and Nordic trails cover more than 50 miles of territory. The longest run is more than 3 miles long and the alpine trails are about 20 percent beginner with the balance split evenly between intermediate and advanced skier levels. Vertical drop here is 2,153 feet, making it one of the highest in New England. All of this territory is served by a multitude of double, triple, and quad chairlifts; moving carpets; a T-bar; and the only aerial Tramway in Vermont. Carrying sixty passengers, it makes six trips per hour. Jay also has off-piste areas that are open to skiers with appropriate skills and good judgment. Jay's rates are reasonable for this quality of skiing, with adult tickets at $65 ($45 ages six to eighteen) and an unbelievable rate of $15 for seniors (Canadians at par). Vermonters get their tickets for $45 ($35 juniors). It is a full-service resort with trailside condos and other accommodation options. Those staying at the resort get free day care for kids aged two to seven, no lodging charge for kids fourteen and under, and a mid-week lesson. One big part of Jay's charm is the influence of its French neighbors who come here to ski in preference to Mont Tremblant and other Quebec areas. On weekends from mid-January to mid-March a luxury ski bus runs from Montreal for $10 round trip (ask about the SDC program). Jay Peak Resort is close to the Jay-Westfield town line, west of Lake Memphremagog, 4850 Vermont Route 242, Jay; (802) 988–2611 or (800) 451–4449; www.jay peakresort.com.

The heavy snows in this region also bring cross-country skiers to the trails of the ***Hazen's Notch Association,*** a member-supported nonprofit corporation dedicated to conservation, environmental teaching, and the responsible use of land. The association maintains 40 miles of trails in winter over conservation lands. During summer 15 miles of these trails are open for hiking and include short trails like the Beaver Ponds Trail and the longer and more strenuous Burnt Mountain Trail, which provides views out over neighboring mountains and valleys. Hiking in summer is free, but there is a charge for cross-country skiing (to defray grooming costs). A contribution to the association at any time of year is welcomed. This is truly spectacular country and there are trails at all skill and difficulty levels. In winter they are open seven days a week 9:00 a.m. to 4:00 p.m., Monday through Friday, and 9:00 a.m. to 5:00 p.m., Saturday and Sunday. They are on Route 58 in Montgomery Center in Hazen's Notch, P.O. Box 478, Montgomery Center, 05471; (802) 326–4799; www.hazensnotch.org.

As you leave Montgomery Center, take a left onto Route 58 East, which climbs and twists and turns into a dirt road about a mile up from town. Great views soon abound. The road follows some parts of the **Bayley-Hazen Military Road,** for which some of the local landmarks are named, including Hazen's Notch State Park. About 5 miles out of the town of Montgomery Center, you'll come across a huge rock outcropping—it looks like you're going to drive right into the mountain. This is **Hazen's Notch,** and Sugarloaf Mountain, with an altitude of 2,520 feet, lies directly behind it.

Past the notch, the second left, where the sign says HAZEN'S NOTCH CAMP-GROUND, leads to **McAllister Pond,** a beautiful body of water for fishing and swimming.

The Champlain Islands

A totally different landscape awaits if you travel northwest from Burlington instead of northeast. At times you'll forget and think it's a seascape, especially if haze obscures the Adirondacks across the lake. North of Colchester, take Route 2 toward **South Hero,** which you will reach via a long bridge. Just before you leave the mainland, you'll pass Sandbar State Park. Even though you're not on the ocean, these island towns have a vague seaside resort feeling, but not quite as crowded.

Vacationing families have been coming here for generations, primarily because not much changes in the islands from one year—or decade—to the next. Moreover, the islands are compact enough that you can spend the day exploring from South Hero to East Alburg, see about everything there is to see, and still have time to return to the mainland—or, after collapsing in one of the inns or B&Bs on the islands, still have enough energy to go for a long bike ride the next day.

If you decide to just stick to Route 2 and its immediate environs, you'll have plenty to explore, from the numerous antiques shops that dot the islands to the various historic sites, from **Ste. Anne's Shrine** on Isle la Motte to the **Hyde Log Cabin** on Grand Isle.

In North Hero, the **North Hero House** is an establishment known for its rooms and its restaurant. It has several different choices for lodging, ranging from the restored inn house to the Cove House, which has rooms with screened porches that directly overlook the lake. These lakeside lodgings are popular with families, since the inn has its own sandy beach below. In the main building, furnishings are often antiques or quality reproductions, and some rooms on the front have delightful screened porches overlooking the lake as well. Mid-week rates begin a $125 during peak season, and include breakfast for two.

If you plan to eat dinner at the North Hero House, either as an inn guest or as a visitor, be prepared for a wait, since the place is popular with locals and with some of the aforementioned families who have been coming here in the summers for decades. What's ideal is to dine on the screened-in porch that faces the Cove House on a late-summer night just as the sky turns to dusk. The menu offers meat, fish, and pasta dishes prepared simply but very nicely, and there's a well-stocked wine cellar. The chef has a way with seafood, especially salmon, and wows everyone with his maple salad dressing. (If you see someone at the next table licking a salad plate, you'll know why.) It's a good idea to reserve a table for dinner on the porch. Entrees are $12 to $25. Breakfast and dinner packages are available with rooms.

Write to the North Hero House, P.O. Box 207, North Hero, VT 05474, or call (802) 372–4732 or (888) 525–3644; www.northherohouse.com.

To explore the islands or delta on a day trip by sea kayak, reserve a space with ***True North Kayak Tours.*** Programs and tours for individuals and groups smaller than four persons are $125 per person. Programs and tours for groups of eight or more are $85 per person. Basic skill instruction for beginners for two hours is $45 per person (equipment not included). Full-day instruction (10:00 a.m. to 3:00 p.m.) is $100 per person. Their summer camp for kids is a five-day program that operates in July and August. Other options include an inn-to-inn paddle, overnight trips, and fall foliage tours. The backdrop for all these trips is Lake Champlain and its surrounding mountains. True North Kayak Tours offices are at 53 Nash Place, Burlington, 05401; (802) 860–1910; www.vermontkayak.com.

TO LEARN MORE IN NORTHWEST VERMONT AND THE CHAMPLAIN VALLEY

Stowe Area Association,
Box 1320, Stowe, VT 05672;
(800) 24–STOWE;
www.stoweinfo.com.

Jay Peak Area Association,
for information on the far north,
R.R. 2, Box 137, Jay, VT 05859;
(800) 882–7460.

More Places to Stay in Northwest Vermont and the Champlain Valley

(All area codes 802)

BURLINGTON

Lang House on Main
360 Main Street
652–2500 or (877) 919–9799
www.langhouse.com
Afternoon tea is served, and breakfast is created by a chef.

The Inn on Trout River
241 Main Street
326–4391 or (800) 338–7049
www.troutinn.com
A B&B in the restored mansion of the owner of the town's first automobile.

STOWE

Edson Hill Manor
1500 Edson Hill Road
253–7371 or
(800) 621–0284
www.edsonhillmanor.com
A summer base for hiking and in winter for tobogganing, sledding, or cross-country skiing. B&B and modified American plans available, as well as special packages. B&B plan rooms begin at $139 in low season.

VERGENNES

Emerson Guest House Bed and Breakfast
82 Main Street
877–3293
www.emersonhouse.com
A comfortable Victorian home in downtown Vergennes.

WATERBURY

Stowe Cabins in the Woods
Route 100, Box 128
244–8533
www.stowecabins.com
Modern, comfortable, and in a beautiful pine-woods setting just off Route 100.

More Places to Eat in Northwest Vermont and the Champlain Valley

(All area codes 802)

COLCHESTER

Junior's Restaurant
6 Roosevelt Highway
655–0000; for the pizzeria, call 655–5555
Southern Italian, with excellent zuppa di pesce and moderate prices.

ENOSBURG FALLS

Abbey Restaurant
6212 Route 105
933–4747 or (800) 696–4748
Known for hearty portions and Sunday brunch.

FAIRFAX

The Country Pantry
951 Main Street
849–6364
Open for three meals daily, with enormous breakfasts (the Belgian waffles are wonderful) at $3.75 to $4.00; dinner entrees are all under $13.00.

MONTGOMERY CENTER

Barney's
72 Main Street
326–4682
Three meals daily from 6:30 a.m. to 10:00 p.m. It's inexpensive and reliable and offers interesting dinner entrees.

NEWPORT

East Side Restaurant and Pub
47 Landing Street
334–2340
With a solid menu featuring prime rib, pot roast, and seafood it's also known for its chowder. Their salad bar comes with entrees. It overlooks Lake Memphremagog. Monday through Friday 11:00 a.m. to 9:00 p.m., Saturday and Sunday 8:00 a.m. to 9:00 p.m.

NORTH TROY

North Troy Village Pub and Restaurant
School Street
988–4063
Combines good food with a lot of history, which owner Irene will be glad to share if asked. It's open from 5:00 p.m.; closed Tuesday; in winter, open Thursday through Sunday.

STOWE

Gracie's
1652 Mountain Road
253–6888
A good stop for mega-burgers, lunch sandwiches, and a general menu of moderately innovative dishes. Portions are gener-ous, and they're open from 5:00 p.m. until 10:00 p.m.

WATERBURY

Tanglewoods
179 Guptil Road
244–7855
Off Route 100 north of Waterbury, an outstanding New American menu with a penchant for the South-west is offered here. Opens at 5:30 for dinner, Tuesday through Sunday.

NORTHEAST KINGDOM

All of the Northeast Kingdom could be considered off the beaten path simply because it's so far removed from everything else. Some of the most sparsely populated areas in the east fall within the boundaries of the counties that make up the Kingdom: Caledonia, Essex, and Orleans.

Credit for the coinage of "the Northeast Kingdom" usually goes to Senator George Aiken, one of the most popular leaders in Vermont history (and who also loved to fish in the region.) "Such beautiful country up here," he said in a speech in Lyndonville in 1949, "it should be called 'the Northeast Kingdom.'"

But according to *The Vermont Encyclopedia,* years earlier in the 1940s at least two other men so referred to their region. These were Newport newspaper publisher Wallace Gilpin and former Vermont senator W. Arthur Simpson. Additional legends crop up from time to time as well, a testimony to the uniqueness and beauty of the region, as well as to the fact that no other area of the state has so far been deemed worthy of its own moniker.

The Kingdom contains three of the four grants and gores in Vermont, land parcels that were left over when town

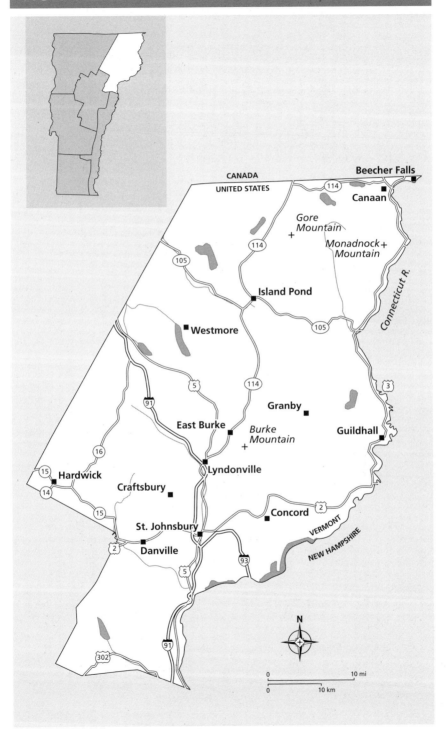

boundaries were set. The three—Warners Grant, Warren Gore, and Averys Gore—are nestled side by side in the extreme northeast, one town south of the Canadian border. Both Warners Grant and Averys Gore contain no roads, although Route 114 does cut through Warren Gore. All three, along with the adjacent town of Lewis, add up to a population of zero. In fact, most of the towns in the Kingdom have populations in the three figures, and sometimes less than that.

Towns in this northeastern frontier were settled later than towns in other parts of Vermont. While parts of southern Vermont attracted pioneers from "overcrowded" Connecticut and Massachusetts as early as 1764, much of northeastern Vermont was settled after 1785 and even well into the nineteenth century.

Some farms in Kingdom towns that front the Connecticut River—towns like Lemington, Guildhall, and Brunswick—still follow the boundaries of the settlement grants and charters of their first settlers. Farmland was laid out in long, narrow strips to allow every settler to have a little of the rich, fertile land that bordered the river, which also served as a water and transportation source.

The Kingdom holds a way of life that disappeared from other parts of the country long ago. Cherish this as you drive over its back roads.

Route 14 North

Route 14 gently climbs out of Montpelier and twists past farms and pastures, while the Kingsbury Branch River plays tag with the road, appearing first on the east side of the highway, then on the west, and finally feeding into Sabin Pond at the northern end of Calais (pronounced CAL-us) and the southern border of Woodbury.

' After a gradual climb (this, by the way, is what Vermonters call flat), Greenwood Lake appears, its shoreline a bustling community in summer

AUTHOR'S TOP HIGHLIGHTS

Architecture on Main Street,
St. Johnsbury

Fairbanks Museum and Planetarium,
St. Johnsbury

St. Johnsbury Athenaeum and Art Gallery

Burke Mountain Ski Area,
East Burke

and all but dead in winter. Here and there you'll see old abandoned houses, sagging barns, and granite block walls, remnants of earlier, more prosperous times. **Woodbury** holds at least two distinctive claims in the Vermont Hall of Fame: (1) The town affirms it sent more soldiers per capita to the Civil War than any other Vermont town, and (2) of the twenty-eight lakes and ponds found in Woodbury, all of their streams and brooks flow out of the town, not into it. (Farther north in Vermont, many of the rivers flow north into Canada, although the Lamoille recrosses back into Vermont farther west.)

By contrast, **Hardwick** is a relatively busy center of commerce in the Kingdom. Hardwick served as the final destination for the Hardwick and Woodbury Railroad, which was built in 1896 to transport the mammoth blocks of granite from the quarries in Woodbury north to the mills in Hardwick. The railroad had the distinction of the steepest grades and most hairpin turns in the East. The tracks were taken up in 1940 when the quarries were abandoned. In 2008, Hardwick landed on the national radar through a town-wide move to create a sustainable economy based on local food production. Heart of that effort is the nonprofit Center for an Agricultural Economy, the backers of which intend to spread this model beyond Hardwick's borders.

The **Brick House Shop/Perennial Pleasures** off Route 16 in East Hardwick is an extensive English herb garden with everything from catnip and lemon thyme to shrubs, roses, and lilies, all clearly marked.

According to local legend, in 1796 pioneer Samuel Stevens was exploring what a year later would become the town of Hardwick, named after Hardwick, Massachusetts. He stabbed a spot in the ground with his walking stick near where the house currently stands, and the stick grew into a willow tree.

There's a tea garden with a gazebo, and afternoon tea ($8.00) is served Tuesday to Sunday, Memorial Day through Labor Day from 12:30 until 4:30 p.m. Reservations are appreciated. Cucumber sandwiches on thin whole-wheat bread with a cream cheese dressing made with mayonnaise, horseradish, dill, and pepper are served, along with scones, homemade jams, cakes, and a variety of teas. The gift shop has many garden-related items and such kitchenware as teapots, honey dippers, twig baskets, oils, ceramics, and both marble and wooden mortar-and-pestle sets.

The nursery is open from May through late September, Tuesday to Sunday from 9:00 a.m. to 5:00 p.m. (it's closed Monday). Brick House, Brick House Road, East Hardwick; (802) 472-5104.

To drive along a piece of Revolutionary War history, take Route 16 north for 3 miles until you see a road on the left with a sign for Greensboro.

ANNUAL EVENTS IN THE NORTHEAST KINGDOM

Early January: Northeast Kingdom Sled Dog Races, held at Island Pond. For dates and locations, call (802) 723–6300; www.islandpond.com.

Late May: Annual Spring Festival in Hardwick Village, with parade, horse pulling, and a barbecue; (802) 472–6555.

Mid-September: Oktoberfest at Burke Mountain Ski Area, with German food, music, dancing, and beer; (802) 626–3322.

Late September to Early October: Northeast Kingdom Fall Foliage Festival, throughout the towns of Cabot, Peacham, Barnet, Groton, Plainfield, and others, with one day's festivities (crafts shows, village tours, flea markets, community suppers) in each town; (802) 563–2472.

New Year's Eve: Torchlight Parade, with the Burke Mountain staff skiing down the trails with lighted torches, followed by dinner and dancing at the base lodge; (802) 626–3322.

The Northeast Kingdom Chamber of Commerce has an excellent Web site at www.nekchamber.com, with monthly guides to activities such as public skating, winter tracking, and snowshoeing in winter; the annual woodsman competition in fall; and the annual Kingdom Triathalon in August.

Follow this road for 2 miles and continue straight past Tolman Corner until you see ***Caspian Lake*** on your right. This stretch of road is part of the ***Bayley-Hazen Military Road,*** a 55-mile-long road originally authorized by George Washington in 1776 so that Revolutionary War troops could have easy access into Canada to launch surprise attacks against the British. A monument can be found on the east side of the road, overlooking Caspian Lake and just past the first road on the left past Tolman Corner. Colonel Jacob Bayley of Newbury directed 110 workers in building the road from his hometown on the Connecticut River to the town of Cabot, 20 miles away, in forty-five days. He paid the laborers $10 a month and half a pint of rum per day.

After one month construction was halted when Washington realized that if the road made it easier for the colonists to reach Canada, then the British would reach the colonists quicker as well.

In April 1779 construction on the road began anew. This time Colonel Moses Hazen led his road builders 35 miles farther into Westfield. But work ceased again six months later when Hazen thought the Brits were gathering steam, and construction that was planned to go through Swanton and up to St. John, Quebec ended for a final time. Two years later the war was over, and the road was used as a major artery for development by settlers.

Willey's Store on Main Street in Greensboro Village has frequently been called the quintessential Vermont general store, as have many others around the state. Once you step inside, you'll see that it's the clear winner.

Willey's has camping gear, nails, hinges, fishing lures, greeting cards, toiletries, trashy summer paperbacks, a deli department, a selection of wines, phyllo pastry, and, of course, maple syrup and Ben & Jerry's. Open 7:00 a.m. to 5:30 p.m. Monday through Friday, and 8:00 a.m. to 5:30 on weekends. Willey's Store is on Main Street, Greensboro; (802) 533–2621.

Many consider *Craftsbury* to be the gold medalist in the picture-postcard division of Vermont attractions. But back in 1781, when the town was first chartered, not many of the original grantees could envision the town's promise. In fact, the grantees of most Vermont towns were residents of Massachusetts and Connecticut; a relatively tiny number of them actually acted on their land grants—typically one hundred acres. Most sold the land to people who had little to lose by heading north and settling the wilderness. The original grantees were moderately wealthy men who did not want to forgo the luxuries of "civilization" for unknown territories.

The founder of Craftsbury, however, was one of the few exceptions. Ebenezer Crafts, one of the original grantees of Craftsbury, was from Sturbridge, Massachusetts, and served as an officer in the Revolutionary War after graduating from Yale University. He founded the village in 1788 (seven years after the town was chartered) and sent his son, Samuel, to Harvard. After Samuel graduated, he returned to Craftsbury to serve as town clerk and later was governor of the state for two terms.

People still follow Samuel Craft's example by returning to Craftsbury, but unlike Sam, they stay only for the summer. North of the village center is Craftsbury Common, where the *Inn on the Common* offers lodging, along with breakfast and dinner for in-house guests.

The inn is an amalgam of new and old: antique beds and claw-foot tubs together with VCRs and tennis courts, giving guests the best of new and old Vermont. The inn's eighteen rooms are scattered throughout several buildings on the grounds, on both sides of the main thoroughfare through town. There's an old, immaculately kept cemetery right next to one of the buildings. The gravestones of both Ebenezer and Samuel Crafts are in the graveyard, right up near the front. On summer evenings after dinner, stroll through the cemetery and read the inscriptions, some of which date from 1790.

WORTH SEEING

Cabot Creamery,
Main Street, Cabot. You can tour their cheese-making operation and sample Vermont cheddars; (802) 837-4261; www.cabotcheese.com.

Groton State Forest,
Groton, where you'll find camping, recreation areas, hiking, geological and natural points of interest, and plenty of the great outdoors.

The Inn on the Common offers a modified American plan, which includes breakfast and dinner. Rates for their doubles start at $165 in summer and $145 in the winter. Nearby activities include swimming in either a pool or a lake, tennis, croquet, and hiking. For more information and for special packages, write to the Inn on the Common, 1162 North Craftsbury Road, Box 75, Craftsbury Common, 05827, or call (802) 586–9619 or (800) 521–2233; www .innonthecommon.com.

The *Craftsbury Outdoor Center* was begun in 1976 in a defunct private boys' school. A variety of sports weeks are held here year-round, from running and sculling camps to walking weeks. You can stay here without enrolling in one of the special programs and participate in all sports. There are 140 acres, with 600 more acres serving as a nature preserve. Currently, 65 miles of trails exist for skiers and hikers to explore, with a few more miles to be added during the next several years. The rooms are what you would expect of a former boys' school, but it hardly matters, since most of the guests spend their time outside being active. The daily rate includes a room, some sports fees, and three meals a day. The food is delicious and served buffet-style, with the emphasis on complex carbohydrates to fuel all the exercise you'll get at the center. Vegetarians are amply accommodated, and during summer the vegetables are from the center's own gardens.

The center is open year-round, and the room rate starts at $98 midweek in winter, and $102 in summer for two, and includes three meals and the use of ski or snowshoe trails in winter, the beach and canoes in summer. Rooms with private baths are available for an extra fee. Special multiday programs are priced according to their length and the recreation activities included. For more information, write to the Craftsbury Outdoor Center, Lost Nation Road, Craftsbury Common, 05827, or call (802) 586–7767 or (800) 729–7751; check www.craftsbury.com for details and special packages.

Newport, just south of the Canadian border on Lake Memphremagog, is a utilitarian kind of town, blending touches of the twenty-first century and bilingual traffic signs with the ambience of an old Vermont town. Even though Newport has always depended somewhat on border trade, it's not especially geared to tourists; it's more for Canadians and Vermonters who need to get their business done as quickly and cheaply as possible.

The town—it's actually a city, the only incorporated city in the Kingdom—rises from the shore of Lake Memphremagog, which means "beautiful waters" in the Algonquin language.

St. Mary Catholic Church has a fine view of Lake Memphremagog from its commanding position high on Prospect Street, on the west side of town. This church with twin granite towers is a mariners' church, uncommon so far inland. The dedication stone reads may 1904, and an inscription reads *Ave maris stella,* a statement that combines Mary and the nautical reference point of the North Star. An anchor is carved into the stone, and a lighted figure of Mary stands between the two towers. This landmark is visible from most of the town at night. The church is open to the public only for Saturday and Sunday services. Call (802) 334–7371 for hours; 5 Clermont Terrace, Newport.

Since 2001, **Lago Trattoria** on Main Street in Newport has earned three *Yankee Travel Magazine* Editor's Picks in a row. All of the pasta, bread, sauces, and dessert items are homemade and scrumptious. Says *Ski Vermont* magazine, "Chef Frank Richardi has quickly become a ski country star for his thin-crust grilled pizzas, homemade ravioli, and signature dishes like shrimp and clams Amalfi with linguini, dramatically served right in the pan." The seafood is fresh; and all Italian products are imported. A different steak is featured every night. Entrees range from $16 (a pasta quattro formaggio, for example: a bit of Gorgonzola, fresh Parmigiano Reggiano, Romano, and fontina, served with fresh baby peas, cream, and fresh herbs); to $28 (maybe the rack of lamb: marinated with a little Vermont maple syrup, fresh rosemary, Dijon mustard, and grilled to perfection). Frank offers not only specialty martinis, but an extensive wine list, featuring many fine Italian wines. Open seven nights a week, 5:00 p.m. until closing. 95 Main Street; (802) 334–8222; www.lagotrattoria.com.

The Northeast Corner

Snuggled into the far corner of the state, this region north of St. Johnsbury and bordered by Canada, New Hampshire, and I–91 is to many people the heart and soul of the Northeast Kingdom. While its border with New Hampshire is pretty easy to identify—in all but one tiny spot, you must cross a river to change states—crossing into Canada is less obvious.

What about border guards? When you cross on a road that actually goes somewhere in Canada, there will be the usual border formalities. But at other places, back roads may stray across the line and back again without your even being aware of it. The rule is that if you can't get anywhere from the road, no one cares much. Or so it seems. In reality, however, the entire boundary between the two countries, which is the longest undefended international boundary in the world, is closely watched. Surveillance cameras alert authorities on both sides to any unusual crossings, even on foot. These illegal crossings are investigated, so the casual appearance of the border on remote roads is misleading.

The border is even more fun in **Derby Line.** As you might guess from its name, the town sits right on the boundary line, with residential streets wandering back and forth randomly. The colors of street signs change at the line, but it is otherwise invisible. The town's opera house and library is an impressive building that ties Derby Line firmly to its neighboring town in Quebec. The international border is marked by an inlaid wooden strip across the center of the reading-room floor. You can read a book there while sitting in two countries.

Upstairs, the theater has the stage in Canada, while the audience applauds from the United States. Anyone who plays there instantly becomes an international star. Some homes sit astride the line, too, so you can imagine what fun this was for revenue men during Prohibition. Guests could enter through a "dry" front door and drink quite legally in the kitchen.

Westmore is a popular summer camp area. Westmore was chartered in 1781, but its grantees decided not to organize until twenty-three years later. Since then, the population has grown at a snail's pace, still totaling only a few hundred. **Lake Willoughby** has a lot to do with it; virtually all of the tiny town's industry is geared toward summer visitors, from the campground and two restaurants to the six inns and clusters of cottages that overlook the lake.

For all its proximity to tiny Vermont towns—East Haven and Victory— **East Burke** is a relatively sophisticated area, with a high-quality restaurant and shopping. Nearby Burke Mountain Ski Area doesn't hurt, but those who come to ski the big mountains and do the Vermont nightlife in places like Killington, Stowe, and Stratton usually ask, "Where's Burke?" when the topic of Green Mountain ski areas comes up.

Between West Burke and Burke Mountain Ski Area, you'll drive for 5 miles through the West Burke Municipal Forest as well as on some pretty back roads. Before you make the left to head to Burke Mountain, drive into the downtown area of East Burke, making a sharp right-hand turn where you see the sign for the **Friendly Art Gallery,** aka **The Art Cache.**

This gallery exhibits established artists' works in oil, watercolor, acrylic, pen and ink, and prints. Every June the Art Cache has an Annual Sports Art Show, with art themed around golf, tennis, water sports, equestrian activities, and, of course, skiing.

Down the main road of East Burke is **Bailey's & Burke Country Store,** an institution for decades for skiers and snowmobilers. If you've ever had any desire to furnish your entire house in Vermontiana, you can do your one-stop shopping here. Household goods, clothing, toiletries, toys, stuffed animals, knickknacks, wicker furniture, live bait, groceries—these are just a few of the items available. In fact, you can't drive through East Burke or go skiing at Burke Mountain without stopping at Bailey's—it's physically impossible. And Bailey's is the reason there's no mall within a good two-hour drive of here, for it goes one step beyond a mall by filling a number of rooms, balconies, and alcoves with souvenirs and necessities alike.

Along with the groceries, fresh bagels, trendy condiments, and decorator items for those who want to make their home look "Vermont-y," you'll find tucked into a back corner, next to the nail-and-screws bin, a community bulletin board with menus from area restaurants and other useful information. Bailey's has achieved the perfect blend of serving both the local residents and the great variety of travelers and skiers who pass through. The store's hours testify to the owners' dedication to being there when townspeople need them: Sunday through Thursday, 7:00 a.m. to 7:00 p.m.; Friday and Saturday, 7:00 a.m. to 8:00 p.m. Bailey's & Burke Country Store, 466 Route 114, East Burke, or call (802) 626–9250; www.baileysandburke.com.

Burke Mountain is a family-friendly ski area where Olympians train, but intermediate and beginning skiers can find plenty of comfortable runs, including a novice trail from the top. Facilities are low-key and good, not flashy or "Ye Olde Swisse," as has become the trend farther south. Burke's forty-five alpine trails are only 7 miles from exit 23 of I–93, and there is lodging available

Visit an Artist

The Vermont Crafts Council sponsors an annual Memorial Day **Open Studio Weekend**, which gives visitors an opportunity to go into the studios of more than 120 artists and fine craftspeople all over the state. In addition to artists in many media, studios include those of makers of fine reproduction and contemporary furniture, potters, and photographers. You can get a map of the arts tour from the Vermont Arts Council, 1344 State Street, Montpelier, VT 05602, and from any state welcome center, or call the council at (802) 223–3380 or check out www.vermontcrafts.com.

in the nearby area. Although Burke has an average of more than 250 inches of snow per year, they have snowmaking capacity that exceeds 80 percent, and it is constantly growing. A quarter of the trails are novice, 45 percent intermediate, and the balance expert. Burke Mountain's cross-country area has 50-odd miles of trails through mixed forests and across meadows with mountain views. It begins right at the base of the ski slopes, handy for families who have both kinds of skiers. Rentals and lessons are available at either. For the downhill area, call (802) 626–3322; for cross-country, best information as at www.kingdomtrails.org; Burke Mountain Ski Area, P.O. Box 247, East Burke, 05832; www.skiburke.com.

In the summer and fall, you can drive to the top of Burke Mountain on the Toll Road, which is the other use for that long novice ski trail from the top. At any time of year, the view is lovely and includes the ridges of Mounts Pisgah and Hoar, with Lake Willoughby between them. From this distance, they look like a single ridge with a giant bite chewed out of the center.

When the O'Reillys, who had several children, tired of being consigned to look-alike motels when they traveled with their family, they resolved to create a fine inn where children were not only welcome but could also pursue their own pleasures without interfering with adult guests' enjoyment of theirs. They have succeeded admirably with the warm and hospitable ***Wildflower Inn,*** on a hilltop with views over the mountains. Stunning gardens frame every view in the spring, summer, and fall, while autumn brings a panorama of brilliant foliage. The swimming pool is set in the gardens, with a view of its own.

Kids of all ages get a lot of attention—teddy-bear-shaped pancakes at breakfast (parents get a full hot breakfast, too, starting with homemade granola chock-full of giant pecan pieces), a barn full of baby animals to pat and watch, bunk beds in many of the rooms, a sledding hill (with sleds) and lighted skating rink, playground equipment, a batting cage, a pitching machine, a basketball court, a playhouse, and a playroom with games and a trunkful of costumes. Mealtimes are planned so parents can have an early prelude while kids eat dinner (from a separate menu filled with their favorites, complete with drink and dessert), then enjoy their own dinner later while the kids are entertained elsewhere—or are sound asleep.

Guests without children are just as much at home in these well-decorated rooms and suites, the latter with kitchenettes. We liked the Old Schoolhouse, a separate building that's perfect for a honeymoon suite. A dozen miles of cross-country ski trails (free to guests) wind through the property, and weekend winter carnivals in March bring skating parties, contests, and dogsledding. Sleigh rides and hayrides are available regularly. Room rates start at $130, summer or winter, with only a modest increase during foliage season, and include a hearty breakfast.

The dining room, which overlooks impeccably kept gardens and mountain views from a glass-enclosed porch, has an eclectic and creative menu. Grilled chicken breast is served with a tomato salsa or marinated in lemon and dill, with Vermont chèvre over a coulis of blackberries. Shrimp and scallops are blended in a Thai curry, yellowfin tuna is topped with tequila-lime butter, and salmon is glazed in orange and basil. The wine list is reasonably priced, and the dining staff can describe preparation details. Have you guessed yet that we've had some great meals here? Dinner is served to guests and the public, with entree prices ranging from $12 to $28.

The Wildflower Inn is at 2059 Darling Hill Road, Lyndonville; (802) 626–8310 or (800) 627–8310; www.wildflowerinn.com.

On the same property is **Vermont Children's Theater,** which for over twenty years has produced two musicals each summer, one a Broadway show and the other written especially for eight- to thirteen-year-old actors. Performances are held in mid-July and August; tickets are inexpensive, or you can watch rehearsals in the afternoons in the 200-seat barn theater on Darling Hill Road. Call (802) 626–5358 for information on current productions and summer workshops.

The entire property was once part of the 8,000-acre farm of Elmer A. Darling, an enormously successful hotelier in New York and a major benefactor of the town. You can see his mansion and huge main barn farther up the road, both privately owned. Beyond the mansion, and also part of the original farm, you'll find the **Inn at Mountainview Farm.** Although it no longer produces cream, butter, or crops on what was once the largest farm in Vermont with 953 acres, its 440 intact, quiet acres of farmland hold farm buildings that will entice you to explore them.

The stately brick main house, which once served as the creamery for the farm, is now a fourteen-room B&B, with each room or suite named after a local town: Sutton, Sheffield, and Wheelock are three of them. There's an understated, casual elegance to the inn that owner Marilyn Pastore has worked hard to attain. There are several sitting rooms downstairs, an ice chest in the lobby, and braided rugs on all the floors, which are painted cement. The breakfast room still contains the old steam engine that provided the power to run the creamery machines; today antique furnishings are found in the common areas and in each bedroom.

A number of restored farm buildings are scattered across the land, and the weather vane atop each tells its purpose: The dairy barn has a cow weather vane that measures 5 feet in length, and on top of the creamery is a butter churn. The clock on top of the 1912 post-and-beam barn chimes on the half hour, and the structure was a model for nineteenth-century agricultural efficiency. Upstairs, hay was stored. Farmhands would spread hay evenly throughout the barn, almost up to the rafters. When it was time to feed the horses, they'd rake the hay over to what looks like half-moon hot-tub structures at the sides of the barn, lift up the covers, and let the hay drop. The horses kept here were about sixteen hands high, and you can see where they chewed on the bottom of the barn's windows.

Rates at the Inn at Mountainview Farm start at $195. Some pets may be allowed by advance permission. Open May through October. You'll find the inn on Darling Hill Road, East Burke; (802) 535–7617; www.innmtnview.com.

South of the Burkes, you'll find another cluster of villages, all some variation on Lyndon, around the town of **Lyndonville.** You can't just buzz through this town because Route 5 makes two abrupt right-angle turns in the center of it. That's okay, since you'll want to look at some of the interesting architecture in the downtown business blocks, not to mention stopping for ice cream at Carmen's.

The **Miss Lyndonville Diner** on Route 5 (Broad Street) is related to the **Miss Vermonter Diner** down in St. Johnsbury, but it's not as big as its sister, and there are fewer out-of-state plates in the parking lot.

The original dining car has been enclosed but is still very much in evidence. The just-greasy-enough burgers are served plain and simple or as the Vermonter, a hamburger-and-thick-steak-fries combo with gravy spooned over both, with a side of slaw. Locals on lunch break hang out at the counter, read the paper, and catch up on local news and the weather.

The Miss Lyndonville is open from 6:00 a.m. until after supper, whenever the last person leaves. Call (802) 626–9890 for information.

We're not sure how **Trout River Brewery** got its name, since there is no Trout River that we know of in East Burke, where the brewery used to be, nor in Lyndonville, where it is now. But the name inspires some clever titles for the excellent brews: Hoppin' Mad Trout, Rainbow Red, and Rising River. Hoppin' Mad is an IPA, and Rising River is a seasonal ale made from rye but tasting very much like a wheat. Scottish Ale is always on their list, as is the Chocolate Oatmeal Stout, which is hearty enough to substitute for dinner. Speaking of which, the brewery serves good pizza from 4:00 p.m. to 9:00 p.m. on Friday and Saturday evenings. They serve pints and sampler trays Friday and Saturday from 11:00 a.m. until 5:00 p.m. at their brewery at 58 Broad Street, Lyndonville; (802) 626–9396; www.troutriverbrewing.com.

If you need to walk off the pizza or the ale, go to White Market on the green (open daily from 8:00 a.m. to 10:00 p.m.) and ask for the directions to the 6-mile **Lyndon Covered Bridge Walk.** If you are a member of the American Volkssport Association or IVV, its international counterpart, you will quickly recognize this as a sanctioned Volkswalk (and you can get credit if you pay a $2.00 fee), but anyone can take the walk free, any time between May and October. Simply sign in at the beginning and follow the directions through four covered bridges, past the Lyndon Institute, the college, a small museum, and some fine mountain and valley views. Other Volkswalks are sponsored by the Kingdom Kickers, the area's very active Volkssporting group, which also sponsors cross-country ski events and an Oktoberfest (see annual events listing on page 43). To learn more about Volkssporting, contact Merrily Wieland, P.O. Box 17, East Burke, 05832.

Three miles north of West Burke on Route 5 in Sutton is **Laplant's Sugar House,** where you'll find an old-fashioned 1,000-bucket sugar bush. During sugaring season you can visit the sugar bush and sample some syrup. Laplant's Sugar House, Sutton; (802) 467–3900.

Orleans is a village within the borders of **Barton,** and the two villages have shared an intense rivalry, ranging from good-natured athletic contests to outright fistfights. Orleans was originally settled as Barton Landing in 1821, and the rivalry started soon after. The final straw came in 1909, when the people of Barton Landing decided to change the name to Orleans, so as not to appear as an underling of Barton. In the past few decades, however, the rivalry has been changed to almost a friendship, since the two villages decided to build a union school together.

The town of Glover, to the south, was settled in 1797 by General John Glover, who was granted the town in gratitude for his service in the military during the Revolutionary War. But today Glover's most popular residents are a 180-degree turn from the town's military founder. Near the Glover General Store, turn onto Route 122 to find social commentary at the **Bread and Puppet Museum,** less than a mile up the road on your left.

Bread and Puppet is a theater troupe that travels all over the world presenting its political ideas to eager audiences. It was begun in 1963 on New York's Lower East Side by an artist-actor named Peter Schumann. He began Bread and Puppet by traveling around New England with a stick-puppet show telling stories from the Bible. Then the organization became more radical, using life-size puppets and performing in parades in New York. Schumann moved his troupe to Plainfield, Vermont, in 1970, then to its present location in Glover in 1974.

You'll never mistake them for conservatives, but all types of people used to show up at Bread and Puppet's annual Domestic Resurrection Circus, a two-day event that thousands of people participated in on the theater's pastures.

The Pond That Isn't There

The well-named Mud Pond was the source of the Barton River, which flowed north, providing power for the grist- and sawmills of Barton and Glover. But in dry summers, such as that of 1810, even the mud dried up, and the mills lay idle. About a mile south, but almost 100 feet higher, was the larger Long Pond, with plenty of water year-round. With his mill idle, owner Aaron Wilson did a little investigating in the mile of marshy brush between these ponds and discovered that their ends were really only 700 feet apart.

A little information can be a dangerous thing, so Wilson persuaded the men of Glover to dig a trench between the two, allowing some of the ample water in Long Pond to spill out and fill Mud Pond, providing water to run the mills downstream. Enough were convinced (possibly by his promise of a keg of rum when the work was done) that a group assembled on June 10 with picks and shovels. By noon, a trench was finished through the soft sand, and most of the men were sampling the rum as a few dug through the last few feet at the north end of Long Pond.

What no one knew was that inside the mound of fine sand holding the lake's end was a lining of packed clay, like the rim of a pottery bowl. When the first pickax broke that rim, the water quickly washed away the supporting sand, and the rim shattered. By the time the one billion or so gallons of water had reached Lake Memphremagog seven hours later, only one house was left in Glover, a few more in Barton, and the fields and pastures were 6 feet deep in sand and mud. Wilson's mill and all the other mills were gone. Trees and boulders were swept away by the wall of water, along with houses, barns, mill machinery, dams, and livestock. Water rose as high as 75 feet above river level in narrow places.

When the pond broke loose, several men ran ahead to warn people to run for high ground, so not a single life was lost. Everyone lost crops and livestock, but they had more than five tons of fish to salt for winter, which they found stranded along the shore, pulled from the mud, or caught in tributary streams into which the fish had fled as the turbulence entered the lake.

Foundations of the church and other buildings you see in Glover are built of stones cut from a 100-ton boulder swept into the village by the flood. And up on Route 16, look for a small sign on the west side of the road marking the low muddy area that was once the 300-acre surface of Long Pond.

But the big annual show, so famous that several alternative restaurants as far away as Brattleboro used to close for "Bread and Puppet Day," is no more. Instead, smaller shows are performed at 3:00 p.m. on Sunday afternoons in July and August. Call for a schedule of other performances and events. The museum is open all summer through October, and if you've never seen the theater's actors in performance, the museum can be a little overwhelming. The sign reads ENTER AT YOUR OWN RISK. Don't say you haven't been warned.

Bread and Puppet makes its point using 12-foot-high, larger-than-life-size puppets with huge heads and tiny bodies. But the exhibits do what a museum should do: make you think. Downstairs in the former horse stable—this was the former Dopp Farm—are montages of previous performances.

If downstairs is striking, then upstairs is an absolute assault on the senses, for everything hangs from the ceiling—a visual cacophony of papier-mâché globes, 12-foot-tall Ben Franklin look-alikes, and more. There's also a box of puppets for adults and kids to play with if inspiration hits. Across the road is the ***Cheap Art Bus,*** an old school bus filled with art and prints ranging from 10 cents to $15.00, though most go for around $5.00. The museum and shop are open every day from 10:00 a.m. to 6:00 p.m. June through October, and the museum is open the rest of the year by appointment. Bread and Puppet Museum, 753 Heights Road, Route 122, Glover; (802) 525–3031 or (802) 525–1271; www.theaterofmemory.com/art/bread/bread.html.

St. Johnsbury

St. Johnsbury developed as a busy northeastern Vermont outpost due to its location at the confluence of three major waterways: the Passumpsic, Moose, and Sleeper's Rivers. The Fairbanks family from Massachusetts also influenced the growth of the town—despite its appearance, St. Jay, as it's commonly called, is a town, not a city. By building a factory, Thaddeus Fairbanks, inventor of the lever scale, made good on the initial patent he was awarded in 1830.

Today the town seems to have two separate parallel main streets running through it, each with a totally different atmosphere. The lower one, Railroad Street, is the commercial area with facing rows of brick business blocks. Up the hill is ***Main Street,*** an avenue of fine Victorian residences, churches, and public edifices, several of which were designed by the architect Lambert Packard. Some of these are based on the Richardson Romanesque style (which Bostonians know well from the imposing Trinity Church on Copley Square). The centerpiece is the red sandstone ***Fairbanks Museum,*** a classic of Richardson style, which contrasts with the Victorian (and also Lambert Packard) but much more perpendicular Gothic style of the North Congregational Church opposite it. These and other outstanding Victorian buildings on Main Street—including Grace Methodist Church, which has a large Tiffany window—are described in a flyer mapping a thirty-minute walking tour of the street.

You can get this map and other fascinating brightly colored information sheets from the ***Fairbanks Museum and Planetarium,*** where you will

They Carried It to the End of the Earth

When Albert Bierstadt's monumental painting *The Domes of Yosemite* was brought from New York to St. Johnsbury in 1873 to be displayed in its specially built gallery, New York critics lamented it as a "profound loss to civilization." The 10-by-15-foot painting is one of the largest landscapes in the United States and is appropriately (well, maybe not, according to nineteenth-century New Yorkers) housed in the country's oldest Victorian art gallery still in its unadulterated original form. Most other galleries have been modernized, but like the neighboring Fairbanks Museum, this building remains a pristine monument to the age of great public museums.

This appropriation of things from the Big Apple didn't end with the painting, however. The street clock at the corner of Main Street and Eastern Avenue in front of the Athenaeum was formerly in the old Grand Central Station and was placed here in 1910, where it has told time (but not always the correct time) ever since.

certainly want to stop. This wonderful Victorian "cabinet of curiosities," which began as the private collections of the town's favorite son and benefactor, has an oak barrel–vaulted ceiling with an arcade of cherry and oak display cases forming an upper gallery. The building is as fascinating as its exhibits, which range from an interactive examination of Vermont's wetlands and the creatures that inhabit them to a bizarre collection of Victorian "bug art" portraits of Washington, Lincoln, and others. Be sure to stop at the wildflower identification table, where you will see fresh examples of wild plants in bloom locally during the current week. The requisite stuffed birds are from all over the world, as are the other natural history collections, although the wildlife displays concentrate on Vermont habitats.

Upstairs are old toys, dollhouses, books, and stone tools from an Abenaki grave in Swanton. The "Vermont in the Civil War" exhibit shows everything from medical and dental implements to a saddle used in battle. Downstairs is for the kids—a hands-on nature center complete with wasp hives, frogs, iguanas, and turtles, as well as machines that show some of the basic properties of physics. The museum also serves as an official U.S. weather observation station, and its planetarium offers in its fifty-seat theater informational programs on the weather and sky above St. Johnsbury.

The museum is on Main Street and is open year-round. Its hours are from 9:00 a.m. to 5:00 p.m. Tuesday through Saturday and from 1:00 to 5:00 p.m. Sunday. In July and August the museum is open 10:00 a.m. to 6:00 p.m. and is open regular hours Monday from May through September. Planetarium shows are scheduled during open hours, but you should call ahead for the times.

Admission is $6.00 for adults, $5.00 for seniors and ages five through eighteen. A family rate is available. For more information, write to the Fairbanks Museum and Planetarium, 1302 Main Street, St. Johnsbury, VT 05819, or call (802) 748–2372; www.fairbanksmuseum.org.

Although Lambert Packard did not design the *St. Johnsbury Athenaeum and Art Gallery,* he did supervise the building of the art gallery, which was constructed to house Albert Bierstadt's *The Domes of Yosemite,* still displayed there.

The building, which is a National Historic Landmark, serves as the town's public library, but visitors are welcome into the athenaeum, an immense dark room with a lone skylight overhead and quietly whirring ceiling fans. The sign at the door says WELCOME TO THE NINETEENTH CENTURY, which is true if you ignore the current best-sellers out in the main part of the library.

The paintings include several religious subjects from the Italian school, as well as classic ships-at-sea and others. The art is a mix of American and European styles, and the collection, as well as the building, was financed by Governor Horace Fairbanks. The showcase at the entrance has books and ephemera from the early days of St. Johnsbury.

The athenaeum is open Monday through Friday from 10:00 a.m. to 5:30 p.m.; and Saturday from 9:30 a.m. to 5:00 p.m. St. Johnsbury Athenaeum/Art Gallery, 1171 Main Street, St. Johnsbury; (802) 748–8291; www.stjathenaeum.org.

One of the more interesting dining spots in St. Johnsbury is *Kham's Thai Cuisine.* The chef/owners are from Thailand, and the dishes they prepare are wonderful. They use really fresh veggies and you have your choice of vegetarian, chicken, fried or steamed tofu, beef, pork, shrimp, squid, or scallops in all of the dishes served. You also have a choice of degrees of "hot"—one to four stars—one of the few restaurants anywhere that will actually make it hot enough for our friend Mike Hern, who travels here regularly from Sugar Hill, New Hampshire. Lunch specials include soup, jasmine or brown rice, spring roll, and crab Rangoon and a large choice of entrees. Prices for lunch are from $6.50 to $8.95, dinners from $7.95 to $12.95. The atmosphere is pleasantly upscale. It's open seven days a week for lunch and dinner. The restaurant is at 1112 Memorial Drive (Route 5), St. Johnsbury; (802) 751–THAI (8424).

If you are in St. Johnsbury on a Monday night from June through the end of August, you can attend the *Courthouse Park Band Concerts* held in the town center. If you thought these outdoor band concerts had gone the way of the Edsel, guess again, because you'll be able to hear everything from oompah bands to Glenn Miller tunes. For more information and a calendar of upcoming performers, call (802) 748–4331.

Molly Newell's **Broadview Farm Bed & Breakfast** is on a quiet side road that was once part of the Boston Post Road. In fact, the house itself, which is on the National Register of Historic Places, once served as a stagecoach inn on the route.

The road doesn't see much traffic, but Molly Newell doesn't mind; her bed-and-breakfast brings her plenty of company from Memorial Day weekend through October, which is when it's open.

theartistwillnot seeyounow

In the nineteenth century, a self-educated artist named Russell Risley lived in the town of Kirby, which lies north of Route 2 as you head east out of St. Johnsbury. Russell and his sister devised a series of levers, pulleys, and trapezes to transfer full and empty milk pails between their house and the barn. They lived as virtual hermits; instead of visiting with real people, Russell painted pictures of neighbors and prominent figures on the side of his barn. Although people came from all over to see his creations, Russell was, after all, a loner at heart; thus, he painted a sign that said SMALLPOX and thereby solved his problem.

The four guest rooms up a steep flight of stairs are filled with the artifacts of the lives of Molly's relatives. In what she calls the Children's Room, there's a picture of her father and his twin sister as children in front of the farmhouse. A pair of Molly's aunt's shoes hangs above the bureau, and in the Whittier Room, named for her opera singer–aunt, Harriet Whittier, a pair of old pointe shoes and old silver brushes and combs rest on the table. Outdoors, guests can swim or fish in the pond Molly's children have built for her. Write to Broadview Farm Bed & Breakfast, 2627 McDowell Road, Danville, 05828; (802) 748–9902; www .bedandbreakfast.com.

Lower Waterford lies close to the Connecticut River along Route 18, a meandering country road between I–93 exits 1 and 44 (in New Hampshire). It's attractive hilly country, and another good place from which to explore the Kingdom. Lower Waterford is a cozy, small settlement of very few buildings and the location of **Rabbit Hill Inn,** one of the premier small inns in the state, and indeed the entire country, as well as one of the friendliest. Its white columned facade dominates the town and is perhaps why the town is reputed to be the most photographed in the state. The inn is country elegant, beautifully appointed but as comfortable as a visit to your best friend's house. Each room is furnished with quality antiques or reproductions and plenty of reading lights. Little details include lighted vanity mirrors, a silent heating system (no roaring blowers or clanging radiators), and coffeemakers. Most have spacious sitting areas (the smallest room has space for two large wing chairs), and each is different in style.

The public rooms for guests are just as comfortable and are plentiful. A big fireplace invites guests to curl up in front of it, an intimate lounge is well stocked with wines as well as a full bar. Hospitable innkeepers Brian and Leslie pay attention to every detail and always seem to have time to chat unhurriedly with guests and suggest places for them to visit in the area. This thoughtful couple has assembled neat packets of brochures to accompany travel instruction sheets for a variety of special interests, from antiques and shopping to outdoor sports.

Rabbit Hill excels at working with local attractions and businesses to give guests real Vermont experiences, several of which they offer as mid-week or weekend packages. A ski package, for example, included two nights' lodging, lift tickets at nearby Burke Mountain, and breakfast, dinner, and afternoon tea daily. In other seasons, an adventure weekend includes hikes to waterfalls and two mountain-top experiences, one by aerial gondola and the other on a 4x4-truck safari, along with lodging and dining. Kayaking adventures on the Connecticut River begin on the riverbank, within sight of the inn, and are suitable for beginners or experienced paddlers.

The inn's restaurant is one of the many reasons for staying here, and our favorite special package offers a chance to learn some cooking secrets from Executive Chef Matthew Secich. "Inn Good Taste" cooking classes are two memorable days of cooking and dining, each exploring a specific topic, covering both the basics and the creative side. Only eight guests are in each class, so there's an opportunity for questions and discussion. On the first evening the group dines together on a five-course tasting dinner paired with wines.

Really Do Be Wary of Moose

As you drive in this part of the state, especially along Route 114, which parallels the international border, you'll see an increasing number of signs warning MOOSE CROSSING or MOOSE NEXT 12 MILES or MOOSE NEXT 5,000 FEET. These are not tourist advertisements to tell you the best sites for wildlife watching. They are serious warnings to sharpen your peripheral road-scanning skills in order to avoid a collision with the most dangerous animal in the northern woods. Slow down when you see these signs, and be especially watchful on overcast days, in the early morning and evening, after dark, and early in the spring. Moose don't dent cars, they total them and often the driver and passengers as well. Nearly everyone up here knows a family that has lost someone to a moose collision, a more frequent occurrence as the moose population increases. Take a good look at the stuffed moose in the Fairbanks Museum in St. Johnsbury, and picture it flying over the hood of your car. You'll understand why you should slow down in moose country.

On the second evening, participants enjoy an intimate dinner for two. With or without the cooking class, the dining experience is first rate, with noted chef Secich committed to using the freshest seasonal ingredients from the best local sources. The creative menus are posted seasonally on the Web site with the early winter entrees including Rabbit Five Ways, accompanied by sun chokes, mustard greens, and brettone ronde onion.

Contact Rabbit Hill Inn at 48 Lower Waterford Road, P.O. Box 55, Lower Waterford, 05848; (802) 748–5168 or (800) 76–BUNNY (762–8669); www.rabbit hillinn.com.

Concord, on Route 2, claims the distinction of being home to the first school in America specifically founded to train teachers. The *First Normal School,* as it was called, was founded in 1823 by the Reverend Samuel Read Hall. The house is 2.5 miles south of Route 2; follow the signs to Concord Corners. The house is not open to the public.

From Route 2, follow signs to Granby and Victory, a left turn as you're headed east. The first few miles of the route are paved, and lots of young hardwoods line the road, which follows the curve of the Moose River. At the Victory town line, the road turns to dirt as you enter the *Victory Bog Wildlife Management Area,* almost 5,000 protected acres where deer, bear, grouse, and woodcock roam freely. There are 5 miles of old logging roads and unmarked trails to explore, as well as several parking areas.

A couple of miles into the bog, if you're sharp-eyed, you'll see to your left a boulder with a plaque that reads: IN MEMORY OF FRED MOLD, WHO WORKED TO PRESERVE VICTORY BOG. IN HIS ROUND OF DAILY LIFE, HE GAVE OF HIMSELF. HE CARED ABOUT THE 'LEAST OF HIS BRETHREN' AND TOOK THE TIME TO EVEN FEED THE BIRDS. WHERE HE MET A STRANGER, THERE HE LEFT A FRIEND. 1921–1975.

It's a nice place for a picnic, surrounded by a quiet pine forest and giant spruce trees. You'll have no doubt that you're in a bog, with the wetlands and stands of ghostly trees that line both sides of the road.

On the other side of the bog, a right turn in the village of Gallup Mills (which is still part of the town of Victory) brings you through little Granby, the last town in Vermont to get electricity. That was in 1962. As you head on toward Guildhall, watch the right-hand side of the road for an old garage covered with license plates, literally covered. There are plates from Vermont and other states and from many years—1962, 1959, Maine, California, New York, New Hampshire, Nevada, Connecticut, Washington. Old vanity plates read SALTY, TOPCAT, TEACH, CHESS. The sign on the garage reads NO TRESPASSING.

Guildhall is the only town in the world with this name. The Essex County Courthouse is here, along with more houses than you've seen for many miles if you arrived here via Victory Bog. Route 102 wends its way north, playing tag with the Connecticut River to the town of Maidstone. This is prime hunting country, and landowners are pretty liberal about allowing hunters on their land. Instead of the posted NO TRESPASSING/NO HUNTING signs that are common in the southern part of the state, HUNTING BY PERMISSION signs abound. Often the landowners offer themselves out as hunting guides to people who don't know the territory.

The entrance to **Maidstone State Park** is in the town of Brunswick. The 5-mile dirt access road proceeds to Maidstone Lake and the park, which even in summer is uncrowded throughout its 469 acres. There are eighty-three campsites, rental boats, fishing, swimming, and plenty of picnic tables. Listen for the loon cries from the lake. The park is open daily Memorial Day through Labor Day from dawn to dusk. For more information, call (802) 676–3930, or write to Maidstone State Park, Box 185, Guildhall, VT 05905; www.vtstateparks.com/htm/maidstone.cfm.

In Lemington, the **Columbia Covered Bridge** crosses over into Colebrook, New Hampshire. This is sparsely populated land, which appears to revel in its isolation. It's thrived for years, hidden away from the rest of the world and from most human influence, with scarcely more than 100 residents in the 20,532-acre town.

This makes **Canaan,** the next town north, seem like a metropolis by comparison, with a number of Christmas tree farms, dairy farms, and a couple of restaurants in town.

At **Beecher Falls,** just north of Canaan, is the one tiny place where New Hampshire and Vermont share a land border. The Connecticut River turns due east at Beecher Falls, while the border continues to run generally north. Canada is directly north, and although the line of the U.S.-Canadian international boundary was set in the 1800s by the Webster-Ashburton Treaty, the two states continued to dispute the exact location of the line for many years. The issue finally went to the supreme court of the U.S. Boundary Commission in 1934, and the definitive line was drawn.

youmightaswell hearitfromus

It's a classic border tale, one of many told along the Connecticut River, and you're bound to hear it if you hang around long enough. When the exact location of the border was finally established, the local selectmen went to visit an elderly Vermonter whose home, according to the new line, was now in New Hampshire. They feared that the shock would be too much for him and took the local doctor along just in case. But they needn't have worried. A happy smile broke out on the old gentleman's face at the news, and he replied with fervor: "Good, b' God, I don't think I could've survived another one of those Vermont winters!"

You can cross it on a road that leaves Beecher Falls and follows the river to the right, while the main road continues left to the international line and the customs control point. The river is a lazy stream here, and as you follow it, you can see cars on Route 3 in New Hampshire on the other side. After the pavement ends, and just as you're sure you must have strayed over into Canada by mistake, you'll see a **granite boundary marker** set at an odd angle on the left side of the road. Its position is skewed because it sits directly astride the border, and on one half is carved: Town/Canaan, Vermont and on the other, Line/Pittsburgh, New Hampshire. Cross that line and you'll need a copy of *Off the Beaten Path New Hampshire* to guide you.

About 3 miles north of the center of Canaan on Route 114, **Wallace Pond** is on the right. The Canadian border is somewhere in the middle of the pond. If you can find the exact point with a boat, you can fish in two countries at once. The boat access ramp is located just off the road. There are a couple of camping areas nearby with good views of the pond.

Averill is large, with an area of 24,320 acres, and was one of the first towns in the Kingdom—not to mention the state—to be chartered, in 1762. But the town was never organized and today has only a dozen or so year-round residents.

Quimby Country is a rustic, sixty-two-acre resort tucked into the woods on the shore of Forest Lake. The best way to describe it is as a summer camp for families. Guests are also close to Great Averill Pond and Little Averill Pond, remote bodies of water that are superb for fishing, swimming, and boating. Meals are family-style; lodging is either in the big lodge or in one of twenty cabins.

Quimby's motto is "Where nothing ever changes," and apart from the addition of a more dependable electrical system, that's quite true. During the summer, rates (which include meals) are about $205 per adult, with lower rates for children based on their age. In spring and fall (Quimby's is open from mid-May to mid-October) cottages with kitchens begin at $97 per person with significantly reduced rates for each additional guest, but without meals. In the spring, these cottages are popular with fishermen and birders, who enjoy seeing the migrating flocks that stop around the lake. Wildflowers are at their best in June, with lady's slippers carpeting the ground in places. In September the lakeshores are painted in bright leaves. All the boats, tennis courts, and other facilities are there off-season, but you have fewer people to share them with.

In the summer Quimby's rates also include a full program for children, with counselors. For more information, call (802) 822–5533 or go to www .quimbycountry.com.

Norton's claim to immortality is that, while it was the first town to be granted a charter in the state, it was among the last to be settled, in 1860. To reach Norton from any other part of Vermont, travelers first had to go into Canada and then come down south into the town center, which straddles the international boundary line. This route caused the delay in settlement.

Brighton incorporates the village of *Island Pond*—a place with quite an illustrious past. A religious group lives in town, and after some initial tensions between the group and the townspeople, both groups now live side by side, some say peacefully, others say by merely tolerating each other. Mystery writer Archer Mayor, who lives down near Brattleboro, based his 1990 novel *Border-lines* on the religious group.

Right in the center of Island Pond, you'll find ***Jennifer's Restaurant,*** where you can get hot sandwiches with gravy and fries for $4.95, a BLT packed with bacon for $2.75, or full dinners for $8.00 to $12.00. A fisherman's platter is $14.95. It's casual and friendly, and you'll overhear a lot of local news while you eat. Jennifer's also serves breakfast, and only a truck driver from Quebec could finish off a platter of their pancakes. Jennifer's, Cross Street, Island Pond; (802) 723–6135.

Lakeside Park is right on the village's namesake, Island Pond. In the middle of the pond is a twenty-two-acre island, which measures 1 mile wide by 2 miles long.

Stand on the shore of Island Pond, close your eyes, and listen for the long-ago bustle of a town where the most valuable resource in the midst of the Industrial Revolution was this body of water. The pond once served as the outlet for the tributary off the Pherrins River that was used as a transport for floating logs from Norton and Canada. Island Pond—the village—was also known as the halfway point between Montreal and Portland, Maine, on the Grand Trunk Railway, where the lumber from the Great North was transferred to the railway.

South of St. Jay

The valley south of St. Johnsbury is a pretty, rural area where many artists have been inspired to call such towns as Peacham and Barnet home. Farms are interspersed with crisp white Capes and rolling vistas of the mountain ranges and lakes that characterize Vermont.

At the *P&H Truck Stop* in Wells River, on Route 302 in the north end of the town of Newbury, thick is the watchword, whether you order omelets, meat loaf, pork chops, fish chowder, or onion rings. This is an old-fashioned kind of truck stop where locals, truckers, and travelers all converge to chow down on delicious and hearty real food. The truckers have their own section upstairs to eat in and relax, while families sit downstairs.

The menu is written in both French and English. Don't pass up some of the homemade bread at P&H: white, oatmeal, whole wheat, or cinnamon raisin. P&H Grill is open from 6:00 a.m. to 10:00 p.m., seven days a week. More than a few southern Vermonters have been known to drive up to Wells River for a piece of Reese's Pie—made with chocolate cream, chocolate pudding, and peanut butter, an exact replica of the candy—or maple cream pie. Call (802) 429–2141.

The **William Scott Sleeping Sentinel Monument** is just down the road west of the village. During the Civil War, Groton native William Scott enlisted in the Union army. He drew night duty one evening, then stood in again the next night for a fellow soldier who was ill. Scott fell asleep and was court-martialed; however, President Lincoln stepped in and pardoned him, rescuing him from the firing squad. Scott went back into battle, and not too long after his pardon, he was killed in Virginia.

Route 232 North cuts through **Groton State Forest** just west of the village. Old railroad lines within the forest are now hiking trails.

In **Danville** is the **American Society of Dowsers,** which is open to the public. Dowsing is the ancient art of locating underground water sources, and you can take free lessons here Monday through Friday between 9:00 a.m. and 5:00 p.m. There are also weekend workshops; call for a free information packet. The society's annual convention is held in late July or early August at Lyndon State College, where you can sit in on basic, expanded, and specialized classes and a wide variety of lectures on dowsing and related topics, including earth energies, feng shui, and labyrinths. Behind the headquarters building is a labyrinth that you are welcome to visit whether the society headquarters is open or not. The society's store, at 430 Railroad Street in St. Johnsbury, carries tools and books on dowsing and other New Age subjects. The store is open from 10:00 a.m. to 5:00 p.m. Tuesday through Saturday; (802) 748–8565. For a free book catalog, classes, or convention information, call (802) 684–3417 or (800) 711–9497; www.dowsers.org.

If you leave Danville on Brainerd Street, where the Society of Dowsers is located, you will see some of the state's finest views of its neighbors, the White Mountains of New Hampshire. To the left is the Killkenny Range; to the right is Cannon Mountain and Franconia Notch, where Mounts Lincoln and Lafayette are located, with Loon Mountain showing in between their peaks. If you continue straight at the fork, along the top of the ridge, you will enjoy more mountain views before dropping to the **Greenbanks Hollow Covered Bridge.** Built in 1886, it spans a rushing river that drops a significant distance as it cascades past the stone foundations of old mills. The sides of this small, one-lane bridge are open, not enclosed, as most others are.

If, you bear left onto Joe's Brook Road, however, you will come to the **Danville Morgan Horse Farm,** stretching along a hillside with more White Mountain views. You can visit the farm any day between 9:00 a.m. and 3:00 p.m. Small signs point the way from Danville or from Route 5, where you will end up if you continue along Joe's Brook Road. The address is 1906 Joe's Brook Road, Danville, 05828; (802) 684–2251; e-mail: dmhf@kingcon.com.

More Places to Stay in the Northeast Kingdom

(All area codes 802)

Information on local B&Bs is available at www.travel thekingdom.com.

EAST BURKE

Bed & Breakfast at Moose Crossing
2171 Route 114
(802) 626–0989
www.moosecrossingbb
.com
About 2 miles from Burke Mountain, the B&B has two guest rooms with private baths in a renovated farmhouse. Rates are very reasonable, especially so close to a ski area.

GREENSBORO

Highland Lodge
1608 Craftsbury Road
533–2647
www.highlandlodge.com
Comfortable, homey rooms, good food (have lunch on the veranda overlooking Caspian Lake), and an accommodating staff. The lodge is open from mid-December until mid-March (when they have cross-country skiing) and from Memorial Day to Columbus Day.

ISLAND POND

Lakefront Motel
127 Cross Street
723–6507
Overlooking Island Pond, in the center of town, this is a nicely kept property where snowmobilers congregate in the winter, and people who enjoy water sports can moor their boats or beach their canoes.

WESTMORE

WilloughVale Inn
Route 5A South
525–4123 or
(800) 594–9102
http://willoughvale.com
Views from each of its seven unique rooms and four lakefront cottages, all furnished in handcrafted Vermont furniture. The inn is closed in November and April. Overlooking Lake Willoughby.

More Places to Eat in the Northeast Kingdom

(All area codes 802)

DANVILLE

The Creamery
Hill Street
684–3616
An upscale restaurant open for lunch and dinner Tuesday through Saturday.

Danville Restaurant and Inn
86 Route 2 West
684–3484
A family-run dining room that has long been a local favorite. Breakfast is served Monday through Saturday, lunch Monday through Friday, and dinner on Friday and Saturday.

TO LEARN MORE IN NORTHEAST KINGDOM

Northeast Kingdom Travel & Tourism Association,
P.O. Box 465, Barton, VT 05822; (802) 525–4386 or (800) 884–8001; www .nekchamber.com

EAST BURKE

Old Cutter Inn
Mountain Access Road
626–5152 or
(800) 295–1943
www.oldcutterinn.com
Highly recommended by local people for its continental menu. It's closed in November and April and on Wednesday.

River Garden Cafe
427 Vermont Route 114
626–3514
www.rivergardencafe.com
In the center of East Burke, the cafe serves lunch and dinner year-round Tuesday through Sunday (closed Tuesday in winter) in an upbeat setting. Jamaican jerked chicken with black beans, fajitas, pesto salmon, or lamb may be on the menu.

CENTRAL VERMONT

Central Vermont has long been defined by its massive granite quarries. This is true partly because of the many Scottish, Irish, and Italian granite workers who flocked to the area during the last half of the nineteenth century. Just as important, though, was the rough topography, which determined where residential areas cropped up, where the best access routes to the quarries were, and where the railroad tracks were laid. Vermonters in this central area had to learn to rely on themselves to a greater extent and in different ways than people in other parts of the state.

But this region of Vermont also has its own particular rugged beauty that is unlike the Green mountain range to the west or the almost-nautical air of the towns that skirt Lake Champlain. Central Vermont's beauty stems from the rocky riverbeds of the first, second, and third branches of the White River, branches that eventually wind their way down and through the mountains to empty into the Connecticut River. The region's beauty also comes from the stands of second- and third-growth forest that line the sides of the state highways through towns such as Chelsea and Corinth. And it's hard to miss the beauty in the wide valleys that cut a swath along

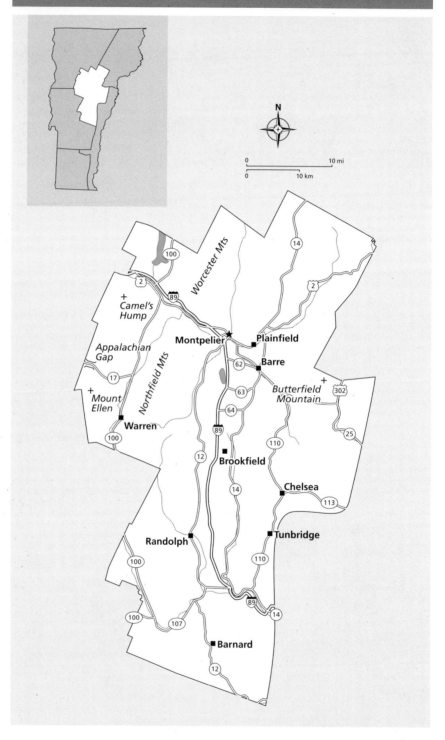

Route 12 in Braintree and Brookfield. Only occasionally does a house pop up in some of these spots.

So drive down an unmarked dirt road on impulse, or follow the signs to the quarries in Barre, to see a part of Vermont that is unlike any other.

Barre/Montpelier

The Barre/Montpelier area is the thriving, active heart of this central region and of the state. Barre has been home to thousands of immigrants over the years, from the Italian stonecutters who came to Vermont via Ellis Island to work in the granite quarries to the Irishmen who were recruited in droves to work on the railroad, first to lay track and then to operate the trains.

The granite quarries were founded shortly after the end of the War of 1812. Three grades of granite are still taken from the mountains: a coarse stone ideal for millstones and doorsteps; a less sandy stone for house foundations, much like the stone used to build the state capitol in Montpelier; and the beautiful, almost flawless stone that is used for gravestones and monuments all over the world.

Despite the retail development both downtown and on the Barre-Montpelier Road, Barre has managed to retain its working-class, melting-pot flavor for more than a century.

Hope Cemetery, a seventy-five-acre cemetery that dates back to 1895, is on Route 14 just north of Route 302. The cemetery is known for its elaborate carvings of Vermont's early-twentieth-century stonecutters. New stones are interspersed with old ones, and Italian names are plentiful. When you first enter Hope Cemetery, turn right and drive around its perimeter to see some remarkable granite statuary stones.

The lifelike sculptures of some of the grave markers are the attraction at Hope Cemetery. Far left and back look for the Brusa stone: A brooding angel, with legs crossed, trumpet on lap, sits beneath a Greek pillar and balustrade sculpture. Here, so as not to detract from the elegance and detail of

AUTHOR'S TOP HIGHLIGHTS

Hope Cemetery

Brookfield Floating Bridge

Covered bridges
Tunbridge and Randolph

Population Burst

Barre holds the distinction of having the largest increase in population in Vermont to occur within a decade: With the opening of Ellis Island in New York City and the great influx of skilled granite workers from Scotland, Italy, and Scandinavia, the population of Barre increased from 2,060 in 1880 to 6,812 in 1890. Social unrest soon followed, when the underpaid granite workers got together to demand better working conditions and higher pay.

Though today Barre looks like the solid, conservative, working-class town that it is, back in the late nineteenth century the politics in town were quite radical. Long before Vermont sent Bernie Sanders, the only independent in the U.S. House of Representatives (and later, the U.S. Senate), to serve in Washington, D.C., Barre elected a socialist mayor to serve its people. Early-twentieth-century anarchist Emma Goldman was arrested in Barre and charged with aiding and abetting the murder of a mayor.

monuments, small stones with the name of each family member are placed in front of the sculpture.

Also look for Elia Corti's stone, a life-size monument at the crossroads near the back of the cemetery. Corti was a stonecutter who died in 1903. His stone shows his full-size likeness sitting and gazing at the surrounding forest. A few stones away from Corti's is the Cole/Spence stone, complete with contemplative Greek goddess.

Another Brusa monument—located in another patch of stones downhill and secluded from the main yard—depicts a wife comforting her dying husband, who succumbed to silicosis, a lung disease many stonecutters contracted from exposure to stone dust. Directly in front is a sculpture of Gwendolyn and William Halvosa, a husband and wife holding hands, with the inscription, SET ME AS A SEAL UPON THINE HEART, FOR LOVE IS STRONG AS DEATH.

Heading back out of the cemetery, stop to walk among the stones that don't face the road. Look for a chair that serves as a grave marker, a soccerball stone, and another with a classic Green Mountain view—complete with fence posts, a rifle, a fishing rod, a dune buggy, and lots of trucks. One shows a Shell Oil truck driving through the mountains; another serves as a belated advertisement for the Benedini Well Company, depicting a truck in the process of digging an artesian well.

You will notice a number of Art Nouveau and Art Deco influences in the designs on stones and on the bronze doors of the family vaults along the back row. On the Calcagni monument, an Erté-like angel stands in a colonnade. You will also notice that all the flowers are fresh, not plastic. Bouquets of cut flowers and carefully tended blooming plants decorate many of the burial places, and on weekends you're likely to see families tending these. Since people from the area still bury their loved ones here, Hope Cemetery is not a historical icon from bygone days. It is an active cemetery where Vermont-ers come to remember their dead, whether they died a century ago or last week. A cemetery is a place to pay one's respects, so remember to show courtesy to people who might not like to be reminded that visitors are taking a casual, interested stroll through the cemetery's grounds.

As you might expect, Barre has a lot of public statuary, from the traditional monuments to a war memorial—granite, of course—in 1930s heroic Realist style. In Dante Park, in honor of the contribution made by Italian Americans to the city, region, and state, is a large statue

that'ssomerock band

Rock of Ages quarry in Barre is 550 feet wide, ¼ mile long, and 450 feet deep, the largest in the world. The high-quality granite is used for monuments and head-stones because its exceptionally fine grain makes it the perfect medium for finely detailed but long-lasting, durable outdoor sculpture. The quarry is the basis of a $200-million-a-year industry that employs more than 1,500 Vermonters.

of a gentleman with a kindly face, so well sculpted that his character seems to shine from within the stone. You will also notice a lot of business signs—real estate offices, the credit union—carved in granite.

Speaking of granite, on Granite Street in downtown Barre, about a mile from Hope Cemetery, is the **ReStore.** This is a shop that recycles a bit of everything and sells it to local craftspeople, schoolteachers, and others with a little imagination.

Everything at the ReStore is considered to be clean industrial scrap from Vermont businesses. And since the ReStore receives new shipments every week, the inventory is always changing.

All types of fabrics, wooden beads, polished marble bases, packing materials, and clay flowerpots are accepted from businesses. The ReStore also accepts items from local homeowners—old lamps, bubble wrap, magazines, cookie tins, office supplies, and the like, items that would otherwise end up in Vermont landfills. Most of the items are unpackaged and displayed in large bins so that you can pick as few or as many as you need.

The ReStore is open Tuesday through Saturday from 10:00 a.m. to 5:00 p.m. ReStore, 34 Granite Street, Barre, 056411 (802) 477–7800. www.therestore.org.

In East Barre you can visit quarries; the hills that surround the town are actually tailing piles from the quarries. In the center of this town, where the quarry workers lived, is a large antiques mall, a craft center, and the factory store of Vermont Flannel, where you can get good bargains on flannel clothing and fabric. They have a half-price sale in April.

East Barre also has one of the largest multidealer shops in the state. The **East Barre Antique Mall,** with more than 12,000 square feet of display space, features antiques and collectibles from glass to furniture, which is one of their strong points. A basement-level area is set aside for bargains. Open Tuesday through Sunday 10:00 a.m. to 5:00 p.m. The shop is at the junction of Routes 302 and 110, 133 Mill Street, East Barre; (802) 479–5190.

musicalcapitals

Montpelier was established as the state capital in 1805, with the first statehouse completed in 1808. Previously the capital had rotated throughout the state, its legislators meeting in towns from Burlington to Randolph. In 1838 another, more regal statehouse was constructed and Vermonters thought the matter was settled. But the debate flared up again in 1859 after the second statehouse burned down, leaving only the shell. Montpelier remained the capital, however, rebuilding the statehouse in the same location.

Though they're joined at the hip, Barre and Montpelier could never be mistaken for twins, fraternal or otherwise; they're hardly even siblings. Their temperaments are too different. From January through April Vermont's state legislature is in session in Montpelier. Elected representatives from all over the state come to the capital to decide how their state will run for the rest of the year. Then, in May, representatives in both the House and the Senate turn back into their regular selves for the rest of the year—farmers, office workers, and homemakers among them.

Montpelier is a dynamic state capital and the smallest in the nation, with a population of under 10,000. Several colleges are located here; and students, teenage skateboarders, conservative lawyers, and activists who live on nearby communes all know one another and frequently share a dish of Ben & Jerry's on Main Street. It's not unusual to see men with long hair and batik clothing sitting next to women in suits and high-heeled shoes.

The **New England Culinary Institute** (www.necidining.com) is one of the foremost in the country, and as part of its training program, it operates three dining rooms in Montpelier: **Main Street Grill and Bar, Chef's Table,** and **La Brioche Bakery and Cafe.** Main Street Grill and Bar and Chef's Table are at 118 Main Street, the former on the street level and open for breakfast, lunch, and dinner and the latter on the second floor and open for dinner only. La Brioche is diagonally across the street at 89 Main Street.

Main Street Grill and Bar's dining room is sleek, modern, and attractive, with big sliding windows overlooking the street and alfresco dining on the portico in good weather. As expected from a culinary school, the menu is interesting and the fare well prepared. Soups and starters include New England clam chowder at $3.95, potato gnocchi with dried plums, forest mushrooms and Madeira sauce at $6.50, and balsamic onion tart at $7.95. Entrees are equally intriguing, and evolve regularly. Lunch is served 11:30 a.m. to 2:00 p.m. (seatings at 11:00 a.m. and 1:30 p.m.) Tuesday through Saturday, and dinner from 5:30 to 9:00 p.m. Tuesday through Sunday. Sunday brunch is served from 10:00 a.m. to 2:00 p.m. 118 Main Street, Montpelier; (802) 223-3188.

Chef's Table is the domain of second-year students. A bit more formal, its innovative menu is always changing to incorporate the freshest in-season ingredients with an emphasis on Vermont products, including native lamb, duck, hams, and cheeses. Chef's Table is open seven days a week, 8:00 a.m. to 9:00 p.m. 118 Main Street, Montpelier; (802) 229-9202.

La Brioche is a European-style bakery, a good place for a light continental breakfast, croissant, or baked goody in the afternoon. There are tables indoors and outdoors on a plaza raised just above sidewalk level. Open Monday through Friday 6:30 a.m. to 5:00 p.m., Saturday 7:00 a.m. to 5:00 p.m., and Sunday 8:00 a.m. to 2:00 p.m. 89 Main Street, Montpelier; (802) 229-0443.

Although there are a few motels located in Barre and on the outskirts of Montpelier, a better choice for lodging—one that's not too far removed from the bustle but is quiet enough that you will forget you're in a city—is **Betsy's Bed & Breakfast,** just up a hilly side street from the main street in the capital. During the early 1990s it was a decrepit-looking Queen Anne

ANNUAL EVENTS IN CENTRAL VERMONT

July and August: Free Summer Band Concerts, State house lawn, Montpelier, Wednesdays at 7:00 p.m.

July 4: Annual Fourth of July Parade and Celebration, Warren; (802) 496-3409.

Mid-July: Annual Vermont Quilt Festival, Norwich University, Northfield; (802) 485-7092.

Mid-September: Tunbridge World's Fair, Tunbridge; (802) 889-5555. (Note that about 30,000 people cram into this tiny town, creating the state's longest and worst traffic jams on record.)

December: Live Nativity Pageant, Joseph Smith Birthplace, South Royalton, has live animals; Thanksgiving weekend through New Year's; (802) 763-7742.

home complete with turrets crying out for rescue. Jon and Betsy Anderson, lawyers who work for the state government, have carefully restored the building to its previous glory. They did such a good job, in fact, that the house won the Montpelier Historical Society's award for best commercial renovation in 1993.

Today the B&B occupies two restored Victorian homes and has twelve guest rooms. All rooms have cable TV, telephones, data ports, and private baths. The plentiful and delicious breakfasts feature cereal, compote, blueberry pancakes, and omelets.

For more information, write to Betsy's Bed & Breakfast, 74 East State Street, Montpelier, 05602, or call (802) 229–0466; www.betsysbnb.com.

The **Vermont State House** is interesting with its ornate halls and floors of—what else would you expect?—marble. Flags from the Civil War decorate the walls, along with portraits and other paintings. You can wander on your own or take a more formal tour with a guide, offered weekdays July through mid-October on the half-hour from 10:00 a.m. to 3:30 p.m. and Saturday from 11:00 a.m. to 2:30 p.m. The building, on State Street, Montpelier, is open weekdays from 8:00 a.m. to 4:00 p.m. year-round, and admission is free; (802) 828–2228.

State Street presents a remarkable architectural heritage, and a walking tour is the best way to admire all the buildings that line it. As you leave the State House, look to the right, across State Street, at number 128, the Edward Dewey House. It's as Queen Anne as you can get, with all the variety this late-1800s style embodied. Notice the different shingles, roof lines, and windows. Turn left and walk down State Street, past the flamboyant Romanesque Department of Agriculture building. Nothing could be further from the simple lines of the farms this agency represents; like the Queen Anne house up the street, it seems never to repeat anything, with a potpourri of different windows and roof styles. A tower, bay, and turret further complicate its design, which is even more embellished with a carved wooden frieze above the front door.

The clean, symmetrical lines of the 1870 building next door are a nice contrast with their tall windows and straight columns. Opposite is the elegant reconstruction of the Pavilion Hotel, which once housed legislators during sessions and now houses state offices and the Vermont Historical Society (see description later in this section). Its bricks were made from molds dating from the 1800s, and some of the original architectural ornaments, such as keystones and spindles on the porch, are originals from the earlier building.

Three buildings on the same side of the street in the next block represent different stages of the Federal period, with its clean, well-balanced shapes based on the Georgian style then popular in England. Number 107, behind

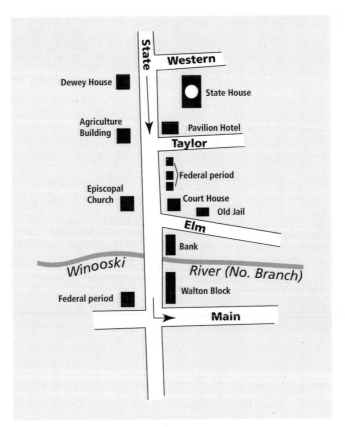

A Walking Tour of Montpelier

the service station, shows more of the Georgian lines in its steep roof and balanced chimneys. Number 99 is more Federal, with the characteristic recessed doorway topped by a fanlight. Number 89, next to it, is quite similar and may have been one of the first houses on State Street. On the corner is the Greek Revival courthouse, and behind it on Elm Street is the old brick jail, which was transformed in the early 1900s to a flat-roofed business block; you can see where the new brickwork began.

Across the street from the courthouse is the Episcopal church, a Gothic design built of local granite. Inside you can see its vaulted ceiling and a rose window. The bank building across Elm Street from the courthouse was built in 1874, but the mansard roof and round dormers were added about twenty years later.

WORTH SEEING

Morse Farm Sugar House and Museum, Main Street, Montpelier; (802) 223-2740.

Rock of Ages quarry, tours and visitor center, Barre; (802) 476-3119.

Sugarbush Ski Resort, Mountain Road, Warren; (802) 583-2381. (The ski area offers 110 trails on three mountains.)

The Walton Block, next to it, is a beautifully restored 1870s commercial building decorated in cast-iron columns and stamped sheet metal, a style popular in that period. Opposite, on the corner of State and Main Streets, is Montpelier's only remaining example of a Federal-period commercial building. You can recognize its Federal lines in the steeply sloping roof and the gables at the ends.

To see more fine examples, most of them Victorian, wander up Main Street to your left, past the residences that show Greek Revival and Federal origins—often mixed at about the same time the earlier Federal homes were modernized. Some of the "newer" homes are more purely Victorian, built after two fires in 1875 destroyed many older ones. To learn more about the distinguished public and business buildings and the beautiful Victorian residences that line Montpelier's streets, seek out a copy of the brochure "Three Walking Tours," published by a local historical group.

One of the structures you will see as you walk up Main Street is a lovely brick Federal building, almost encircled by a veranda supported on delicate columns. This is now the elegant ***Inn at Montpelier,*** its interior also beautifully restored, with fireplaces, fine woodwork, and grand staircases. It is warm and comfortable, with individually decorated rooms furnished in antiques and reproductions, each with telephone and television. Plan to be there long enough to enjoy the wraparound front porch overlooking the shady street. It is one of the nicest you'll sit on anywhere, and the relaxing atmosphere of the inn will make you want to do just that. There's even a little in-house bar, so you can enjoy a glass of wine on the porch. The inn is only a block from the center of Montpelier, but in a town so small, this means you're still in a quiet residential neighborhood. Rooms run from $132 to $229 in high season. The inn is at 147 Main Street, Montpelier; (802) 223-2727; www.innatmontpelier .com; e-mail: mail2inn@aol.com.

Down from the capitol a few doors toward the center of town is the ***Vermont Historical Society,*** with an extensive library and a museum.

Fortunately, you don't have to be a member of the society to visit either the library or the museum—people travel here from all over the country to conduct genealogical research, for which the library has a treasure trove of old papers, letters, and reference works.

The museum also has exhibits about the numerous stages of the state's history, and these exhibits change about once a year. One year the featured exhibit showed how Vermonters coped with the rigors of World War II on the home front. Newspapers, canned goods, and piped-in music helped create the atmosphere.

The museum is open Tuesday through Saturday 10:00 a.m. to 4:00 p.m. and Sunday from noon until 4:00 p.m. Admission is charged to both the museum and library. Vermont Historical Society Museum, 109 State Street, Montpelier; (802) 828–2291; www.vermonthistory.org.

Manghis' Bakery (pronounced "Mang-high") bread is available fresh in general stores and markets around the Barre-Montpelier area, but it's best to buy it direct from the source. Manghis' bakes bread Monday through Friday. The bakery is open from 7:00 a.m. to 5:00 p.m. Monday through Thursday and from 7:00 a.m. until 2:00 p.m. on Friday. The best times to stop in are from noon to closing on Monday, Wednesday, and Thursday, or you can call ahead to order a special loaf. Manghis' offers anadama, maple walnut, six grain, cracked wheat, onion herb, challah, and whole-wheat oatmeal breads, as well as special breads at holiday times, like hot cross buns at Easter and stollen at Christmas. Manghis' Bakery is located off Main Street, 2 blocks northeast of its intersection with State Street. Or just follow the aroma of baking bread to 28 School Street, Montpelier; (802) 223–3676.

The ***T.W. Wood Art Gallery*** was founded to give Vermonters access to the art of their time, and it still fills the mission with changing exhibits of contemporary artists. But you will also see art from earlier times, including the

The Great Green Mountain Pumpkin Show

While most of the spring and summer ***Ellie's Farm Market*** sells plants and fresh produce from their stand on Route 12, south of Montpelier, it is in October that half the population of Vermont (or so it seems) appears at Ellie's. On October 30 and 31 every year, the staff carves more than 1,000 jack-o-lanterns, which are then placed about the property, even in the trees. Come after dark, preferably after 9:00 p.m., to avoid the crowds. Admission is free, but donations are taken to benefit a local charity. It all makes perfect sense. You just have to know the code.

work of the nineteenth-century artist T. W. Wood, who endowed the gallery. Permanent collections feature a selection of Depression-era work. The gallery is open Tuesday through Sunday, noon to 4:00 p.m. and admission is free. It is part of the Vermont College campus on College Street; (802) 828–8743; www .twwoodgallery.org.

Montpelier is nothing if not compact; everything is either within a long 2-block or a short 2-block radius of everything else. Tucked away a few steps from the main drag is *Angeleno's,* a local favorite for pizza and pasta. Situated in an old Victorian house, Angeleno's makes the best pizza in Vermont. The pizza has a thin crust, and the tomato sauce is just a little bit spicy. You can choose from thirty-one different toppings, with the more obscure ranging from peanut butter and pickles to turkey and eggplant.

All the pasta is homemade, and daily pasta specials include baked mostaccioli and linguine tossed with olive oil and shrimp; one side of the menu is devoted to heart-healthy dishes and suggestions for diabetics. Wine and beer are available, and the desserts are variations on traditional Italian themes. The frozen tortoni is made from a slice of rum-soaked pound cake with vanilla and chocolate ice cream and rum custard between the layers and a thick, hot, bittersweet fudge sauce ladled on top.

And, of course, Angeleno's has cannoli, a crunchy shell with a light ricotta filling that tells you it was prepared seconds before arriving at your table.

Angeleno's is open at 11:00 a.m. Monday through Saturday, closing at 9:30 p.m. Monday through Thursday and 10:00 p.m. Friday and Saturday. They are open 1:00 to 9:30 p.m. Sundays. The restaurant is at 15 Barre Street, Montpelier; call (802) 229–5721 for reservations or takeout.

Sarducci's overlooks the river, with an enclosed porch for dining on the water side. Low walls separate the large dining room into several smaller areas without obscuring the view of the big wood oven or the flamboyant chefly show with the pizza dough in the open kitchen. But pizza, however good and tender of crust, is only part of the menu. Pasta dishes usually have more meat than pasta, a refreshing change from the usual. Nice pairings may include mussels and Italian sausage with roasted onions in a white-wine sauce or sea scallops with tomatoes and asparagus in a basil broth. The menu balances well between the haute of northern Italian dishes and the red-sauce circuit. Sarducci's doesn't make pretenses and provides a thoroughly satisfying dinner, cheerfully served in a most pleasant atmosphere at a very reasonable price. Who can ask for more? Sarducci's is open daily, with lunch entrees at around $7.00 and most dinner entrees $8.00 to $16.00. Monday through Saturday 11:00 a.m. to 9:00 p.m. Sunday 4:30 p.m. to 90:00 p.m.; 3 Main Street, Montpelier; (802) 223–0229.

It's Really Not Sugar

Although it's called sugar-on-snow, it's really hot syrup they pour onto the snow, causing the syrup to solidify quickly into a sticky strip of sweet, chewy candy. It's so sweet in fact, that the traditional accompaniment for it is sour pickles. Sugar-on-snow is a New England rite of spring, and it should not be confused with a maple snow cone, a warm-weather treat at county fairs that involves pouring cold syrup over finely crushed ice in a paper cup.

Maple syrup and its relatives—maple sugar, candy, and cream—are perhaps the quintessential Vermont products. A good place to see these made the old-fashioned way and to experience the pleasures of a maple grove is ***Bragg Farm Sugarhouse and Gift Shop.*** Take the personal guided tour of the operation, or watch it all on the video. The shop sells candy, syrup, and even maple soft ice cream. On Saturday and Sunday in March and April, Bragg's makes sugar-on-snow from noon until 5:00 p.m. The farm, open daily November through April from 8:30 a.m. to 6:00 p.m. and May through October 8:30 a.m. to 8:00 p.m., is a mile north of the village on Route 14, East Montpelier; (802) 223–5757 or (800) 376–5757; www.braggfarm.com.

Winter has other pleasures in Montpelier, one of them at the ***Morse Farm Ski Touring Center.*** Main Street in town passes the Culinary Institute of America buildings and shortly thereafter becomes County Road. Two and a half miles from the roundabout you will find Morse's, a beautiful location with views of Camel's Hump and the Hunger Mountain Range, and 20 km of professionally designed and machine-tracked trails for all levels of experience. Of these, 15 km are suitable for skating. Facilities include a warming hut where skiers can enjoy cider and coffee, and they have a well-stocked rental shop. If you are skiing in late February and March, look into their maple syrup Sugar Shack. Rates are $10.00 adults, $8.00 seniors and ages seven to twelve. Snowshoeing (with snowshoe rental) is also available. Morse Farm, 1168 County Road, Montpelier; (800) 242–2740; www.skimorsefarm.com.

North of the Capital

The town of ***Plainfield,*** on Route 2, is home to the progressive Goddard College and many of its graduates. Because of the college, which has retained its bohemian and independent reputation, Plainfield was a mecca in the 1960s for communes and hippies of all stripes, some of whom are still here. Town kids and adults hang out on "the Wall," a few doors up and across the street from the Winooski River Valley Co-op, while dogs run leashless in the street. A visitor might have to check a calendar or newspaper to be sure of the year.

The ***Maple Valley Café and Gift Shop*** only enhances this aura. Locals come here, including those who commute from St. Johnsbury, about 25 miles away via Route 2, to Montpelier or Barre—a not-uncommon routine in these parts. They'll stop in for coffee and a pastry on their way to work.

At Maple Valley you'll find locally made greeting cards, books, candles, incense, and Ben & Jerry's ice cream. The cafe has hummus, corn chowder, vegetarian chili, sandwiches, and cappuccino, all available to go or to eat there.

The store is open in summer from 5:30 a.m. to 5:00 p.m. every day but Wednesday. It closes down Christmas Eve, and opens again the first week in May. The Maple Valley Café & Gift Shop is on Route 2, Plainfield; call (802) 454–8626.

Up at the town's main attraction, "Camp Goddard"—as Goddard College is referred to by some—does indeed resemble a camp in certain ways, and students carry on the school's traditions of participating in a certain number of chores each day and in group meetings.

On Route 2 east of Plainfield, near the Maple Valley Country Store, Hollister Hill Road heads up the hill to a long ridge. Some of the oldest families and houses in town are on this road, not to mention a one-room schoolhouse that is furnished and offers the public an opportunity to peek inside the windows for a glimpse of how education in Vermont used to be run.

A mile and a half up from Route 2, the road will fork. Bear left. A half mile later is an intersection with a red barn on the left and a white farmhouse on the right. Go straight and you'll immediately see the white schoolhouse on the right, the former ***Hollister Hill School.*** Arnold L. Tibbitts, the present owner, occasionally changes the messages on the blackboard. Old gaslights and the original desks and woodstove are still there. The school dates from 1856, and the "lesson" Tibbits records on the blackboard is intended to put history in context. As he explains, the white farmhouse that immediately precedes the schoolhouse was built during the presidency of John Adams, the second president. The addition was put on when James Polk was president, and the schoolhouse was built during Franklin Pierce's term. You can't go in, but you can see the entire school through the large windows.

Back on Route 2, continue east into Marshfield and ***Rainbow Sweets*** in the village. Ask owner Bill Tecosky if the empanadas have just come out of the oven. These Mexican turnovers, stuffed with onions, green and red peppers, raisins, and spicy beef, all wrapped up in a slightly sweet, flaky crust, come with a side of chips and hot salsa. Rainbow Sweets also offers stuffed brioche, which is its trademark; smoked salmon; and gnocchi.

People of lesser willpower and greater determination come in, sit down, and cut right to the sugar. The chocolate tart is light, sweet, and chocolaty, a three-layer cake liberally strewn with almonds and cocoa-butter cream. The almond meringue tart is mild, with a thin layer of sweet almond filling on top. There's a big display case filled with that day's desserts, and the staff patiently describes each one to you.

For those who visit and can't wait until next time, several offerings can now be shipped to your door. Linzer torte, walnut caramel kirsch torte, English fruitcake, almond chocolate butter crunch, and chocolate cherry almond torte are the delectables from Rainbow Sweets that travel well on a UPS truck, and many patrons take advantage of this service.

Rainbow Sweets is open summers from 9:00 a.m. to 6:00 p.m. Monday, Wednesday, and Thursday and from 9:00 a.m. to 9:00 p.m. on Friday and Saturday. On Sunday the restaurant is open from 9:00 a.m. to 3:00 p.m.; it's closed March and April. During the winter, they are closed Monday and Tuesday, opening at 10:00 a.m. the rest of the week, closing at 5:00 p.m. on Wednesday and Thursday, 9:00 p.m. Friday and Saturday, and 3:00 p.m. on Sunday. Write to Rainbow Sweets, Box 98, 1689 U.S. Route 2, Marshfield Village, 05658, or call (802) 426–3531.

From the town center of Marshfield, take the road west that leads to East Calais and Route 14. Follow the signs to Kent's Corner. At the Kent's Corner crossroads, turn right onto Robinson Cemetery Road. A short way up on the left is *Robinson Sawmill,* a reconstructed sawmill with original parts that were used to build the mill back in 1803. A display gives the history of the mill and shows the development of the area with photos that date from 1875. Set on the Aldrich Nature Preserve at Mill Pond, the sawmill still has its old turbine, saw blades, and machinery intact.

Robinson Sawmill was a busy place. One miller wrote out his invoices on shingles that were milled here, kids floated on sap pans in the pond, and local farmers and merchants traded gossip and news. The mill sits on extremely thin fieldstones as pilings, one atop another. You're almost afraid to sneeze, lest the impact set the mill tumbling down. But the mill can take a lot more than is obvious, as it was in full operation from 1803 to 1958.

If you're in central Vermont in late October, don't miss the Halloween-night display at the *1782 Settlement Farm* on Route 2 in Middlesex. Driving south on I–89, you'll see the glow from hundreds of pumpkins illuminate the dark autumn night; the pumpkins rest on platforms out in a field, showing off their last rays of glory before being consigned to the compost heap.

The whole area, including local schools, becomes involved in the carving, scooping, and setting up that this massive operation entails. Political messages declaring vegetation will save the nation cover one of the displays; animal faces, tombstones, flowers, and fish are other examples of the separately themed exhibits, each of them expressed through the pumpkins. For sale inside the farmhouse are cider, syrup, fruits and vegetables, cookies, and, yes, pumpkins. Don't park on the interstate, though; state troopers are out in throngs on this night. Instead, head south on I–89 and take the Montpelier exit. Follow Route 2 heading west for a few miles, and the farm will be on your left.

The Mad River Valley

Camel's Hump, a 4,083-foot mountain that straddles the borders of Duxbury and Huntington, is the third-highest mountain in the state, after Mount Mansfield and Killington. It has variously been known through the years as the Sleeping Lion, the Couching Lion, and Camel's Rump. The Long Trail passes by Camel's Hump, and trails to access the mountain's summit run through Huntington and Duxbury.

South of Duxbury on Route 100 are Waitsfield and Warren. This is prime tourist country, very busy in summer and winter. The ski resorts **Mad River Glen** and **Sugarbush** are in the area.

To say that Mad River Glen is a skier's mountain is a bit of an understatement; it is, in fact, the only ski mountain in the country that is actually owned by the skiers. Founded in 1948 by Fred Palmedo, it was not primarily a business but rather a place for people who loved the sport. That philosophy stuck with the next owners, Truxton and Betsy Pratt. When Betsy decided to retire, she almost closed the place down because she didn't want it to become like the other areas. That's when the skiers who loved it got together and bought it.

The vertical drop of about 2,000 feet is among the greatest in the state. Mad River has such a reputation among avid skiers that many beginners hesitate to try it. That's a mistake, because beginners have their own separate section of the mountain with their own lift. Intermediate trails run from the tops of two of the peaks of the ridge, as do expert trails. One of the really nice things about the trail layout here is that you won't get a nasty surprise if you start down a beginner or intermediate trail. Trails here either keep their own rating or merge into trails of the next lower category, so you won't suddenly find yourself over your head (literally or figuratively). For experts, the terrain here is probably the most challenging anywhere in the East, over natural snow covering wild bumps and down through narrow trails and glades. Located on 3,600-foot General Stark Mountain, the annual average natural snowfall is about 250 inches per year, which tends to keep the forty-seven trails at Mad River well covered. Ten of the trails are novice, sixteen are intermediate, and twenty-one are expert. Most of the trails are groomed, but the snow is all natural.

Their "ski it if you can" motto ought to tell you something. Remember, this place is for skiers—there's no huge lodge with a big bar and lots of snow bunnies. But if you like it, you can become an owner for $1,750 (800–850–6742). If you're a snowboarder, however, pass this one by, because snowboarding is not allowed, a policy that suits most skiers just fine.

Day rates begin at $39 midweek, and multiday rates are excellent. Student passes are a bargain, as is a midweek season pass, and skiers under twelve get free season passes. Check Web site for other rates and for daily updates on snow conditions. Mad River Glen, P.O. Box 1089, Waitsfield, 05673; (802) 496–3551; for snow reports, (802) 496–2001; www.madriverglen.com.

notacornerto hidein

Designed by the Shakers, round barns are a classic example of the Shakers' inventive and practical improvements on farming. The farmer could drive a team in, load or unload, and circle around and drive out. The raceway, a ramp to the loft, led directly into the top, where hay was stored. The middle level was for dairy cows, which were also easier to herd in and out in a circle and whose straw litter and manure could be removed by trapdoors to the ground floor. There it could be removed easily— or even allowed to fall directly into the wagons.

Palmer Sugar House looks a lot like it did in 1840, when it was new. Open for visits to the working sugar house in late February and early March, Palmer's sells syrup at the farm year-round. Palmer's Sugar House, Palmer Lane, Waitsfield; (802) 496–3696.

The great round **Joslyn Barn,** overlooking the valley from East Warren Road, is a local landmark, one of very few remaining in the state of the twenty-four known to have been built. After the Simcoes renovated the family farm into the **Inn at the Round Barn Farm,** they tackled the restoration of the 1910 barn. But more on that later. The inn fits so well into the rambling home with its attached carriage sheds that you'd never guess what guest luxuries await inside. The large rooms are beautifully designed and furnished, with windows big enough to make the mountain views part of the decor. Hearty breakfasts are filled with home-baked breads and served in a bright sunporch overlooking the gardens below. In the winter the inn has its own cross-country ski center for guests and the public. Hosts are relaxed about everything but the maintenance of the inn, which is meticulously cared for, and they enjoy conversations with their guests. Inn at the Round Barn Farm, 1661 East Warren Road, Waitsfield; (802) 496–2276. www.theroundbarninn.com; e-mail: info@innattheroundbarn.com.

Back to the barn. It took the Simcoes two years to restore it, from the time they began jacking up the entire structure and pouring a new foundation until it was insulated and reroofed. Then they had to decide what to do with it. When a couple asked to be married at the inn, they had part of their answer. The rest of it came when they held a music festival there, and it was a success, and the **Green Mountain Cultural Center** was born. Now with more than 200 members, the barn is a venue for performing and visual arts and hands-on workshops year-round, with the Vermont Mozart Festival, soloists, ensembles, and an annual art show filling its schedule.

itmadesense atthetime

The tiny town of Washington is part of Orange County but not of Washington County, its immediate neighbor. Washington—the town—was named for George Washington. Washington—the county—comprises the towns of Barre, Montpelier, Plainfield, and Waitsfield, among many others, and was originally called Jefferson County (in 1810) after Thomas Jefferson. Four years later, however, the locals and many other Vermonters turned against Jefferson for his influence on the Embargo Act and the War of 1812. The name of the county was therefore changed, but the name of the town—which again, is in Orange County—wasn't. Got it?

On Route 100 in Waitsfield cross-country enthusiasts will find Ole's Cross Country Center, with about 50 km of trails traversing gently rolling hillsides, forests, and fields with views of Sugarbush. Group and individual lessons are available, as is equipment rental. Snowshoe rentals and trails add another dimension of snow sports. All of the trails are machine groomed and tracked, but ski skating is available as well. Warm up in the hut with hot beverages, fresh soups, and sandwiches. Adult rates are $16 and ages seven to twelve and seniors are $13. **Ole's Cross Country Center** is on Airport Road, Waitsfield; (802) 496–3430; (877) 863–3001; www.olesxc.com.

To get off the beaten path around here, head for the **Warren-Sugarbush Airport,** a bucolic area where you can take gliding lessons or have one of the airport's experienced pilots fly you over the valley in a sailplane.

The airport is perfect for a day's outing. You can enjoy the swing set, an outdoor barbecue, a volleyball net, a gazebo for contemplation, and a feeling of being on top of a mountain. There's even a snack bar, the Diner Soar Restaurant, where you can grab a sandwich or bowl of soup, sit outside on the second-floor deck, and watch the gliders soar in and out of the fields. Decades ago people sometimes spent the entire day at an airport, picnicking, visiting with friends and family, playing games, and watching the planes fly in and out. You can spend a similar day at the Warren-Sugarbush Airport.

The airport is the home of **Sugarbush Soaring,** a flying club that uses sailplanes to better experience the **Mad River Valley.** Flight in one of these sleek, long-winged beauties is unlike any other flight experience. It's soundless and has the sensation of freedom from the earth. A 20-minute flight (The Mad River Valley) is $129 and the Top Gun at Sugarbush (about 30 minutes) is $169. But the best deal is the introductory flight lesson that includes flight instruction and flight with a certified instructor for only $160, and you get to fly. Sugarbush Soaring also offers multiday, learn-to-soar camps. Another offering is a three-day soaring package, which includes eight training flights. The ultimate indulgence, however, is the sixteen-flight package. The soaring season at Sugarbush begins in Mid-May, and ends the last week in October. For more information, call Sugarbush Soaring at (802) 496–2290 or visit www .sugarbushsoaring.com.

If you're at the Warren Airport around lunchtime, try the **DinerSoar Deli,** under the management of Dino Valadakis. Dino specializes in a unique stuffed baked bread sandwich that is delicious. There are also Boar's Head products and other fine offerings.

The White River Valley

The first and second branches of the White River rise in the hills south of Barre, paralleled by Routes 110 and 14, respectively. Either route takes you through rolling farm country, and at the southernmost end of each, past covered bridges. A third north-south road, Route 12, parallels these to the west of I–89. To make the choices even more varied, Routes 64, 65, and 66, as well as several unnumbered back roads, go east-west between these. You could spend a couple of days wandering about in these hills and valleys and see a Vermont that even most Vermonters have never explored.

Route 12, the westernmost of these roads, goes through Northfield Falls, where four covered bridges cluster in a group, then drops into Northfield Gulf, one of several gulfs in Vermont. The easternmost, Route 110, goes through Washington, and from here it is only a short trip east—on unpaved but good road—to East Orange and its unique **Mosaic Church.** A needlelike spire, pointed windows with stained glass framing the panes, and a riot of fancy-cut shingles identify this structure as atypical of Vermont village churches. A nice four-bay carriage shed and a small schoolhouse complete the ensemble in the center of this tiny town.

Route 14, the center option, passes through Williamstown, where you should look on the southern end of the village for a sign to **Knight's Spider Web Farm.** One day Will and Terry Knight decided to maximize the beauty of the spiderwebs they saw in their barn. Both artists, the Knights devised a system of spraying a spiderweb with a combination of white paint and glue before mounting it on a wooden plaque and allowing it to set.

The Knights initially scouted out webs in their own and neighbors' barns, then opted for mass production by constructing a series of frames protected by a roof where spiders could spin their webs in peace and where you can watch them at work. Some of the Knights' designs incorporate painted flowers onto the plaque for an additional decorative touch. The gift shop is open year-round, but to see the web-creating process, go from mid-June to mid-October.

coolfacts

It took 5,000 pounds of ice a year to cool food for an average family.

It took 1,500 pounds of ice to cool the milk produced by a single cow during a year.

A cube of ice measuring 1 square foot weighs about fifty-seven pounds.

Brookfield ice was so clear that people claimed they could read the *Boston Herald* through a piece 16 inches thick.

Ice blocks stored in sawdust would keep through the summer.

Knight's Spider Web Farm is open from 9:00 a.m. to 5:00 p.m. daily mid-June through mid-October, and then weekends until Christmas. They ship a 7-by-9-inch web portrait for $25.00, plus $7.00 shipping. Write to Knight's Spider Web Farm, 124 Spider Web Farm Road, Williamstown, VT 05679, or call (802) 433–5568; www.spiderwebfarm.com; e-mail: webfarm@together.net.

Farther south on Route 14, a right turn onto Route 65 will bring you to the town of **Brookfield,** home of the 320-foot-long **Floating Bridge.** To reach the bridge, you'll first come to a dirt road, then take a right. Floating Bridge is a one-lane bridge that floats on 380 tarred wooden barrels and is connected to the land by hinges that allow for variations in the water's depth. Still well traveled by local foot and auto traffic, Floating Bridge spans what is called at various times Sunset Lake, Mirror Lake, and Colts Pond. When you walk on the bridge, there's a certain buoyancy to it, which becomes more obvious when a car crosses.

The bridge, which is part of Route 65, is located in a tranquil spot with lots of trout. As if to attest to the bridge's popularity as a fishing spot, fishing lines and sinkers hang suspended from the phone lines and power lines that cross over the lake, parallel to the bridge. There are some boggy areas to the lake. When a car passes over the bridge, the water comes up between the wooden planks. Puddles of water gather in strategic spots on the bridge. Because of this, it's often under repair, or might be closed due to high water.

In the late 1800s and early 1900s, Brookfield was known as one of the best sources of high-quality ice, and harvesting ice from Sunset Lake was one of the town's primary businesses. The general store had a large icehouse near the floating bridge and stored enough ice there to supply the town. The rest was sent to nearby Randolph, where it was used to cool the milk train to Boston.

For more than a quarter century, the people of Brookfield have revived this industry for one day each winter. On the last Saturday in January, they haul out all the old ice-harvesting tools and equipment, which visitors and townspeople alike can use to cut, saw, and haul ice blocks. As one local told us, "After you see all the work involved, it makes you want to go home and hug your refrigerator." So unusual is this activity, which takes place at the Floating Bridge, that 200 people may show up to watch.

Within a stone's throw of the bridge is *Green Trails Inn,* whose several buildings range from Federal to Greek Revival style. Of the thirteen guest rooms, some have private baths, some shared, some with whirlpool baths. Trails originally cut for the inn's stable of riding horses now serve as hiking trails in summer and cross-country and snowshoe trails in winter. Winter also brings sledding and skating, and on the last weekend of January, inn guests join in the annual Ice Harvest Festival at nearby Sunset Pond, reliving a tradition that dates from 1875 or earlier. Green Trails Inn, P.O. Box 484, Brookfield, 05036; (802) 276–3412.

Farther south and on the west side of I–89 is *Randolph,* a busy, thriving town with farms and manufacturing plants, and home of Vermont State Technical College.

Randolph was chartered in 1781, and the origin of its name is somewhat confusing. General John French, an early settler in the town, was born in Randolph, Massachusetts, but the town was not named by or for him. The first settler in Randolph was known to be from New Hampshire; although there is a Randolph, New Hampshire, as well, local history has it that Randolph, Vermont, was named by Vermonters, without any outside influence. Incidentally, early towns in Vermont were named by the governor of New Hampshire, Benning Wentworth, when Vermont was part of the New Hampshire grants.

In the village of Randolph, the ***Chandler Art Gallery and Music Hall*** serves as the area's cultural oasis for locals who don't want to travel to either Montpelier or Dartmouth College in Hanover, New Hampshire, for their dose of art.

The music hall holds several performances each month, ranging from works by local theater groups and children, to swing bands, to the acclaimed folksinger Odetta. The gallery next door holds exhibits centering on the history of Vermonters' use of art. Past offerings have included displays of decoys, children's art, antiques, stenciling, and art from the Abenaki; workshops and demonstrations are often conducted on the theme of a given month's exhibit. The Music Hall box office is open 3:00 p.m. to 6:00 p.m. Monday through Friday, and 11:00 a.m. until one hour before the show on the day of performance.

The Chandler Art Gallery (802–728–9878) opens when there are performances at the Music Hall. It is also open Saturday and Sunday from 1:00 p.m. to 3:00 p.m., or by appointment during the week. The Music Hall season begins in September and runs through May with concerts generally held Friday and Saturday evenings and Sunday afternoons. In August look for a multiday Chamber Music Festival, and on the last Sunday before Labor Day the New World Festival, an all-day event. The Music Hall Box Office can be reached at (802) 728–6464; www.chandlerarts.org. They are on Main Street in Randolph.

Route 12 leads from Randolph to Bethel, a town that was the first town chartered by the erstwhile Republic of Vermont. One of the most unusual street signs in the state is located in Bethel. If you're headed north on Route 12, the state highway makes a sharp left turn over a bridge. If you miss the turn and instead go straight, you'll soon discover your error, for there is a big red-and-white sign on the right that says THIS IS NOT ROUTE 12. The residents got sick of answering travelers' questions after too many wrong turns and remedied it with the sign.

On Route 107 West is the ***White River National Fish Hatchery.*** If you go fishing in Vermont, chances are that the next salmon you catch will have originated in Bethel. The best time to visit the hatchery is in November. It is then that two million Atlantic salmon eggs are hatched in the incubation room that the visitors room overlooks. The sight is something out of a sci-fi movie: huge, circular tanks that look as if they're ready for takeoff.

The fish are transferred to outdoor tanks before they're let loose to stock the Connecticut River and its tributaries in spring and again in fall. Also at the hatchery are displays of old photos that show how incubation and stocking were done in former times and how the breeding of salmon occurs without human interference. The hatchery is open daily from 8:00 a.m. to 3:00 p.m. For more information, call (802) 234–5400, or write the hatchery at Route 107, Box 140, Bethel, 05032.

The Brick Store, 235 Main Street in Bethel, has a 1930s soda fountain, along with penny candy. It also carries items made by nearby Johnson Woolen Mills, including vests, coats, hats, backpacks, and ladies' bags. The adjoining *Specialty Shop* represents over one hundred exhibitors, with quilts and other crafts; (802) 234–5378.

If you follow Route 107 east from the village of Bethel, you'll reach *Vermont Castings* on your right. You've probably heard of this maker of woodstoves, since the company ships its stoves all over the world. Some of its models—the Defiant, the Vigilant, and the Resolute—have been responsible for Vermont Castings' reputation for powerful, reliable stoves that go all night. The company has kept up with technology by introducing gas-powered stoves as well as the pellet stoves that cut down on pollution and wood use.

If you've never considered owning a woodstove, a visit to the Vermont Castings showroom will make you yearn for a cold winter's night even if it's the middle of summer. For information, write to Vermont Castings, Route 107, Bethel, 05032, or call (802) 234–2300.

South of Bethel, as Route 12 heads toward Woodstock, Barnard sits on the shore of Silver Lake, with a quintessential village store in its center. *Barnard General Store* has stood on this corner since 1832. Locals call it the "glue that holds the community together," and it's certainly the place to find part of the town's population at breakfast. If you stop by to sample the pancakes ($1.25 to $1.50, with Vermont maple syrup), you may meet nonagenarian Bucky Joy, custodian of the morning coffee there for more than twenty years—so long that the town's favorite coffee blend is named "Bucky's Brew." At other times of day, you can sit on the chrome counter stools and eat a made-to-order sandwich. The store is open in winter from 6:00 a.m. to 6:00 p.m. Monday through Thursday, 6:00 a.m. to 9:00 p.m. Friday and Saturday when they serve pizza, 8:00 a.m. until 4:00 p.m. on Sunday. In the summer the store stays open two hours longer each evening. On Monday nights, monthly in the winter and more frequently in the summer, the store hosts "Karmic Café," a community dinner featuring a local cook. Anyone is welcome, but reservations are essential; call (802) 234–9688; e-mail: barnard@vaics.org.

The store is also a good place to provision for an impromptu alfresco meal, with picnic tables on the lakeshore and in the Dorothy Thompson Memorial Common, on the other side of the store. A sign on the common remembers a longtime Barnard resident, journalist Dorothy Thompson. The road beside the store leads to the entrance of **_Silver Lake State Park,_** with a campground and water-sports facilities on the lake.

Just up the street (which in this case is Route 12) from the lake and general store is a charming small B&B, **_The Fan House._** Our room there had an indefinable Tuscan feel, despite the wide-board floors, Victorian claw-foot tub, American antiques, and oriental rugs. The low ceiling had been opened up to reveal every quirky angle of the eaves, but the space overhead was relieved from any cavernous feeling by cappuccino-colored paint and a skylight over the bed, through which we could count stars in the night sky. Gallery lights illuminated an original Gobelin tapestry on one wall. On the opposite wall a wood mantel, stripped of a century of paint layers, surrounded a working fireplace. There was no artifice, and no decorator-magazine Tuscan embellishments, but the feeling was unmistakable. With large down pillows and a substantial comforter on the king-size bed, it was one of the most appealing rooms we have ever opened our suitcases in. Each of the three rooms (one is a family suite) is different, and the others have a slight aura of provincial France. The well-traveled owner has restored and decorated this Victorian Revival house skillfully, incorporating family heirlooms with art that she has collected in her travels. Very knowledgeable about this area of Vermont, she can guide your travels well and help you plan your day over a full country breakfast. Rates begin at $160. The Fan House, Route 12, Barnard; (802) 234–6704; www .thefanhouse.com.

For those who enjoy wildlife, The Fan House has teamed with a local Audubon Society leader and an expert animal tracker to introduce guests to local birds and animals. These wildlife walks can be planned for a half or full day, with snowshoe rentals available locally for winter tracking trips. Seasonal birding events include hawk-watching in September, the breathtaking sight of thousands of snow geese migrating in October, and the Christmas bird count in December. May is the prime month, however, with sightings of as many as fifty species possible in an afternoon ramble.

Even smaller than Barnard is East Barnard, which is reached by an unpaved road a short distance past the entrance to Silver Lake State Park. The well-known artist Sabra Johnson Field has a studio on the road between East Barnard and South Royalton, where she works and sells her prints from a small gallery. Many of her themes are inspired by Vermont's landscapes, and the Vermont Land Trust commissioned her to create a commemorative poster. Be sure to call first if you plan to visit the gallery, since it is not always open; (802) 763–7092; www.sabrafield.com. Her work is also shown at Woodstock Folk Art Prints and Antiquities in Woodstock; (802) 457–2012.

Just east of Bethel, Routes 14 and 110 follow the respective branches of the White River, joining in the Royaltons, where their streams also meet the main body of the White River. A trip up either one of these or, better yet, a loop that combines the lower ends of each by a road over the ridge that lies between them will show you one of the heaviest concentrations of covered bridges in the state. Heading up Route 110 you will pass five, all but one within sight of the road (and that one's close, but hidden in a little hollow).

You will pass, in turn, the Howe Bridge (on the east side of the road), the Cilley Bridge (on the left), and the Larkin Bridge (on the right). The next is the Flint Bridge, on the right, which you can cross to find the ***Morgan Horse Cemetery.***

After you go through the Flint Bridge, turn right and follow the dirt road up the hill until you come to a small grassy triangle at a fork. To your right, beside the right-hand road (which turns into a driveway here), you'll see a granite stone marking the grave of the Morgan horse Lippitt Mandale. What you may not see, unless you look downhill from the first, is the other stone monument, which reads as follows: ON THIS FARM LIES THE BODY OF JUSTIN MORGAN, FOALED 1789 DIED 1821 PROGENITOR OF THE FIRST ESTABLISHED AMERICAN BREED OF HORSES. On the stone is a portrait of the famous horse.

The next bridge is not visible from Route 110, but you can cross it if you follow the riverside road instead of recrossing the Flint Bridge. You will cross the 1883 Moxie Bridge and return to Route 110, just before the left turn that will take you over the ridge (with nice mountain views) to Route 14 at East Randolph. About a mile south of the intersection is Braley Covered Bridge Road on your right, at the bottom of which you will find a small covered bridge. Farther along Route 110 is the Gifford Bridge on the left and the Hyde Bridge on the right. Not far south of the last bridge, Route 14 joins Route 107 to complete the loop.

As you travel along Route 110, you will pass through the town of Tunbridge, site of the ***Tunbridge World's Fair,*** which has been going strong since 1867. It missed only twice, in 1918 because of the terrible influenza epidemic, and during World War II, when so many men were away that it was impossible to run the agricultural events. It's an old-fashioned agricultural fair, with rows of jellies, plates of perfect vegetables, and vases of garden flowers hung with blue ribbons. Entertainment is family oriented and fun, such as the illusions and hijinks of Tom Crowl and the Mrs., and a contra dance group that has demonstrated their fancy steps there since the 1930s.

In the center of the fairgrounds is an entire museum building, filled with an impressive display of antiques and old agricultural equipment collected from central Vermont. Amid these fascinating artifacts, craftsmen demonstrate skills that range from rug hooking to violin making. It's worth a trip to the fair just for this museum, which is open only during fair week in mid-September. Demonstrations of cider making and many other rural skills are going on constantly, and most of the performances and grandstand events are free. Tickets can be purchased at the gate or by mail from P.O. Box 152, Tunbridge, 05077; (802) 889–5555; www.tunbridgefair.com.

More Places to Stay in Central Vermont

(All area codes 802)

BARNARD

Barnard Inn
Route 12
234–9961
www.barnardinnrestaurant
.com
Fine dining (by reservation) or informal bistro-style menu in the pub, with good American dishes, such as bowls of plump mussels. Moderate prices.

WAITSFIELD

Lareau Farm Country Inn
Box 563, 35 Lareau Road,
Route 100
496–4949 or (800) 833–0766
www.lareaufarminn.com
Has thirteen homey rooms with private or shared baths in a rambling farmhouse.

More Places to Eat in Central Vermont

(All area codes 802)

BROOKFIELD

Ariel's Restaurant and the Pond Village Pub
Stone Road and Route 65,
Brookfield Village
276–3939
www.arielsrestaurant.com
Fine dining in a nineteenth-century farmhouse or a bit more casually in the pub.

TO LEARN MORE IN CENTRAL VERMONT

Central Vermont Chamber of Commerce; (802) 229–5711; www.central-vt.com.

Central Vermont Event Listings; www.centralvt.org

MONTPELIER

McGillicuddy's Irish Pub
14 Langdon Street
223–2721
Pub fare, with hot and cold sandwiches at about $5.00 and a selection of ales.

WAITSFIELD

American Flatbread
Lareau Farm, Route 100
496–8856
www.americanflatbread
.com
Bakes pizzas in a wood-fired oven and serves them in an informal setting on weekends only.

WARREN

The Common Man Restaurant
3209 German Flats Road
583–2800
www.commonman
restaurant.com
Offers an uncommon menu of New American and European dishes, expertly prepared.

CONNECTICUT RIVER VALLEY

The Connecticut River cuts a wide swath between Vermont and New Hampshire—at least in this area—as though underscoring the differences between the two states. Beside it, and in sight of it for much of its route, runs Interstate 91, high along a shoulder of the hills that rise on the river's western bank. The views are among the best from any interstate highway in the country, over rich fertile farmlands, the wide winding river with its oxbows and tributary streams, and the hills and mountains of New Hampshire across the river. It's New England scenery at its best at any time of year, and a spectacular panorama in the fall.

Route 5 also parallels the river, often weaving back and forth across the straighter interstate, and passing through some of the most fertile farmland in New England as it strings together the towns from Brattleboro to Newbury—and beyond to an area you've already read about: the Northeast Kingdom.

Early settlers homesteaded along the river so that they could easily receive supplies from their previous homes in Connecticut and Massachusetts. They weren't dissuaded by the countless bends in the river that are especially common

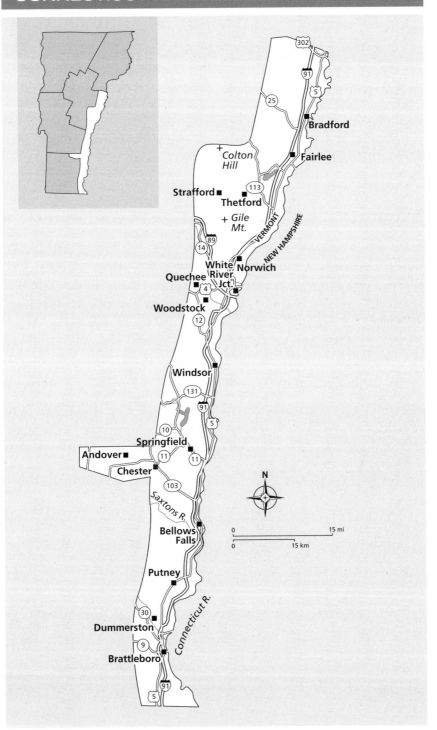

between Thetford and Newbury. In fact, Bradford's high school is called Oxbow.

In some towns in the Upper Valley—the towns that fall between Springfield and Newbury—the line between Vermont and New Hampshire across the river begins to blur. A phone call from Norwich to Hanover, even though it's from Vermont to New Hampshire, is not a toll call; there are ample bridges for residents to travel from one state to the other. Since the area is touted as a region and not two different states, the line gets even fuzzier. In fact, the Norwich/Hanover school district is the only multistate local school district in the country.

White River Junction

White River Junction, in the center of the valley, is an old railroad town that, like many others, had its heyday when the trains made the air thick with smoke. Today the town still has many thriving retail stores, a food co-op, and a couple of restaurants. And, yes, White River Junction still serves as a stop for Amtrak.

The *Vermont Salvage Exchange* is funky and utilitarian at the same time, a used-house-parts store where you can find everything from stained-glass windows to doors, wainscoting, and heating grilles, all in one place.

Amid the three floors of boxes of doorknobs, light fixtures, and gargoyles are creative decorating hints intended to help you make the most of your purchases. A hand-printed sign atop a cart of old solid oak doors asks, HAVE YOU EVER THOUGHT OF MAKING WAINSCOTING FROM 5-PANEL DOORS? The decorator-in-residence then offers drawn diagrams to help you envision this unusual wainscoting and offers three or more doors at $25 apiece to help you out.

The store is open Monday through Friday from 9:00 a.m. to 4:30 p.m. and from 8:00 a.m. to 3:00 p.m. Saturday. Vermont Salvage Exchange, Railroad Row, White River Junction, 05001; call (802) 295–7616 for more information about what's come in on a given day; www.vermontsalvage.com.

AUTHOR'S TOP HIGHLIGHTS

The Montshire Museum of Science	Justin Smith Morrill Homestead
Chester	

In the center of town, within sight of both the Briggs Opera House and Vermont Salvage, stands steam locomotive ***Engine 494*** with its tender and caboose, a reminder of the days when as many as fifty trains a day brought passengers to and from the depot here.

North of White River, off Route 5, the town of Hartford has established the ***Hurricane Forest Wildlife Refuge,*** thanks to a gift from Windsor and Bertha Brown. The entrance to the 142-acre tract is off of Old King's Highway. Four trails are from ²⁄₁₀ mile (Pond Loop) to ⁸⁄₁₀ mile (Beacon Hill Loop) in length. Benches are placed at strategic points for resting or observing nature. Look for the turn on the left, close to the I–89 underpass on Route 5. For more information, contact the Town of Hartford Parks and Recreation Department at (802) 295–9353, ext. 31.

Norwich–Strafford

Visitors to Norwich, just north of White River Junction, frequently marvel that on their approach to Hanover, New Hampshire, and Dartmouth College just across the Connecticut River at how courteous Vermont drivers are. As you approach the Ledyard Bridge, there's a left-turn-only lane that—would you believe?—drivers use only to make left turns. A more common response might be to seize an advantage over fellow drivers by squeezing into the adjacent lane. Not here, though, for whatever reason.

It's a Long Way to White River Junction

Boston & Maine Railroad's Engine 494 is not just any old steam locomotive; it has a unique history of its own. Built in Manchester, New Hampshire, in 1892, Engine 494 hauled passengers on the company's Eastern Line, then was used on the uphill run from Fabyan Station to Marshfield Station, 2,700 feet up the side of New Hampshire's Mount Washington. It hauled coal to fuel the Cog Railway, which ran from Marshfield to the summit. Over its lifetime, many improvements were made in train construction, and with each, Engine 494 was modernized to keep up with the times. It was retired in 1938.

But not quite. In 1939 Engine 494 was chosen to represent Boston & Maine at the New York World's Fair, and it was unmodernized, its steel cab replaced with wood, its electric headlamp replaced with an oil light. After the fair it was stored and almost scrapped, but a group called the Railroad Enthusiasts was unwilling to see this unique example of a restored nineteenth-century locomotive die, and a new home was found for it in White River Junction.

ANNUAL EVENTS IN THE CONNECTICUT RIVER VALLEY

Late February: Winter Carnival, Brattleboro, one of New England's oldest, with events for all ages; (802) 254–4565, www.brattleborochamber.org.

First week in June: Strolling of the Heifers, Brattleboro, kicks off National Dairy Month as salute to family farms and their contributions to Vermont's agricultural heritage; www.strollingoftheheifers.com.

Late June to early August: Yellow Barn Music Festival, Putney, brings a series of concerts by well-known musicians; (802) 387–6637.

Mid-July: Cow Appreciation Day, Billings Farm Museum, Woodstock, where you can try your hand at milking and enjoy freshly churned butter and hand-cranked ice cream; (802) 457–2355.

Mid-July to mid-August: Marlboro College Music Festival, Marlboro, features professional and student musicians who perform for the public on weekends; (802) 254–2394.

Early August: Annual pilgrimage to Rockingham Meeting House, Rockingham, where for more than ninety years this fine example of an early meetinghouse has been commemorated annually with music and historical programs on the first Sunday in August; (802) 463–3941.

Late August: Annual Scottish Festival, Quechee, with bagpipes, dancing, foods, Rugby, sheepdogs, and massed bands, held the fourth weekend of August; (800) 295–5451.

Mid-October: Annual Heritage Festival, Newfane, featuring crafts, Vermont products, a flea market, and entertainment on the common; (802) 365–7855.

Mid-October: Harvest Celebration, Billings Farm Museum, Woodstock, when the fall activities of a nineteenth-century farm are demonstrated and celebrated: cider pressing, the pumpkin harvest, a husking bee, preserving, and more; (802) 457–2355.

Late October: Apple Days, Brattleboro, with crafts, foods, art and musical events, orchard tours, and cider pressing; (802) 254–4565.

Early December (usually the first Saturday): Brattleboro Farmers' Market Annual Craft Show, Congregational Church, Main Street, Brattleboro; (802) 254–4565.

Norwich is home to hundreds of Dartmouth College employees, professors, and students, as well as a number of eighth-generation Norwichers. The town has a countrified, genteel air, from the Montessori school to the green that serves as playground for the town's elementary school. Norwich is a curious blend of culture and country.

Located right on the banks of the Connecticut River, the ***Montshire Museum of Science*** is a place where both adults and children can let loose the kid inside. "Montshire" is an amalgam of Vermont and New Hampshire.

The first Montshire opened in Hanover, New Hampshire, in January 1976 in an abandoned bowling alley as a community museum for the public—which was a novel idea at the time. From the beginning it was operated as a learning center instead of a museum. Montshire moved across the river to a new facility in Norwich in November 1989 and was designed top to bottom to be a hands-on science museum, from the color-coded ventilation systems to the exposed trusses.

Kids may take a few minutes to make the transition from a world of "Don't Touch" to the freedom of the Montshire, where even adults feel as if they're getting away with something. You can play with light switches, shoot baskets, blow bubbles, and splash around in soapy water.

Parents especially like the Montshire because the only snacks offered are apples, yogurt, trail mix, and Gatorade.

Upstairs are a variety of beetles (dead ones) and boa constrictors (live ones). There's also a dinosaur-size ant colony with hundreds of thousands of ants climbing through eleven Plexiglas chambers. Even if you had an ant colony as a kid, the Leafcutter Ant Colony will make your skin crawl. The Montshire also hosts a number of traveling exhibits—one year it was a collection of dinosaur eggs—so you'll never know what you'll find when you visit.

hailtheking!

In the 1920s, when barrels of King Arthur Flour were delivered throughout New England by truck, the company's advertising consisted of a white truck with a life-size wooden statue of King Arthur on his horse. It was a three-dimensional version of the logo used today, complete with standard flying over his head. Just in case no one noticed this king and his horse hitching a ride through town, the white truck was equipped with a calliope to draw attention to the royal visit.

The Montshire is open from 10:00 a.m. to 5:00 p.m. seven days a week. It's closed on New Year's Day, Thanksgiving, and Christmas. Write to the Montshire Museum of Science, Montshire Road, Norwich, 05055, call (802) 649–2200 for information on special programs and daily highlights, or visit www.montshire.org.

On Route 5, just south of the I–91 exit, is a mecca for home bread bakers. ***The Baker's Store*** is the walk-around version of the King Arthur Flour catalog, which supplies bakers all over the country with everything from the right pan to the right type of yeast and plump dried currants for real scones. Here you can see it all and taste the breads that the catalog only gives you the recipes for (we wonder if they've thought of a scratch-n-sniff patch so readers will have the aroma of fresh-baked bread to inspire them). The store would inspire anyone to get elbow-deep in bread dough, and it offers some specialty items not shown in the catalog. You'll never again think of King Arthur as just flour. The store is open from 7:30 a.m. to 6:00 p.m. Monday through Saturday and 8:30 a.m. to 4:00 p.m. Sunday; Route 5, Norwich; (800) 827–6836 or (802) 649–3361; www.kingarthurflour.com.

On your left just past the three-way stop in the village is **Dan & Whit's,** a country store that's unusual even by Vermont standards. Whenever anyone in Norwich gives out directions, the inevitable benchmark is: "Oh, go a mile past Dan & Whit's, turn left onto Turnpike Road, and keep going."

The immense outdoor bulletin board on the front of the building serves as the contemporary version of a town crier. Notices about everything from rooms for rent to goat's milk for sale to pancake suppers are posted here. Inside, Dan & Whit's is the antithesis of the modern-day supermarket. No scanners here, just shelves with loaves of locally baked bread next to boxes of doodads. Wander around the aisles up front, but the real treasure is through the door next to the meat counter, a door that looks like it should have an employees only sign hanging over it. The hardware department is in here. Stovepipes, birdseed, shovels, sleds, and inner tubes compete for space and more often than not haphazardly spill onto the cement floor.

Dan & Whit's General Store is on Main Street; the hours are generally from 7:00 a.m. to 9:00 p.m. seven days a week. Call (802) 649–1602 for information.

Look for signs opposite the common at Main and Elm Streets directing you to the almost-hidden **Allechante.** Sandwiches are built on slabs of crusty sourdough bread, or ask for a baguette packed with imported cheeses and exotic cold cuts. A few small tables in the cafe provide a place to perch while you eat. We like to stop there in the morning to prepare for the day's picnic with a loaf of bread and a rondel of cheese, which might be a local chèvre or a complex vintage cheese from a remote valley in France. It's one of the best selections of hard-to-find and rare cheeses in New England. Allechante is open Monday through Friday 7:30 a.m. to 6:00 p.m., and Saturday until 5:00 p.m.; Main and Elm Streets, Norwich; (802) 649–2846.

If you continue on Main Street heading west, the road ascends, climbing up into the mountains from the Connecticut River basin, winding past working farms. Some 5.5 miles from Dan & Whit's, the road forks. Bear left onto Route

132 and about 8 miles from the fork take a sharp right. You'll be in the village of South Strafford.

If instead of continuing west on Route 132, you bear right at the T on the Justin Smith Morrill Highway and drive 2 miles, you'll be in the Strafford town center. Justin Morrill served Vermont in the U.S. House of Representatives from 1855 to 1867 and in the U.S. Senate from 1867 to 1898. He is remembered for the Morrill Act of 1862, which provided land grants to help found state colleges to promote agricultural, mechanical, science, and classical studies. He is often called "the Father of the Agricultural Colleges." It's hard to miss his home, now a museum dedicated to his memory. The *Justin Smith Morrill Homestead* is a large, peach-colored Victorian fantasy with steep gables and generous gingerbread trim, sitting on a hillside along the road in the center of town. The seventeen-room mansion was built in the Gothic Revival style and remains as it was designed, complete with original furnishings, gardens, outbuildings, and an exquisite handpainted window in the ceiling of the library. It's open from 11:00 a.m. to 5:00 p.m. Wednesday through Sunday from Memorial Day through Columbus Day. Justin Morrill Highway, in the center of the village of Strafford; (802) 765–4484.

Facing the green is the *Stone Soup* restaurant. There isn't any sign for the restaurant—the laws of Strafford place certain restrictions on the types of signs that retail establishments can hang outside—so the owners decided to buck the trend and not have any sign at all. Look for the picket fence surrounding a house on the left side of the green. Gardens out back provide many of the vegetables served in the restaurant.

The menu changes nightly and includes a fish entree, poultry, and meat. Some of the possibilities are turbot with three-peppercorn shallot butter, roasted hens with a sauternes glaze, and lamb tenderloin with a cabernet

WORTH SEEING

The Billings Farm & Museum, Route 12 and River Road, Woodstock; (802) 457–2355.

Basketville, Main Street, Route 5, Putney; (802) 387–4351.

Green Mountain Flyer Scenic Train Ride, P.O. Box 498, Bellows Falls; (802) 463–3069.

Quechee Gorge, Route 4, Quechee (east of Woodstock); (802) 295–7600.

Vermont Institute of Natural Sciences and Raptor Center, Church Hill Road, Woodstock; (802) 457–2779.

sauce. All entrees are served with fresh vegetables in season, and if you're lucky enough to get there in the spring, more likely than not your plate will include a few precious fiddlehead ferns—a Vermont delicacy that gets Vermonters' attention because its presence in markets and restaurants signals the end of winter.

Stone Soup is open Thursday through Sunday from 6:00 to 9:00 p.m. all year. Reservations are a must, as is saving room for dessert. Stone Soup is at 7 Brook Road, Strafford; call ahead at (802) 765–4301 for the nightly specials.

Norwich to Fairlee

Route 5 North out of Norwich parallels the Connecticut River and the old Boston & Maine tracks. This is a route that's popular with bicyclists, and on the river you may see the Dartmouth sculling team.

About 10 miles north is Route 113 West. Just north of the turnoff on the right is *Pompanoosuc Mills* in East Thetford. Pompanoosuc Mills produces and sells finely designed furniture at its seven stores located throughout New England. But all the furniture is made here.

Dwight Sargent is a native of the area. He attended Dartmouth both as an undergraduate and as an MBA candidate at Dartmouth's Tuck Business School. While he was at Tuck, he decided that starting up Pompanoosuc Mills was the best way he could apply what he had learned about furniture making from his grandfather.

Dwight proved to be a good student. The East Thetford showroom is spacious and airy and shows off Pompanoosuc's beds, tables, cabinets, and other furniture to their best advantage via decor suggestions and floor layouts. Each piece of furniture is available in cherry, oak, maple, birch, walnut, and occasionally bird's-eye.

Got Milk?

The old joke about Vermont having more cows than people, although once true, has gone the way of the family farm. Over the past decades, Vermont has been losing dairy farms at a rate of about 4 percent a year. But the trend seems to have slowed, then reversed. Not that you can expect to find an overflow of cows grazing on the State House lawn in Montpelier—the increase amounts to fewer than a dozen new farms a year. But it's progress in keeping the dairy farmer from joining the piping plover on the endangered species list.

Head upstairs to another showroom and a picture window that looks out onto the mill floor, where you can see workers sanding, shaping, and creating the furniture. Several times a year Pompanoosuc Mills conducts tours of the mill for the public. Call for the dates of its next tour.

Write to Pompanoosuc Mills, Route 5, East Thetford, VT 05043, or call (802) 785–4851 or (800) 841–6671; www.pompanoosuc.com. Pompanoosuc Mills is open Monday through Friday from 9:00 a.m. to 6:00 p.m., Saturday 9:00 a.m. to 5:00 p.m., and Sunday from 11:00 a.m. to 5:00 p.m.

Route 113 heads west, through several of the villages of Thetford. At Thetford Center you'll see a cluster of nice brick homes, and if you turn left there, you'll drop into a little hollow with a covered bridge, waterfall, and old mill foundations. Farther along Route 113 is Post Mills Airport, where Post Mills Aviation offers scenic balloon and glider rides over the Connecticut Valley. You might see their brightly colored balloons drifting above the treetops as you drive along the interstate.

From Post Mills, Route 113 wanders on to West Fairlee. Less than a mile past the village center, take a left where the sign reads SOUTH VERSHIRE AND STRAFFORD. This road is known in various parts as Beanville Road, Copper Mine Road, and, farther west, Algerin Road. The road parallels Copper Creek on the left and follows several of the river's twists and turns. Stay on this road, and $\frac{3}{10}$ mile from Route 113 you'll see copper-colored rocks on the left in the creek. Just $\frac{1}{10}$ mile later is a reddish parking area on the right that is the entrance to what used to be the ***Vermont Copper Mining Company,*** an old copper mine. Pull in here and walk in at the gate to see the rusting and crumbling remains.

Vershire was first known as Ely, and this area was called Copperfield. This road used to see a lot of traffic. At its height in 1880, there were 600 miners and 225 horses working here at the mine, which produced more than 60 percent of the copper in the United States.

Vegetation grows to the left of the road, but other sections remain spookily barren. The fumes and smoke from the copper smelter and the roasting beds up ahead killed off most of the area's vegetation by 1875, after only twenty years of operation. No vegetation meant that the thin layer of topsoil was easily washed away, and the land is still recovering.

Scraps of iron and slag are scattered throughout the old roasting beds. Straight ahead 100 yards or so is the path the old tramway took to bring the copper ore down from the mines. There's an old cellar hole, quite elaborate, that, judging from old maps, photographs, and descriptions, was the smelter. Parts of the wall still stand, and where the bricks lie used to be the furnace. If you go back a little farther, about 50 feet or so, you'll see what looks like a heap of copper-colored dirt with large spidery cables sticking out of it. A couple of huge rusted bolts and nuts also stick up out of the concrete walls.

There are plenty of trails to explore at the mine, summer or winter. In fact, local snowmobile clubs and cross-country skiers use the trails in the winter.

Fairlee, on Route 5, is blessed with two sizable lakes that have attracted summer visitors for almost as long as Vermont's been a state. Fairlee can become quite congested during July and August, but at any time of year it's a pretty detour from Route 5 to drive around the wooded shore of *Lake Morey.*

If Fairlee is known by a few for the first steamboat, *Bradford,* the next town north of Fairlee, is known for James Wilson, who created the first geographic globes sold in the United States in the early part of the nineteenth century.

Bradford is also an important early mill town. Lots of the old mill buildings have been converted for new businesses and residential use. But there's no mistaking them.

At *Colatina Exit* you can enjoy Italian veal, chicken, and seafood entrees and your choice of spaghetti, linguine, or fettuccine heaped with a thick tomato sauce that's made fresh every day. Antipasto and good, hearty soups such as an Italian white-bean-and-sausage soup with a touch of tarragon are among Colatina's appetizers.

But most people come here for the pizza, available in four sizes with every topping imaginable and even some you never thought of before. Chopped onions are free. The one room holds twenty tables, but if you want to hear quiet local music while dining on pizza and sandwiches, Colatina has a bar upstairs that's open till late.

Wouldn't That Steam You?

Originally from Orford, across the river in New Hampshire, *Samuel Morey* invented a steam engine and used it in a tiny skiff that he operated on the Connecticut River on a quiet Sunday morning in the early spring of 1793. Morey later moved to Fairlee, Vermont, and worked on his invention while plying the waters of the nearby lake that bears his name. There is a strong tradition that says that somewhere on the bottom of Lake Morey are the remains of the very first steamboat, and it wasn't invented by Robert Fulton. Robert Fulton reportedly visited with Morey in New York and at Orford, and with another Rhode Island steamboat inventor, years before he built his own steamboat and claimed the patent on steam navigation, denying Morey recognition as the inventor of steam propulsion for boats and ships.

He Sure Pulled the Wool over Their Eyes

One of the better-known residents of Corinth, west of Bradford, was Horace McDuffee, who lived here in the late 1800s. He had a graduate degree in engineering from Dartmouth and compensated for his small stature by wearing many layers of overalls. Another Corinthian was Daniel Flagg, who loved animals so much that he didn't wear shoes because they were made out of leather; he wouldn't ride a horse; and he invented the cowcatcher because he felt sorry for the cows who were speared when trains came roaring through the valley. And Orson Clement, still another Corinth native, raised sheep to such an extent that he stored the wool anywhere he could on his 600-acre farm: in the barn, the house, the granary basement, the stables. Clement was the equivalent of the man who saved every piece of string to make into a big ball. He never sold any of his wool until he was forced to do so by the federal government, which needed wool for uniforms during World War I. Even then, Clement managed to keep a sizable cache for himself that wasn't discovered until his death.

Colatina's main dining room is open from 11:00 a.m. to about 9:00 p.m. seven days a week. Call (802) 222–9008.

If you're an antiques buff, you already know Vermont is filled with lots of shops and malls that offer some items you'd shake your head at, while others will cause you to take out your wallet and ask how much.

Happily, the owners of many antiques shops have pooled their resources to produce brochures and directories that point out all of the antiques shops and malls within a particular region. At the junction of Routes 5 and 25 in Bradford opposite the Hungry Bear is the rustic collaborative ***Bradford 4 Corners Antiques.*** Here some vendors have shops with storefronts, while others just set up their tables in the parking lot. Then there's the auctioneer in the large hall in between all of the other shops who conducts auctions every Friday at 6:30 p.m. and Monday at 6:00 p.m. sharp. The auctioneer is Ernie Stevens, and you can reach him at (802) 222–5113 or (603) 989–5809 for more information on the auctions, or write to him at Bradford, 05033. But the best way to go antiquing in Bradford is to just show up.

Boston University alumni may be surprised to learn that their alma mater began just north of Bradford, in the tiny town of Newbury. Originating in 1836 as a school for the classical education of Methodist clergy, the Newbury Biblical Institute (as it was first called) was in a four-story brick building overlooking Newbury's common, next to the white Methodist Church, which was also part of the school. In 1846 the institute moved to Concord, New Hampshire, then to Boston in 1849, when it was renamed Boston University. A 1913 fire destroyed the original brick building, but the white **Old Village Church** still stands, restored by the Newbury Women's Club.

The Southern Connecticut River Valley

I–91 roughly parallels the Connecticut River until just south of St. Johnsbury, providing elevated river and valley views that the slower, lower Route 5 can't match. But Route 5 winds through a series of very interesting towns that I–91 travelers will miss. Other numbered routes branch off from Route 5, most heading northwest—Route 30 in Brattleboro, Route 103 in Rockingham, Route 108 in Springfield, Route 12 in Hartland, and Route 14 in White River Junction. Routes 9, 11, 131, and 4 head west, connecting Route 5 to Route 100, which runs up the center of the state.

Each of these roads leads through small towns and long stretches of rural landscapes marked by mountains and narrow valleys. Take any of these, and wander deeper into rural Vermont on the unnumbered roads that branch off of them. Don't worry (except in mud season) about leaving the pavement behind. Vermont has many unpaved roads, a wise decision in a climate where frost makes smaller paved roads look like fruitcake with all the nuts pulled out. These unpaved roads are usually smooth to travel and are easy to repair in the spring by simply running a road grader over them.

Quechee and Woodstock

Route 4 crosses over the deep and dramatic **Quechee Gorge** in the town of Quechee, well worth a stop to walk along the rim and down to the base on the southern side of the road. The village of Quechee is heavily developed, but if you pass through the covered bridge and turn right, you'll soon be out of it and find the peaceful setting of The Quechee Inn at Marshland Farm.

Family-friendly and comfortably warm and casual, and with one of Vermont's finest dining rooms, the inn offers twenty-two nicely decorated guest rooms, with pieced quilts, wide-board floors (some as wide as 24 inches), and views of the pond, the river, and the woodlands that surround the property. Rates, which include a substantial buffet breakfast, begin at $90. Children are more than welcome, and a family suite is located on the lower floor with no surrounding guest rooms, perfect for parents who worry that other guests may not enjoy their children's enthusiasm. The inn is at 1119 Main Street, Quechee; (802) 295–3133 or (800) 235–3133; www.quecheeinn.com.

Todd Murphy got it right, and despite those who said it would never work, it does. Todd's ***The Farmers Diner*** in Quechee serves "food from here"— not in capital letters, just a plain fact. A farmer himself, he worried about the decline of family farms in Vermont, but he also worried about all the greater issues that the globalization of food brings with it—stale ingredients, picked green and loaded with preservatives or genetically mutated for shelf life, instead of flavor and nutrition. The premise of his restaurant is deceptively simple: offer people a choice of imported and tasteless or local and tasty at the same price, and they'll choose the second every time.

So you can eat well and feel good, knowing that the food is healthy (he uses organic and sustainable growers whenever available), and economics of it are preserving local landscapes and a way of life. Begin your day with a three-eggs-and-cheese omelet with an additional side, plus toast, $9.50. Then for lunch, try the Smoking Boar, a club sandwich with Vermont & Cure ham, turkey, bacon, with Cabot cheddar, tomato, and lettuce on La Panciata wheat bread, for $11.00.

And if you can't live without more of the bacon, they'll ship it to you. Find The Farmers Diner in the Quechee Gorge Village on Route 4, a quarter-mile east of the Gorge bridge. They are open seven days a week, 7:00 a.m. to 3:00 p.m. Breakfast and lunch are served all day. (802) 295–4600; www.farmers diner.com.

The ***Quechee Inn Restaurant*** is outstanding. A casual-dining supper menu includes sage-rubbed pork tenderloin seared and sliced over apricot brandied butternut leeks with cheddar potato croquettes and a port wine peppercorn reduction for $18. If you're driving through, the luncheon is delectable with offerings such as a fresh sandwich buffet and a choice of two salads at $14.95, or marinated beef tips with sautéed wild mushrooms, onions, and egg noodles, at $17. There is a comprehensive wine list and a range of decadent desserts. Entrees on the "fine dining" menu begin at $23, but we never got past the supper menu, which is always available. The chef's own pâté was buttery smooth and fine flavored, served with dried cherries plumped in cognac. The gingerbread served with port-poached pears for dessert was so dark and rich that it could have been chocolate. The talented chefs are passionate about using locally grown and produced ingredients whenever they can, and they combine them brilliantly. This is a restaurant to travel far for. For reservations, contact them at (802) 295–3133 or (800) 235–3133; www .quecheeinn.com.

The inn offers guests a wide range of outdoor sports for all age groups in their ***Wilderness Trails*** program, among them: flat-water and white-water paddling through the waters of the neighboring wildlife sanctuary, a fly-

the movable bridge

Lincoln Bridge used to be in the middle of Woodstock, where the Billings Bridge is now. But in an 1869 flood, the entire structure was washed some distance downstream, where it came to rest, intact, on an island. Charles Lincoln's bridge had also been washed away by the flood, but it was completely destroyed. Lincoln waited for a heavy winter with a hard freeze and plenty of snow, and hauled his newfound bridge up Route 4 on a sled. It's been at its present location, through hail and high water, since 1877.

Its ability to withstand being ripped from its moorings and carried by floodwaters is a testimony to its design, patented by T. W. Pratt in 1844. Its vertical posts and crossed iron rods were to become the prototype for hundreds of steel railroad bridges built with the growth of the railroads, but this one is the only remaining original covered bridge of this design.

fishing school, mountain bikes, cross-country ski trails alongside Quechee Gorge, ice skating, and snowshoeing, all with or without guides, instruction, and equipment—even ice-skate rentals. Wilderness Trails has 18 km of groomed cross-country ski trails, over rolling terrain and past beaver lodges, waterfalls, and the fields and woods of Marshland Farm. Four km of the trails are suitable for ski skating. Access Wilderness Trails via the **Quechee Inn at Marshland Farm,** Main Street, Quechee; (802) 295–7620, www.quecheeinn.com.

Woodstock is unquestionably pretty, especially around its green, from which a covered bridge is visible. It is also well aware of its own charms, and is perhaps the state's most pernicious speed trap. That said, there is a lot to see and do here, and tourism has been a part of the town's history for at least the last century, so the tourists who fill the little boutiques are authentic, too.

Woodstock can thank the late Laurance Rockefeller for a great many things, not the least of which is preserving its early village landscape by burying telephone and electric lines. Woodstock's history as a retreat for the wealthy has left it a legacy of fine homes and estates, one of which has become the nucleus for an unusual national park.

In addition to its great wealth, the Rockefeller family is well known for its deep commitment to conservation, an interest that first took shape in Woodstock. At the **Marsh-Billings-Rockefeller National Historic Park,** visitors can discover how the ideas of the first American conservationist, George Perkins Marsh, were put into action, first by rail king Frederick Billings and later by the Rockefellers. This is the only national park to concentrate on land stewardship and its evolution in America. The park has two separate components to visit. The first is the working farm, which includes visiting the cows in the dairy barn, the farmhouse and dairy, and a museum of New England farm and rural life. The park and museum are open May 1 through October daily from 10:00 a.m. to 5:00 p.m.; weekends in November including Thanksgiving weekend, December weekends and December 26–January 4, 10:00 a.m. to 4:00 p.m.; weekends in January and February, 10:00 a.m. to 4:00 p.m. Sleigh Ride Weekends: Martin Luther King and Presidents' weekends, 10:00 a.m. to 4:00 p.m. Admissionis $11 for adults, $10 for adults over sixty-two, $6.00 for children ages five to fifteen, and $3 for children ages three to four. Major credit cards accepted. 54 Elm Street, Woodstock; (802) 457–3368.

Overlooking the farm from a wooded hill is the mansion, originally a brick Federal-style home but transformed in several stages into a stylish Victorian mansion, with windows, fabrics, and wallpapers by the Tiffany studio. Like the house, the gardens were updated and expanded in stages, each time by a foremost landscape architect. Tours are the only way to see the house and gardens and are priced at $8.00 for adults, $4.00 for children under age sixteen. Reservations are a good idea for the mansion tours. The museum is on River Road in Woodstock; (802) 457–3368.

Woodstock has been selected by the National Park Service as the first of the many parks with a Civil War theme to feature the home front. Park historians schedule and lead *Civil War tours* of sites significant in Vermont's considerable war effort. The tours document the war's impact on small towns in Vermont, examining its effects on places far from the battlefields. Sites on the tours—which you can also visit on your own—include the Congregational Church, where abolitionists met long before the war itself, and the River Street Cemetery, burial site of black Civil War veterans from Woodstock's free African-American community. Tours that include about 2 miles of walking begin at the *Billings Farm & Museum Visitor Center.* The tours are free, but reservations are essential: (802) 457–3368, ext. 22; www.billingsfarm.org.

For a nice view down onto Woodstock and across the valley, follow the *Precipice Trail* to the summit of Mount Tom. It's about 2.5 miles round-trip, part of the network of trails from the village and carriage paths through the Marsh-Billings-Rockefeller National Historic Park.

Love Those Cows

Test your bovine IQ at the "Cowlege Bowl" competition for families and sample Vermont dairy products, from freshly churned butter to hand-cranked ice cream. **Billings Farm & Museum** makes learning about its resident Jersey cows fun for the whole family at the Annual Cow Appreciation Day in late July; (802) 457–2355; www .billingsfarm.org.

Woodstock is unique in many ways, not the least of which is that it is home to more Paul Revere foundry bells than any other town in the United States—a total of five. The earliest, dating to 1818, resides on the porch of the Congregational Church. Another is on a plinth behind the Woodstock Inn, one is at the Masonic Temple, and the remaining two are at the Universalist and Episcopal churches.

The Appalachian Trail crosses Route 12 just north of Woodstock, and you can easily hike a section as a day hike, or begin a more extended trip there. This part of the trail covers fairly gentle terrain, through hillside forests and lowland meadows. Bordered by a strip of public land, this narrow ribbon is home to rare and endangered plants. It also provides a valuable habitat for wildlife, and traverses the headwaters of the White and Ottauquechee Rivers. Volunteers from the Green Mountain Club and the Dartmouth College Outing Club maintain this part of the famous trail, which crosses Vermont on its way from Maine to Georgia.

A few miles west of Woodstock is *Jackson House Inn*, with fifteen richly appointed guest rooms. Each is designed in a different style, ranging from the floral Victorian air of the Mary Todd Lincoln Room to Clara's Corner, which features crisp geometric lines, beiges, and leather with crimson accents. Although most rooms are furnished in period antiques—the inn is listed on the National Register of Historic Places—one room is furnished entirely in original furniture by Charles Shackleton and pottery by Miranda Thomas. Rooms feature massage tubs, individual climate control, sitting areas, gas fireplaces, and other amenities.

There are extensive gardens behind the inn, and the dining room overlooks these through a wall of windows. Room rates begin at $195, including

A Stop for Freedom

The *Kedron Valley Inn* has an interesting history and is one of only a handful of places in the state that can be documented as a stop on the Underground Railroad. The nature of the endeavor—which was illegal—made it important not to keep any written records, so although many homes are thought to have been involved, only a few can be identified for certain. The building, which sits in front of the main inn and is now an annex with more guest rooms, was once a general store, and its owner was very active in helping escaping slaves. One of the guest rooms (and our favorite, not just for its history) occupies two floors, and the stairway between the two was once concealed in a closet. The room above was completely out of sight, an excellent hiding place. General stores made good stations in the Underground Railroad because no one took any special notice when large boxes were loaded and unloaded there.

breakfast and a wine reception in the evening. The inn is at 114-3 Senior Lane (Route 4), Woodstock; (800) 448–1890 or (802) 457–2065; www.jackson house.com.

Kedron Valley Inn is a few miles south of Woodstock, and has an excellent restaurant with a talented culinary team. The menu changes seasonally, and may include an herbed Misty Knoll turkey burger with cranberry sage mayo and sweet potato steak fries at $13, to a filet of beef with a Madeira mushroom demi, parsley oil, Vermont blue cheese mashed potatoes, and seasonal vegetables, at $17. Rooms are well decorated with the owner's collection of antique needlework. More examples decorate the public areas, including some very fine old quilts—each labeled with its history. The inn has a beach on its private swimming pond. Rooms start at $139 midweek. The inn is on Route 106, South Woodstock; (802) 457–1473 or (800) 836–1193; www.kedron valleyinn.com.

Suicide Six sounds fiercer than it is. One of the smaller of the state's ski areas, it is well designed for families and offers adult-and-child ski clinics on weekends, when parents can learn to help their children become better skiers, as well as pick up a few tips themselves. Although the elevation is not as high as many other areas, Suicide Six has an evenly divided mix of beginner, intermediate, and expert terrain. It is under the same ownership as the Woodstock Inn, and the inn offers a number of attractive packages that combine lodging and lift tickets. The ski area is on Stagecoach Road, South Pomfret; (802) 457–6661, (800) 448–7900, snow conditions (802) 457–6666; www.suicide6.com.

Hartland–Windsor

On Route 5 south out of White River Junction, you'll find a relatively large amount of industry in the form of farms, factories, computer-consulting companies, and other businesses. This part of the road is relatively industrial, but farms suddenly appear, along with a sprinkling of motels, campgrounds, and private homes. This state highway is a winding, downhill road.

One of the real joys of summer and fall travel is the chance to find beautiful gardens at their peak. In Hartland we found **Talbot's Herb and Perennial Farm,** where you can see collections of herbs and perennials in attractively arranged show gardens. In addition to many of the more common perennials, there's a good selection of unusual varieties. Patty and David Talbot have developed an excellent reputation for the informative and practical gardening classes they hold in their propagation greenhouse. Much of each class is spent in hands-on activity, and students leave with plants and cuttings and divisions they have made themselves. The only drawback is that you must sign up for the whole series, which covers landscaping, garden design, old-fashioned roses, herbs, perennials, and many other subjects. Talbot's is 3 miles south of Quechee on the Hartland-Quechee Road in Hartland, and is open Tuesday through Sunday from 9:00 a.m. to 5:00 p.m. spring through October; (802) 436–2085.

Route 5 plays tag with parallel I–91, weaving over and under it at various points. As you drive into Hartland proper, Routes 5 and 12 merge. Head north on Route 12 for 2 miles; you'll come into Hartland Four Corners and **Skunk Hollow Tavern,** a neighborhood pub and restaurant with good prices and food, a place where the menu is written on a large slate and where darts fly on Friday nights.

that'salotof baaaaaaa

In 1838 a herd of 18,000 sheep passed over the **Cornish Windsor Covered Bridge,** a predecessor of the one that spans the Connecticut River between the two towns today. Three presidents—Hayes, Wilson, and Theodore Roosevelt—have crossed the present bridge, which was built in 1866 after the earlier bridge was swept away in a flood. Until 2007, the bridge was the longest covered bridge still in use in the United States, at 449 feet, 5 inches. (That honor now belongs to a more recently built bridge in Pennsylvania.) No one has recorded just how many sheep fit onto the bridge at one time, nor what it sounded like in there as they crossed.

The second floor at Skunk Hollow is more formally decorated, but the same menu is served. The downstairs pub fills up most weekends by 6:00 p.m., since the tavern is a favorite local hangout.

Skunk Hollow Tavern is in Hartland Four Corners; call (802) 436–2139—reservations are strongly recommended. Skunk Hollow is open Wednesday through Sunday 5:00 to 10:00 p.m. There is live music Wednesday through Friday evenings.

A few miles south on Route 5 is **Windsor.** A short distance north of town is **Harpoon Brewery,** which offers tastings and tours, the latter at 11:00 a.m. and 1:00 and 3:00 p.m. Tuesday through Saturday. Lunch is served from 10:00 a.m. to 6:00 p.m. Sunday through Wednesday, and 10:00 a.m. to 9:00 p.m. Thursday through Saturday, on the same days in their beer garden. You can get samplers of their ales to taste with your grilled panini sandwiches. It's open seven days a week summer and fall, closed Mondays winter and spring. 336 Ruth Carney Drive, Windsor; www.harpoonbrewery.com.

Route 5 is also the main street of Windsor, and you'll pass between rows of well-kept brick houses and distinguished business blocks, built when Windsor was a major player in the precision tool industry.

Just south of the intersection with Route 44 is a huge brick building, the **American Precision Museum,** on Route 5. The museum is a tribute to a bygone era when automated machines were a wonder to behold. Huge milling machines, lathes, steam engines, and generators fill an entire room, looking every bit the dinosaurs they are today.

Many of the machines here were invented by Vermonters who, far too stubborn to ask for help from the outside world, had to find a way to perform the tasks themselves. It seems strange to see all these machines placed together like some Industrial Revolution graveyard. Glass showcases contain salesman's samples, planes, and levels, some with the original instruction booklets. Other display cases hold the modern calculator of 1903, a cylindrical slide rule, plastic toy molds, and early-model pencil sharpeners.

Cases display miniature models of lathes, presses, band saws, and shapers, scaled to a sixteenth of their true size. They actually run—press a button and the gears spin, just like the real thing. They're built by John Aschauer, a former toolmaker who spent twenty-seven years making these miniature machines. He used his memory to re-create them.

The museum is open daily from May 24 through October 31 from 10:00 a.m. to 5:00 p.m. The admission fee is $6.00 for adults, $4.00 for students, and children under 6 are free. American Precision Museum, 196 South Main Street, Windsor; (802) 674–5781; www.americanprecision.org.

Also downtown, the **Vermont Witch Hazel Co. and General Store** features—no surprise witch hazel personal cleansing products such as soaps, cleansing gel, and distilled witch hazel. Derived from a shrub that grows primarily in the Northeast, witch hazel is reputed to reduce inflammation and pain, soothe rough and raw skin, clean the complexion, and reduce itching and swelling of insect bites. The general store has a large selection of Vermont-made handcrafts and Vermont products that include maple syrup, jams, horseradish, honey, and ice cream toppings. They are open Tuesday through Saturday 10:00 a.m. to 5:00 p.m. 113 Main Street, Windsor; www.vermontwitchhazel.com. (802) 674–5060.

In the 1900 former Boston & Main Depot is the family-run **Windsor Station Pub,** with its many years of paint removed to expose beautiful pine ceilings. Entrees priced from $12 to $25 include tender beef served with creamy spinach, sliced fried potatoes, caramelized onions, and finished in a homemade hollandaise sauce at $22; butternut squash gnocchi, sautéed with mushrooms, oven-roasted tomatoes, brown butter sage sauce, and topped with parmesan cheese, at $16. Open seven days a week, starting at 5:00 p.m. Depot Avenue, Windsor; (802) 674–2052; www.windsorstation.com.

High on a hill overlooking the town stands a mansion built in 1901 during Windsor's glory days, which has been restored as **Juniper Hill Inn.** In the summer its gardens are lovely, and you can enjoy them from a terrace with valley views for a backdrop. Fine paneling gives the large public rooms elegance, but they are still very comfortable, with big windows and well-chosen antiques. Guest rooms are also bright and large, with fireplaces. Dinner is served by reservation in the candlelit dining room Tuesday through Saturday, and they'll bring breakfast to your room if you ask. Rates range from $135 to $325. North of town on Route 5, look for Juniper Hill Road (R.R. 1 Box 79), Windsor; (802) 674–5273 or (800) 359–2541; www.juniperhillinn.com.

Many areas once known only as ski mountains now offer attractions that make them year-round resorts. One of these is **Ascutney Mountain Resort** on 3,144-foot Mount Ascutney. In winter the northwest slopes are a busy ski mountain, especially good for families. A good alternative to the mega-mountains elsewhere in the state, Ascutney is a place where the kids can ski on their own, with slope-side lodging and entertainment facilities. It is a big, compact mountain where it is easy to keep track of the kids while still finding slopes to suit adult needs. There is a nice vertical drop of 1,800 feet, over which fifty-six trails (served by six lifts) descend to a base area with accommodations, shops, and restaurants. Beginner and expert trails each count for 30 percent of the trails, and the balance are intermediate. For bolder skiers, glade skiing offers a challenge. Ascutney has the highest percentage of snow-making coverage in the state, with 95 percent of the trails covered. Rates are mid-range, with weekend adult tickets at $56 ($54 midweek). Special ski and ski-and-stay packages make it even more affordable.

Like other resort owners, the operators reasoned that all these facilities were just as good in the summer, with a little change in focus. In summer you can enjoy the Sports and Fitness Center, indoor and outdoor pools, miniature golf, hiking trails, and racquetball and tennis courts with a resident pro. For traveling families there's also a summer day camp with activities for kids, ranging from art to nature excursions. Special packages allow you to arrange canoeing trips on the Connecticut River or to golf at the Crown Point Country Club in Springfield or the Woodstock Country Club in Woodstock. To reach Ascutney, leave I–91 at exit 8 in Weathersfield and take Route 5 north. Take Route 44A (and Route 44) toward Brownsville; the entrance road will be on the left, well marked by signs. Ascutney Mountain Resort, Brownsville; (800) 484–7711; (800) 243–0011 reservations; www.ascutney.com.

Mt. Ascutney is also one point of departure for the Vermont Hang Gliding Association. On nice days three seasons of the year, as many as 30 hang gliders launch from the two mountain-top sites. They're fun to watch, and if you're there when the last pilot lifts off, you may be asked to assist in the launch. The most successful flights can last 90 miles to the New Hampshire shore.

Springfield–Chester

Route 5 heading south from Windsor into Springfield is a winding road with more farms, where in some spots the forest is so thick, it almost forms a canopy that blots out the summer sun. Just past Wilgus State Park about a mile south of Route 131 in Windsor, rows and rows of corn line both sides of the road from late spring into September. Between Windsor and Springfield lies the town of Weathersfield. As you pass through Weathersfield Bow, where the peninsula juts out sharply to the left, the identity of the land seems to meld with that of New Hampshire, which is visible most of the time from Route 5. Sometimes it seems as if you can wade across the river.

On a blustery winter night, few sights in Vermont are as welcome as that of the *Inn at Weathersfield,* its white clapboard facade aglow across the snow-covered front yard. That's how we first saw it, and even when we arrive for dinner on a summer evening, we remember that first view. The reality is up to the promise at this family-fun inn, and its very hands-on owners make sure of that. So does Chef Jason Tostrup, which is why it's important to make dinner reservations here. Jason believes strongly in local agriculture, and works with local farms to keep his menu filled with Vermont-raised ingredients, from the syrup on the breakfast pancakes (even the eggs they are made with) to the tangy-sweet raspberries that garnish dessert. Did we mention that Jason was named Vermont Chef of the Year in 2008?

The Inn at Weathersfield offers three dining options: The first is an a la carte menu with a variety of entrees both local (Black Watch Farm grass-fed short ribs, $28); and exotic (Moroccan spiced barramundi with cauliflower couscous, $26). The second option is a chef's seasonal, locally based five-course menu, for $57, with optional chef's wine pairing. Your third choice is Lucy's Tavern for lighter fare in a relaxed, informal setting. Black Watch burger, anyone?

With such dining variables as these, it's easy to focus on the food and forget the rooms, but they are as varied as the night's menu. Each is individually decorated, and since the inn's two buildings date from 1792 and 1890, respectively, you know that each will be shaped differently. Taking advantage of the vagaries of historic buildings, rooms are tucked under the eaves (often with skylights) and even on the top floor, where a charming aerie offers a whirlpool tub, fireplace, sitting room, and a private rooftop deck. The luxurious touches, which include terry robes, fine-count linens, featherbeds, and fireplaces in most rooms, suggest higher rates than the inn's modest $149 and up. Such service is one reason this destination was named one of the "Hot Ten Country Inns" nationwide by *Bon Appetit* magazine. Along with Chef Tostrup's

Best Chef award, this made 2008 a good year indeed for The Inn at Weathersfield, 1342 Route 106, Perkinsville; (802) 263–9217; fax (802) 263–9219; www .weathersfieldinn.com.

Route 11 leads from Route 5 to **Springfield,** an old mill town with more than its fair share of ups and downs, but currently well on the up side. There are many towns in the United States named Springfield. All of them were named after Springfield, Massachusetts, and the Springfield in Vermont holds the distinction of being the first of them. In 2008, Springfield also was declared home of television's *Simpsons,* winning a nation-wide contest with the other 12 Springfields that submitted three- to five-minute videos.

The **Eureka Schoolhouse,** located on Route 11 just west of I–91, is the oldest schoolhouse still standing in Vermont. It was used continually from 1785 until 1900 and was reconstructed in 1968 on its current spot.

Inside, the schoolhouse is still set up as though a group of children will walk through at any minute, with desks and slates and quill pens and inkwells. But in a nod to current realities, such modern amenities as a fire extinguisher, telephone, and space heater are inside, too. Smell the old wood siding; the building smells as if it's seen a lot. Each of the old wooden shakes on the roof seems to have a personality of its own, as no two adjacent shakes point in the same direction. The schoolhouse isn't open to the public, but visitors are welcome to walk around and look.

To the left of the schoolhouse is an old covered bridge. It's the last covered bridge in existence in the town of Springfield. Like the schoolhouse, and like many other historical buildings in Vermont, it was moved from its original spot and reassembled on this site.

The **Springfield Art and Historical Society** maintains memorabilia of early Springfield, and its **Miller Art Center** houses a collection of dolls and information on Joel Ellis, America's first doll manufacturer. Born in Barnard, Vermont, in 1830, he was an inventor and manufacturer who started out making baby buggies and tops, and at the age of twenty-eight started a factory for the manufacture of wooden dolls. He took out a patent on his system for the assembly of movable joints. The Miller Center is free and open mid-April to the end of October, Tuesday through Friday from 10:00 a.m. to 4:00 p.m. and Saturday from 2:00 to 5:00 p.m. It's located at 9 Elm Street, Springfield; (802) 885–2415.

For a feeling of upper-crust and intellectual Vermont of the nineteenth century, stay at **Hartness House.** James Hartness's fortune was based upon his invention of the turret lathe, and he held over 120 other patents. With this fortune he built his mansion, Hartness House, beautifully preserved today as a forty-one-room inn. The gracious public rooms are paneled in oak, and antiques furnish rooms throughout the inn. Special midweek and weekend package rates are available.

From the dining room you can look out over the valley as you enjoy a dinner of their very popular shrimp scampi with mushrooms, capers, roasted tomatoes, garlic and herbs, tossed with lemon and Chardonnay wine sauce over whole wheat linguini, at $16.00.

Hartness's avocation was astronomy, so while you are there, ask to see his 600-power, 10-inch lens turret equatorial telescope. It is housed in an unusual structure that is home to the Stellafane Society, an organization of amateur astronomers. 30 Orchard Street, Springfield; (802) 885–2115 or (800) 732–4789; www.hartnesshouse.com.

Springfield is also home to **Wellwood Orchards,** where from mid-June you can pick your own strawberries, raspberries, and blueberries. In early September to November 1, you can either pick your own apples or buy them from the stand. Tour the orchards on a wagon ride, and before picking let the kids enjoy the petting zoo. Among the apple varieties are Macoun, McIntosh, Empire, Cortland, and Red Delicious; there are also a few old-fashioned varieties. The shop has pies, cider, maple syrup and candies, pumpkins, and squash. The farm is 3 miles out Valley Street at 529 Wellwood Orchard Road, Springfield; (802) 263–5200.

Route 11 leads to Chester, 8 miles to the west. Beautifully restored Victorian houses line both sides of the narrow green. Look for School Street, a block off the green, and **Rose Arbour Tea Room & Gift Shop.** This is an old-fashioned kind of tea shop—you thought nobody made finger sandwiches and served fresh berries with clotted cream anymore?—that takes its tea seriously. While cream teas with scones are available anytime, for the full traditional afternoon tea ($17.50) you'll need to give the owner forty-eight hours' notice, so she can prepare the special treats that bring her customers from all over southern Vermont—although the scones are enough to bring us back.

Classical music plays throughout lunch, which may include real English scones, a light herbal chicken salad, or an authentic ploughman's plate, with hearty cheddar, homemade bread, and an apple.

The tearoom is open from 11:00 a.m. to 5:00 p.m. Wednesday through Saturday, November through June and every day July through October.

Upstairs at Rose Arbour are two bed-and-breakfast suites, furnished with four-poster beds, old samplers, and feather duvets. One of these is a large suite with a kitchen; the other sleeps four people. Double guest rooms cost $95, and a three-room suite is $150 ($240 for a two-night snow weekend. Call for other seasonal packages.) When you're not sleeping upstairs or relaxing on the screened second-floor porch, you can play croquet or admire the herb gardens

Say "Cheese!"

As interest in cooking and fine dining has blossomed, so has interest in Vermont's fine farm-made cheeses. Sometimes referred to as farmhouse cheese, these excellent specialty cheeses are made in small lots. One producer is Vermont Shepherd, founded by sheep farmers in 1990 who had to deal with an excess of ewe's milk after spring lambing. When demand exceeded their production capacity, they enlisted other sheep farmers, who now make cheese that is aged in the Vermont Shepherd caves. Other farms to look for are Vermont Butter and Cheese Company, Orb Weaver Farm, Shelburne Farm, and Grafton Village Cheese. The Vermont Cheese Council Web site features a virtual tour of the cheese farms; www.vtcheese.com.

out back. Write to Rose Arbour, School and Canal Streets, Chester, 05143; (802) 875–4767; www.rosearbour.com.

Fine homes, mostly Victorian, line the main street of Chester, which is also Route 11. Just out of the village in Proctorsville is **Baba à Louis Bakery,** best known outside the area for the popular cookbook *Baba à Louis Bread Book,* featuring the chef's best bread and pastry recipes. Breads and cookies are for sale, along with light lunches, in this glistening high-ceilinged bakeshop, where you can buy the book, meet the author, and even get his floury autograph.

Seven miles later, on the north side of the road, you'll see a striking brick building with the word Simonsville printed over its third-story outdoor porch. You've found **Rowell's Inn,** an exquisite original stagecoach stop that is furnished throughout with antiques and plenty of rockers.

The two guest rooms up on the third floor once served—together—as the inn's ballroom and are particularly impressive, with high vaulted ceilings, clawfoot tubs, and heated towel racks.

Four-course dinners are served to guests on weekends by reservation and may feature entrees such as beef bourguignon, cognac-glazed Cornish hens, or pork tenderloin in apple and rosemary cream sauce. The house special dessert is caramel-fudge pecan pie. B&B rates are $90; add $25 per person for dinner. Rowell's Inn, 1834 Simonsville Road (Route 11) Andover; (802) 875–3658 or (800) 728–0842; www.rowellsinn.com.

If you are planning a visit to the Chester area, check the performance schedule of the **Green Mountain Festival Series,** a program that brings top-quality performances to local schools and communities. Six shows are presented to the public each year at Green Mountain Union High School, and they have included the Vermont Symphony Orchestra, the Vermont Swing and

Big Band, and solo performers such as George Winston. Tickets usually range from $15.00 to $17.00, with $5.00 student tickets and family pricing; www .greenmountainfestivalseries.com.

If you leave Chester on Route 103 to head back to Route 5 and the Connecticut River, you'll see *Curtis' All American Restaurant* on the right, just outside of town. Co-owner Sarah Tuff is daughter of Curtis Tuff, whose outdoor barbecue has been an institution in Putney since 1968 (but hardly "off the road," right there on Route 5 as it is). Sarah and her husband, Christopher Parker, apprenticed under the tutelage of the Curtis, the master, for several years before starting out on their own—and they seem to have gotten things just about right. They serve the same succulent ribs and chicken available in Putney (about which *Gourmet* magazine's Michael Stern has rhapsodized: "The meat pulls off in big succulent strips that virtually burst with piggy flavor"), as well as smoked beef brisket, chopped BBQ chicken and pork (to eat in their spacious restaurant or to go, by the pint), nachos, and quesadillas. All meat is served with a wide choice of sides, including baked beans, cole slaw, corn bread, collard greens, potato salad, and corn on the cob. Curtis' All American Restaurant opens at 11:00 a.m. from Wednesday to Sunday, closing at 8:00 p.m. Wednesdays, Thursdays and Sundays, and 9:00 p.m. Fridays and Saturdays. Buffets are served Saturday (4:00 to 7:00 p.m.) and Sunday (noon to 3:00 p.m.) Call (802) 875–6999; 908 VT Route 103, Chester, VT 05143. www .curtisbbqvt.com

If you head out of Chester on Route 35 South, you'll soon enter the village of Grafton, a very tourist-oriented town. Bypass the main village and head west on Route 121. Once you leave the village, the road turns to dirt. The *Grafton Swimming Pond* is a mile up the road on the left. Even on a hot Saturday

Mountain Lions in Vermont?

Catamount is the name given to the eastern native puma by Vermonters. Also known as the mountain lion, this cat is capable of 40-foot leaps and incredible speeds over short distances. The animals were thought to be extinct in Vermont since early in the twentieth century, victims of a bounty imposed to protect domestic sheep and cattle.

Recently, residents of Townshend, Grafton, and Newfane have reported sightings that have raised hopes that there is still a viable population. If you happen to see a big, golden-brownish cat, 4 to 6 feet long with a 4-foot tail, take a picture of it; then call Vermont Fish and Game. They'll probably tell you it's a bobcat, but you'll know the truth. For more information, contact the Eastern Puma Research Network in Baltimore, (410) 254-2517.

afternoon in August, you may find the pond deserted. A field surrounds the pond, which is close to the road, and there's a portable toilet so you can spend the whole day at the pond. The pond has docks and a roped-off area for wading but no lifeguards.

Before leaving town, stop at **_Grafton Village Cheese,_** on Route 35 at the edge of the village. You can see parts of the cheese-making process here, as well as sample the product and buy some to take home. Head cheese maker Scott Fletcher has had 35 years on the job to perfect his craft. P.O. Box 87, Townshend Road, Grafton, 05146; (802) 843–2221 or (800) 472–3866; www .graftonvillagecheese.com.

Next to the cheese "factory" is a covered footbridge, part of Grafton's walking trail system.

Route 35 continues south through the town of Athens. As with Route 121 in Grafton, it's common in Vermont to have numbered main state roads turn to dirt in certain areas. Route 35 is dirt for a few miles, then turns back to blacktop.

In summertime pick-your-own and porch-side farm stands abound throughout the state. There's usually at least one in each town. Also keep a lookout for the ingenious scarecrows people construct to fend off intruders.

Route 35 meets up with Route 30 in Townshend, sitting around its postcard-picture common. The Townshend Corner Store serves breakfast and lunch with old-fashioned counter service. North on Route 30 is the **_Townshend Lake Dam_** over the West River, operated by the U.S. Army Corps of Engineers. The dam was built between 1958 and 1961 to better control flooding of the West River. The dam is 1,000 feet long and 133 feet tall and has a capacity of almost eleven billion gallons of water.

If you drive across the top of the dam, you'll get a strange, vertiginous feeling. There are lots of paths to explore. On weekends the parking lot may be almost full with mostly Vermont plates, but it is usually relatively quiet: no loud radios and just the clink of horseshoes and the sound of people's voices.

The recreational facilities at the dam include picnic tables, horseshoes, boating and swimming areas, volleyball, and several trails, all with a view of the dam. The dam is part of Townshend State Park, which has a total of 856 acres and thirty-four camping sites. Call (802) 365–7500 for more information or write to Townshend Lake Dam and State Park, Route 30, Townshend, 05353.

Scott Bridge, which you can see from Route 30, not far from the dam, is the longest wooden span in Vermont. (Remember the one in Windsor is not completely in Vermont.) Strategically placed concrete blocks prohibit cars from crossing, but you can walk across it. Scott Bridge is 277 feet long and was built in 1870.

Bellows Falls–Putney

As you travel south on Route 5, Springfield melds into Rockingham and the town of **Bellows Falls,** which is actually a village within the town of Rockingham—as is Saxtons River, farther west. Perhaps this habit of having what seems like towns inside of other towns is the most puzzling of all New England's idiosyncracies.

On Route 5 in Rockingham you'll spot **Leslie's,** an informal restaurant with a New American menu based on fresh produce from their own extensive gardens. Many of the dishes are low-fat and heart-healthy as well as delicious. Sunday through Thursday Leslie's offers a bistro menu from $13.00 to $19.00, in addition to the usual entrees—such as the popular roast rack of lamb with mushroom port wine sauce. Dinner is served from 5:00 to 9:00 p.m. Entrees range from $15 to $20. It's close to the interstate highway junction on Route 5; (802) 463–4929; www.lesliestavern.com.

Bear left as you head south on Route 5 to enter the town of Bellows Falls for a cross-section of modern-day Vermont history: The **Miss Bellows Falls Diner** is housed in one of the original Worcester dining cars from the 1920s and 1930s and offers standard diner fare at diner prices. It's at 90 Rockingham Street, just north of the main square; (802) 463–9800.

It would be a shame to pass through here without seeing the falls, just to your left at the square and visible from the tall stone bridge that leads to New Hampshire. Upstream are the dammed falls and another iron bridge, but the best views are of this lower section. These are a raging torrent of

Waste Not, Want Not to the End

Hetty Green, popularly known as "the Witch of Wall Street," was born in New Bedford, Massachusetts, in 1834. She was regarded as the richest woman in America and probably the cheapest, too.

As a young woman and heir to a New Bedford whaling fortune, Hetty Howland Robinson had flirted with New York society and danced with the Prince of Wales. She then multiplied her net worth by acquiring her aunt's sizable fortune as well, and by marrying Edward Green, a wealthy silk and tea trader who grew up in Bellows Falls. She threw him out after he failed to take her advice in business. Her son lost a leg because she was too stingy to take him to a doctor for a kneecap injury; when she finally did, a year later, it was under an assumed name so she could put him in the hospital's charity ward. By the time of her death in 1916, she had amassed a total of about $100 million, but when she had to travel to New York on business, she still stayed in a dollar-a-night rooming house in Brooklyn.

froth in the spring, but impressive anytime, not so much for their height as for the depth of the gorge and the amount of water compressed between the narrow rockwalls. In case you're interested in geology, this is about the only place where you can actually see the seam in the rocks where the two tectonic plates meet—New Hampshire is actually a piece of Africa left off when that plate moved away. If it had taken all of itself, you'd be standing on the Atlantic shore here, and Vermont wouldn't be the only New England state without a coastline.

The first bridge to span the Connecticut River was built from Bellows Falls across to Walpole, New Hampshire. The falls for which the town was named also was the site of the first canal built in the country, completed in 1802.

While in Bellows Falls, take a walk down Exner Block on Canal Streeet (down the hill and to the right off Westminster Street), a historic building beautifully restored to serve as a live/work setting for emerging artists. The structure is charming, with wainscoting, pressed tin ceilings, and traditional hardware. Check out Bellows Falls' growing art scene the third Friday of each month during Gallery Walk.

Visit the galleries and take a break at the delightful *Hraefnwood Café,* where proprietor Eric Jette will prepare for you what he maintains is the best cappuccino in Windham County. We do not dispute his claim. Also available are fine pastries, sandwiches for lunch, and beer and wine for an afternoon Happy Hour best enjoyed at one of the few tables overlooking the historic Bellows Falls Canal. Hours at Hraefnwood (Olde English for "Raven") are 7:00 a.m. to 8:00 p.m., Friday 7:00 a.m. to 11:00 p.m., Saturday 8:00 a.m. to 11:00 p.m., and Sunday 10:00 a.m. to 5:00 p.m. Call (802) 299–7429.

Across the street and a few steps down from the Hraefnwood Café is *Bocelli's on the Canal,* a friendly, funky neighborhood restaurant and specialty grocery store. It features great pastry, organic coffee, and hearty Italian meals, with a selection of wines and micro-brews. It serves lunch and dinner Wednesday through Saturday, 11:00 a.m. until closing. 46 Canal Street; (802) 460–1190.

On Fridays in the summer and fall, from 4:00 p.m. until dusk, visit the *Bellows Falls Farmer's Market,* across the canal bridge just down from Bocelli's. In addition to a wide variety of fresh fruit, vegetables, and baked goods sold by local producers, there are several takeout stalls featuring Thai, Indian, and down home goodies. Live music as well most Fridays.

Be sure to see the huge (32-by-40-foot) wall mural painted by local artists Bonnie Turner and Cliff Clear. It's on Westminster Street and depicts the town square at the turn of the nineteenth century. Many of the same buildings are still there.

In its long history, the town of **Westminster,** south of Bellows Falls, has been variously part of New Hampshire, Massachusetts, New York, and Vermont.

The town was first granted as part of Massachusetts and was known as Number One in 1735. The main village of Westminster lies on Route 5, which was originally constructed as the King's Highway and was built wide to allow for military training sessions by pre–Revolutionary War soldiers.

Westminster was in flux for the twelve years between 1740 and 1752, when the northern boundary of Massachusetts was determined to be farther south, and New Hampshire governor Benning Wentworth regranted the land to New Hampshirites. In 1772, however, New York got into the act by locating a county courthouse in the town. Westminster officially became part of Vermont along with the rest of the state in 1777, when the Vermont government proclaimed itself to be a free and independent republic.

On Route 5 in Westminster you'll see **Harlow's Farm Stand.** After four generations at that location—and beginning as a small roadside shack—Harlow's has grown to become a handsome, modern store—and recognized as one of the earliest organic farms in southern Vermont. It includes a wide assortment of organic vegetables, bedding plants, and a profusion of hanging baskets. Stop in for breakfast or lunch and select a table outside, where you can watch the cows graze in the back fields. Open daily, May to mid-December. (802) 722–3515.

South on Route five for another seven miles or so will take you straight into **Putney** and a slice of life almost frozen in time from the 1960s, when Putney was hippie heaven. As you roam its backroads, you'll still see, mixed in with the trust-fund farms, metamorphosed homes that grew out of the back-to-the-land homesteads of escapees from the draft and the modern world itself. Communes thrived, and while those days have gone, they have left Putney a nice, mellow place to spend time, a haven for artists and craftspeople. In the center of town—the very center of town—owners Stephen and Jeremy of the **Front Porch Café** have worked out a schedule that suits both them and their patrons—town regulars and visitors alike. They get high marks for their breakfasts, whether chosen from a wide variety of baked goods accompanied by an espresso—or less lethal beverage—or a three-ingredient omelet of the day. Take breakfast out on the 30-foot-long porch and watch Putney's version of the world go by. Lunches, the Friday night dinner, and Sunday brunch likewise have folks coming back for more. Breakfast and lunch Tuesday through Saturday, 7:00 a.m. to 4:00 p.m.; brunch on Sunday from 10:00 a.m. to 2:00 p.m.; dinner Friday night. The Front Porch Café, 133 Main Street, Putney; (802) 387–2200.

Sharing the Café's ample front porch is its next door neighbor, **Putney Books,** which specializes in used books but also stocks new fiction and non-fiction. Putney Books is a collective effort that was assumed by a group of town residents who, after the previous bookstore went out of business, took on the responsibility of determining whether the town would be able to support one. So far, so good. Hours are Tuesday through Friday 10:30 a.m. to 5:30 p.m.; Saturday 10:00 a.m. to 4:00 p.m.; Sunday 11:00 a.m. to 3:00 p.m. 133 Main Street, (802) 387–4800.

As the heart of Vermont's back-to-the-land movement, Putney is an appropriate home for an outstanding natural-fiber spinning mill. **Green Mountain Spinnery** processes local wool into knitting and weaving yarns, which you can purchase at their shop. On the first and third Tuesdays of the month, tours of the mill are given, and you can see how the entire process takes place. The mill shop is open Monday through Friday 9:00 a.m. to 5:30 p.m., Saturday 10:00 a.m. to 5:30 p.m., and Sunday noon to 4:00 p.m. Look for it off Route 5 in Putney, at the end of the exit 4 ramp from I–91, opposite Putney Inn, Putney; (892) 387–4528; www.spinnery.com; e-mail: spinnery@sover.net.

Putney Mountain, the 1,600-foot elevation that rises west of town, has a 360-degree unobstructed view of the valley, the river, and the surrounding hills and mountains. It's an easy walk via a trail that begins near the Putney School, a private school on West Hill. At the summit you can sit and watch hawks soaring on the thermals.

Brattleboro

Brattleboro is a large, bustling town (there are only nine cities—by definition—in all of Vermont, and Brattleboro does not enjoy that distinction) that incorporates the best of urban, rural, and even suburban characteristics. It is influenced by the presence both of the Brattleboro Retreat, a highly respected drug-and-alcohol rehabilitation center and one of the largest employers in town, and of the SIT Graduate Institute, formerly known as the School for International Training. With students and faculty from more than thirty nations, SIT prepares students to address the world's critical challenges.

Many of the men and women who came to Vermont in the 1960s to live in communes ended their journey as soon as they crossed the Massachusetts border into Vermont, so the town still has a New Age flavor, as evidenced by the posters on telephone poles that advertise shiatsu, peace meetings, and Brazilian dance lessons.

Downtown Brattleboro—or "Brat," as locals refer to it—is the old section, with relics of factories and hotels from the booming railroad days.

Jumping Off a Mountain

Downhill skiing was still a novelty when Fred Harris started the annual Harris Hill Ski Jump meet in Brattleboro in 1923. As an undergraduate, he had helped start the annual Winter Carnival at Dartmouth College in Hanover, New Hampshire, in 1911. Some of the world's best ski jumpers have competed here, including Torger Tokle, his brother Art Tokle, Art Devlin, Hugh Barber, and Vladimir Glyvka. The contests take place in three-hour segments on each of two days, and usually include present and future Olympians and World Cup contenders. The date may vary, but the event is usually held on Presidents' Day weekend. It's an exciting show, even for the spectators, who cheer the contestants by ringing cowbells. If you don't have one to bring, you can buy a bell there. Applauding with mittened hands isn't very effective, hence the bells.

In 2005, the jump was declared unsafe. After competition that year, no events were held until 2009, after $257,000 had been raised by local residents to help pay for essential renovation. In February of that year, world-class competition again came to Harris Hill. "I think my dad would be totally amazed that this is happening again," said Fred's daughter Sandy. "It's a world-class facility that can now be used to train for Olympic events and other tournaments."

Restaurants, shops, and cultural events abound here. The city's reputation as a top destination for art lovers can be seen in full swing on the first Friday of each month during Gallery Walk. Many studios are open, and artists are in a chatting mood, happy to join you in a glass of wine. There are more than 50 exhibitions to see. It's a great time to stroll around town, enjoy some live music, sample the refreshments and then have dinner at one of the local restaurants. Gallery guides are available in numerous locales around town, or at www.gallerywalk.org.

The **Brattleboro Museum and Art Center,** located on Main Street at the south end of town (at the intersection of routes 119 and 142), is housed in a charming former train station. Featuring compelling exhibits by regional internationally acclaimed artists, it is open every day except Tuesday from 11:00 a.m. to 5:00 p.m.

Drive a few miles out of town. Once you're in the hills you'll feel miles away from Main Street. But when you head west on Route 9 or south on Route 5, all the telltale signs of suburbia are there, from fast-food restaurants to motels and supermarkets.

Brattleboro has no shortage of good places to eat, but for a healthy, delicious lunch at affordable prices, you won't do better than the deli counter and cafe at the **Brattleboro Food Co-op,** where you may spend more time trying to decide what to order than you will eating it. The choices are mouth-watering, and seem endless: custom sandwiches made from nitrite-free meats and artisanal breads, hearty flavorful soups (they're made from the pick of the Co-op's organic fresh produce), salads, and dozens of ready-made dishes, from stuffed grape leaves, curries, and samosas to Thai, Italian, and New England favorites. It's a wonder anyone in Brattleboro cooks for the family with this selection available (and we suspect that quite a few busy people take these home and reheat them in their own pans without ever letting on that they didn't spend all day cooking). Although the deli cafe is probably of more interest to those traveling through, the cheese counter deserves a good look, if for no other reason than to see the diversity of Vermont cheeses. Few places have such a wide and well-chosen variety of small-production farm-stead cheeses. Gather your picnic makings and stock up on healthy snacks for the road here, too. It's right downtown, at 2 Main Street, Brattleboro; (802) 257–0236, and open Monday through Saturday 8:00 a.m. to 9:00 p.m., Sunday 9:00 a.m. to 9:00 p.m.

Still on the Asian end of Brattleboro's culinary spectrum, **Anon's Thai Cuisine** offers selections from the traditional pad Thai and chicken satay to basil calamari and our personal favorite, a salad roll with cilantro, Thai noodles, mint, and carrots with a homemade peanut sauce. The restaurant also has a full takeout menu, and you can find Anon's mobile version on Saturdays in summer at the Brattleboro Farmers' Market (it's easy to tell which stand is theirs—it's the one with the long line). Anon's restaurant is hidden off Canal Street, which is Route 5, close to exit 1 from I–91 at 4 Fairground Road, Brattleboro; (802) 257–1376.

Brattleboro is well supplied with restaurants and cafes, including **Peter Haven's,** right across Elliot Street. There are only ten tables, so you should make reservations on weekends to sample the deceptively simple-sounding menu. Appetizers, all at $10, include smoked salmon fillet with popover and horseradish dill sauce, while the entrees, starting at $25, include fresh sea scallops on a nest of braised spinach with apple brandy and cream sauce, and roast duck with port wine, black current and sour cherry sauce. Dinner is served Tuesday through Saturday from 6:00 p.m. Peter Haven's is at 32 Elliot Street, Brattleboro; (802) 257–3333.

Farther up Elliot Street is the outstanding but tiny **T.J. Buckley's,** with an eclectic menu of only four items, which change seasonally. Everything is strictly fresh (the chef often shops from local farmers at the biweekly farm-ers' market) and flawlessly prepared. If it doesn't put too much of a dent in your wallet, it's worth every penny of the $40 for a main course. The restaurant has such a following that you'd better make reservations well in advance if you hope for a table. Credit cards aren't accepted, but you can pay by personal check. This is one book you can't judge by its cover—it's located in a 1927 Worcester diner at 132 Elliot Street, Brattleboro; (802) 257–4922.

You can shop from the same local farmers on Saturday and Wednesday at the **Brattleboro Farmers' Market,** on Route 9 just west of town. Like so much else in Brattleboro, this is a local institution, where you will find both old-favorite vegetables and the trendiest new varieties. Big truck farms join small homestead farmers here; one stand sells nothing but Asian vegetables and greens. In the spring you can buy plants for your own garden, and all summer you'll find a smattering of crafts (including stunning dried-flower wreaths) and farm-related products, such as herb vinegars, fruit jams, fresh-baked breads, cheese, maple syrup, and organic honey.

Many people go just for lunch and the live music that's often playing on the shaded lawn inside the circle of stands. Several vendors sell only prepared foods, which you can eat at picnic tables or carry off for dinner later. These usually include Japanese *udon* noodles, Lebanese *dolmas* and other dishes, and authentic Mexican and Thai foods. There's a booth with great coffee and tea and freshly baked breakfast goodies and cookies. What you won't find are burgers and fries or hot dogs. At every booth you'll find at least one big smile; it's the friendliest group of people you'll meet anywhere. Open Saturday, May through October, from 9:00 a.m. to 2:00 p.m., and Wednesday 10:00 a.m. to 2:00 p.m.

The **Old Creamery Bridge** is close to the Brattleboro Farmers' Market. Named for the Brattleboro Creamery, which once stood on the far side, it was built in 1879 and has ever since provided an easy route from the west end of Brattleboro to downtown. In 1917 a footbridge was added to one side, allowing pedestrians to cross Whetstone Brook without fighting traffic. This is the last remaining of the four covered bridges that once carried traffic in Brattleboro.

Bogey in a Blizzard

Rudyard Kipling liked Vermont best in the winter, possibly because fewer people tried his patience then by invading his treasured privacy. Sir Arthur Conan Doyle, a frequent guest at Naulakha, gave Kipling a pair of skis, on which he loved to tour the eleven-acre property. He was an early golf enthusiast and is credited by the U.S. Golf Association with inventing winter golf. He painted golf balls red and created holes by sinking tin cans into the snow.

Just west of the farmers' market grove on Route 9 is West Brattleboro, an attractive enclave of distinguished old homes and a tiny business center with several places to eat.

Just before this highway heads over Hogback Mountain is the ***Chelsea Royal Diner.*** The menu is a slightly updated version of traditional diner food, with liver and onions, macaroni and cheese, and meat loaf along with slightly more sophisticated fare. Wednesday through Saturday you'll find a number of Mexican-style dishes, too. Prices are strictly of the old diner tradition, with most entrees around $6.00. Be sure to check out the specials board, which may offer an all-you-can-eat catfish fry with hush puppies and other irresistible deals. Chelsea Royal Diner, Route 9, West Brattleboro; (802) 254–8399.

The ***Bonnyvale Environmental Education Center*** (BEEC) sponsors programs in schools and for the public throughout the area. It offers a busy schedule of outdoor activities, usually hikes and walks accompanied by astronomers, geologists, zoologists, botanists, and other experts to examine some phase of the natural world. Most of the trips are free but require advance registration. The Sunday morning A.M. Ambles, also free, don't require registration; just show up at 9:00 a.m. any Sunday at the appointed place. Past ambles, which last about two hours, have explored Putney Mountain, West River, and Hamilton Falls, a rare patch of old-growth forest, and Mount Olga. To get a complete schedule with the meeting places, contact BEEC, Brattleboro, 05301; (802) 257–5785; www.beec.org.

Hey, It's a Live One!

You never know what you'll find happening in Brattleboro. One Saturday in May, my daughter and I were driving into town to have lunch, and as we came past the small park at Wells Fountain, we noticed a group of young people dressed in white, jingling across the street with bells on their legs. "Morris dancers!" we both said at once, and I quickly found a parking space in front of the library.

We followed them to the park and sat down on the lawn to wait for the dancing. They also sat down, in little groups on the granite steps and on the lawn, and quickly became engaged in animated conversations. Assuming that they were waiting for someone or something, we waited. And waited. Finally, a dancer about my daughter's age noticed her, as young men tend to, and wandered casually toward us and engaged us in conversation. When he learned that we'd come to watch the dance, he looked startled, then quickly called to the others, "Hey, we've got a real audience!" and they all jumped up and took their places to begin.

—Barbara Radcliffe Rogers

On Memorial Day weekend, Morris dancers hop and prance on nearly every open space in town. The annual Morris Ale is held on this weekend each year at nearby Marlboro College, but the dancers perform all over the area, with the greatest concentration of them in Brattleboro on Saturday. After individual groups have danced all over town, they gather for a massed show on Elliot Street at 5:00 p.m. These lively, good-humored dance troupes travel from all over the East for this event.

Two Brattleboro B&Bs are striking examples of the enthusiasm of the 1920s and 1930s for revival architectural styles. Each is located conveniently on a major route into town but within walking distance of the center.

Approaching town from the north on Route 5, just after you cross West River at its junction with the Connecticut, is an eye-catching French château. Its name, which was also its address in the days before Brattleboro changed its street numbers to accommodate 911 identification, is the **40 Putney Road Bed & Breakfast.** Inside the double-thick brick walls are well-decorated rooms awash with thoughtful amenities, such as ironing boards, bathrobes, hair dryers, small refrigerators, queen-size beds, and modems. Most rooms have couches or love seats, and all have modern private baths. A tiny private pub downstairs has an extensive beer and wine for guests, as well as light dishes for those who decide not to sample Brattleboro's ample restaurant offerings. Breakfast is served from a menu—so you can choose your own style—in a sun-filled dining room or under the awning on the terrace, which overlooks a garden with fountains. Rooms run from $120 to $180 for two. Incongruously, 40 Putney Road Bed & Breakfast is at 192 Putney Road, Brattleboro; (802) 254–6268 or (800) 941–2413; fax (802) 258–2673; www .fortputneyroad.com.

You might expect that Rudyard Kipling wrote *Jungle Book* during languid and steamy afternoons of the Raj, somewhere in the India it portrayed, but it was actually written just over the Brattleboro town line in Dummerston. So were *Captains Courageous* and some of the *Just So Stories*. Just as you enter Brattleboro on Route 5 from the north, assuming that you avoid being side-swiped by a truck as you share the ineffective roundabout at the junction with Route 9, turn west (right) on Black Mountain Round and head uphill. There's no mistaking the shingled "cottage," which Kipling referred to as a ship, sailing along the hillside to your left.

You can't take a tour of **Naulakha,** but you can stay there by advance reservation. The house, restored even to the shingled roof, just as Kipling had it built, belongs to Landmark Trust, a British preservation society that restores historic homes in Britain. The group extended its territory to acquire this property because of its connection with British literature. Inside, the home gleams with polished wood; many of the furnishings belonged to the Kiplings. It's entirely self-catering and is big enough for eight people, for three-night minimum stays. For information about the house, call (802) 257–5840 or (800) 848–3747. To make reservations, contact the Landmark Trust, Shottesbrooke, Maidenhead, Berkshire, UK SL6 3SW; 011–44–1628–825–925.

Heading west from Brattleboro on Route 9, past West Brattleboro, the road begins to climb . . . and climb. It winds upward through rock-strewn woods, crests momentarily atop a deep ravine, then climbs again to a ridge with views of distant hills. As you climb, watch on the north side of the road for the Spiral Shop. You'll recognize it by the large front yard filled with an outlandish assortment of lawn art and outdoor sculpture. It's a place for people with a sense of humor.

The final climb takes you to the summit of Hogback Mountain, where the views (there is a pull-off with a telescope) reach into three states. Along with a store selling Vermont cheeses and maple syrup, the summit has a small natural history museum with a collection of local birds.

More Places to Stay in the Connecticut River Valley

(All area codes 802)

CHESTER

The Inn at Cranberry Farm
61 Williams River Road
(800) 854–2208 or
(800) 463–1339
www.cranberryfarminn.com
Built in 1992, the eleven-room inn centers around a room with a 30-foot-high cathedral ceiling and was formerly known as Madrigal Inn. Rates include a full

breakfast, and there is hiking right outside the door. They hold occasional quilting weekends.

Inn Victoria
875–4288 or
(800) 732–4288
www.innvictoria.com
On the Green, a carefully restored Victorian home, thoughtfully translated into lodgings.

NORWICH

The Inn at Norwich
Main Street
649–1143
www.norwichinn.com
A vintage village inn updated and with a good, reasonably priced dining room.

PUTNEY

The Putney Inn
Depot Road (at exit 4 of I–91)
387–5517
Large, well-decorated rooms, each with its own outside entrance. A creative chef prepares favorite New England dishes with artistic flair.

WOODSTOCK

Woodstock Inn and Resort
14 the Green
457–1100 or
(800) 448–7900
www.woodstockinn.com
With a pool, alpine and Nordic skiing, golf course, and indoor sports facilities, the inn is a complete resort in the center of the village.

TO LEARN MORE IN THE CONNECTICUT RIVER VALLEY

Brattleboro Chamber of Commerce, 182 Main Street, Brattleboro, 05301; (802) 254–4565; www.brattleboro.com.

Woodstock Area Chamber of Commerce, 18 Central Street, P.O. Box 486, Woodstock, 05091; (802) 457–3555; www.woodstockvt.com.

More Places to Eat in the Connecticut River Valley

(All area codes 802)

BRATTLEBORO

Sarkis Market
50 Elliot Street
258–4906
A Lebanese cafe that serves authentic Middle Eastern dishes.

SOUTHWEST VERMONT

The southwestern corner of Vermont seems at times cut off from the rest of the state, largely because no interstate highway is within 40 miles of the far reaches of the area. The Green Mountains separate it from eastern Vermont, and Pownal, a town that is as far away from Montpelier, the state capital, as you can get, seems to have more in common with the bordering states of New York and Massachusetts than it does with the rest of its own state.

The landscape here is one of rolling hills and mountains, alternating with wide, flat, fertile valleys. The region is also historically rich, since it served as an early gateway to settlement in the rest of Vermont.

Although at one time or another all of Vermont has fallen to some kind of border dispute with neighboring states—and one foreign country—the southwest corner seems to have seen more than its share of fights over where Vermont ends and Massachusetts and New York begin—and even where New Hampshire ends.

The remote **Tri-State Monument** that marks the exact spot where Vermont, New York, and Massachusetts converge is buried deep in the woods at the southwest corner of the

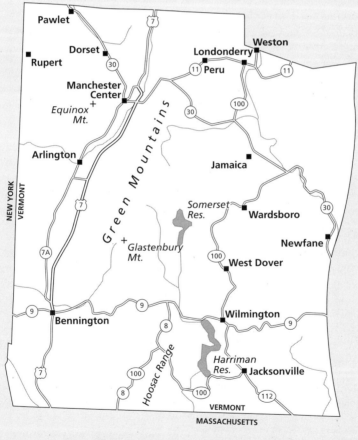

town of Pownal, almost 2 miles from the end of the nearest dead-end road. The granite marker is 8 feet tall and 14 inches square and has four sides, three of them marked with the initials of the state it faces. The final boundary was settled in 1812, but the marker wasn't erected until 1896.

Bennington

Bennington, in fact, is where it all began. It was the first town west of the Connecticut River to be chartered by New Hampshire royal governor Benning Wentworth. The charter was drawn up in 1749, when New York and New Hampshire both claimed the land.

During the American Revolution, the Battle of Bennington in 1777 was fought in lands from Cambridge, New York, to a point about 5 miles west of Bennington in Vermont. This single battle turned the tide against the British and caused British leader John Burgoyne to rethink his strategy in the war. Colonial militia, under the command of General John Stark, discovering General Burgoyne's plans, fought and destroyed British and Hessian forward elements of his army, leading to Burgoyne's retreat. The battle ended British plans to defeat the colonies by splitting them in half, and made the final American victory possible.

After the battle—which is immortalized by the 306-foot-high **Bennington Battle Monument,** visible from most parts of town—Burgoyne wrote a letter describing Vermonters as "the most active and rebellious race on the continent."

The monument, by the way, was built over the course of four years and dedicated in 1891 by President Benjamin Harrison. When an elevator was installed, a few Vermonters balked, believing that if the Green Mountain Boys could prove their valor by fighting the British, then it would be a small task by comparison to walk up the 412 stairs that make up the climb to the top. To visit the site of the actual battle, you'll have to travel into New York, following Route 67A (Northside Drive) to North Bennington, then Route 67

AUTHOR'S TOP HIGHLIGHTS

Equinox Skyline Drive	Green Mountain National Forest
Canoeing the Batten Kill	Bromley Ski Area and Alpine Slide
Magic Mountain Ski Area	Robert Todd Lincoln's Hildene

across the state line to the battlefield, about 5 miles from the center of North Bennington.

The late fiction writer Shirley Jackson, author of *The Haunting of Hill House* and the famous short story "The Lottery," was a resident of Bennington. Jackson's husband taught at Bennington College, and she, formerly from upstate New York, incorporated into her fiction many of her feelings about small-town life in Bennington.

Bennington is home to one of the state's fish hatcheries, the **Vermont State Fish Culture Station.** This is a fascinating place, especially for kids, who will be intrigued by the sight of thousands of trout massing in the tanks. From Route 9 on the east side of town, go south on South Stream Road. The hatchery is open daily from 8:00 a.m. to 3:30 p.m.; (802) 447–2844.

On one of Bennington's back streets is the **Bennington Potters Yard,** a factory store featuring high-priced pottery dinnerware, you also will see swank gift and kitchenware shops. Here you'll find a full range of dinnerware and accessories, along with seconds at lower prices. On the grounds is a shop with fine glassware and a restaurant. At the intersection of East Main Street (Route 9) and North Street in the center of town, take North Street north 3 blocks and turn right onto County Street. Open 10:00 a.m. to 6:00 p.m. daily. The Potters Yard is at 324 County Street, Bennington; (802) 447–7531; www.benningtonpotters.com/potters-yard.

On Route 7, 1 mile north of the junction with Route 9, is the **Blue Benn Diner,** a local institution offering everything from burgers and lasagna to tofu. The jukebox is equally eclectic, and the clientele ranges from Bennington College students to construction workers.

The lines and colors inside are sharp, with neon reflecting off the smooth chrome surfaces of the display cases and milk machine. Despite its 1950s diner look and atmosphere, the Blue Benn serves an updated version of comfort foods, with several Mexican favorites along with the meat loaf.

The Blue Benn is open Monday and Tuesday 6:00 a.m. to 5:00 p.m., Wednesday through Friday 6:00 a.m. to 8:00 p.m., Saturday 6:00 a.m. to 4:00

easycome, easygo?

The most illustrious native of Pownal was born in North Pownal in 1834. "Jubilee" Jim Fisk has been variously described as a railroad magnate, a Wall Street genius, and a playboy. Fisk took over the Erie Railroad and gambled in the gold market against another notorious New Yorker of the time, Jay Gould. Fisk's other accomplishments included purchasing an opera house, spending his fortune as quickly as he made it, and being murdered in a love triangle in what was then the Broadway Central Hotel in 1872.

p.m., and Sunday 7:00 a.m. to 4:00 p.m. It's on Route 7 in Bennington; (802) 442–5140.

The menu is always inviting at the casual ***Alldays and Onions,*** where you can get hefty sandwiches at lunch, stacked onto tasty whole-grain breads. Vegetarians will be comfortable here, with several good choices. The dinner menu offers both traditional and innovative dishes; unfortunately, the service at dinner often lags behind the cuisine, but you may forgive all after one of the chocolate desserts. Alldays and Onions is open Monday through Saturday 7:30 to 10:30 a.m. for breakfast and 11:00 a.m. to 3:00 p.m. for lunch, and from 5:00 p.m. for dinner Tuesday through Saturday. There's also brunch on Sunday from 9:00 a.m. to 1:00 p.m. It's located at 519 East Main Street, Bennington; (802) 447–0043; www.alldaysandonions.com.

The offices of **Hemmings Motor News** are on Route 9 (Main Street) west of town. *Hemmings Motor News,* in case you're not a fancier of old cars, advertises everything from the Volkswagen Thing to Model A Fords, from parts to entire cars and even fan clubs.

This is where it's all put together. A small store in the building sells books on every kind of old car there is, and if you want to sneak a peek at upcoming issues, you can take a tour through the production and subscription

How Vermont Began

Colonial boundaries were determined by royal grants made in London and bore little relationship to land surveys or geographical landmarks. These vague boundaries led to inevitable disputes between colonies, particularly Massachusetts, which claimed areas around Brattleboro, as well as in New York and New Hampshire, which contested all of the area covered by Vermont. To royal governors, the granting of townships was an important source of income, and the governors of both New Hampshire and New York granted townships that often overlay one another, causing violent disputes over title.

The Allen brothers, Ira and Ethan, both highly independent landowners under New Hampshire grants, became ardent champions in defense of the New Hampshire grants, and against the attempts of New York to enforce its grants. Neither state was able to enforce its authority, however, and the residents finally established the Republic of Vermont. During the Revolution, this new republic even flirted with seeking a separate peace with the British.

After the war, New Hampshire and New York continued their tug-of-war over the Green Mountains, and Congress repeatedly failed to accept the Vermonters' application to join the Union. It wasn't until Vermont paid New York $30,000 to give up all claims that Vermont was admitted to the Union as the fourteenth state in 1791.

The Molly Stark Trail

It's ironic that Route 9, the only year-round route across the southern part of Vermont, should be named for a New Hampshire woman. Even more ironic, perhaps, is the fact that it is named not for the heroic leader of the Battle of Bennington, but for the wife he rode home to after the battle. On a simple stone in the cemetery behind the white church in West Bennington, you'll find the carved inscription of General Stark's famous words, which he uttered before the decisive battle: "Boys, yonder are the redcoats, and they are ours, or this night Molly Stark sleeps a widow."

departments during the publisher's regular hours. Back issues, *Hemmings* sweatshirts, fifteen-year subscription pins—they're all here. Vintage vehicles are on display, and the shop sells tools, toys, and models.

Write to *Hemmings Motor News,* Route 9, Bennington, 05201, or call (802) 447–9652. The *Hemmings* shop is open from 7:00 a.m. to 10:00 p.m. daily.

The ***Bennington Interpretive Center/Images from the Past*** is run by interpretive historian Tordis Ilg Isselhardt, an expert on local and New England history. The center is a combination of Isselhardt's expertise in the form of walking tours and slide shows—which she designs for many tour groups—and a small shop where she sells postcards, old photos, T-shirts, cards, and posters. All the items evoke the past of Bennington, Vermont, and the United States.

Isselhardt says that her main task in interpreting history for people is to help them orient themselves in time and space about Bennington and its history, which will then enable them to see the current period in the context of a long continuum of people and events.

She accomplishes this task through the use of a variety of reprints from negatives of photos by the late Robert L. Weichert, who took hundreds of photos of old, craggy Vermonters who wear their entire life histories on their faces.

The center's hours vary, because Isselhardt is frequently out guiding groups on walking tours through the town; you'll catch her in only by chance or appointment. Write to the Bennington Interpretive Center/Images from the Past, 155 West Main Street, Bennington, 05201, or call (802) 442–3204.

Off Route 9 west of Bennington is the ***Bennington Center for the Arts.*** The permanent collection includes Native American pottery, nature art, kachinas, and Navajo rugs. Four galleries host permanent and touring exhibits, including a covered bridge museum. The center is open May through October, Tuesday through Sunday from 11:00 a.m. to 5:00 p.m. It's located at Gypsy Lane, Bennington; (802) 442–7158; www.benningtoncenter forthearts.org.

The nearby **Bennington Museum** has long been a favorite for admirers of Grandma Moses, one of the state's best-known primitive folk artists. The museum's extensive collection of her work, memorabilia, and schoolhouse studio are part of a new Grandma Moses Family Heritage Gallery. An addition has also added more space for displaying the museum's collections of fine art, Bennington pottery, furniture, toys, and colonial and Civil War–period artifacts. The outstanding collections of American glassware and early-to-Victorian quilts have a bit more elbow room now. Even if you saw this museum a few years ago, it is definitely worth another stop. It is on Route 9 west of Bennington and is open daily 10:00 a.m. to 5:00 p.m., year-round except January (closed Wednesdays except September and October). Admission is $9.00 adults, seniors and students $8.00, under 18 free. 75 Main Street, Bennington; (802) 447–1571; www.benningtonmuseum.org.

Green Mountains South

Not long out of Bennington, Route 9 East begins to climb, then enters the **Green Mountain National Forest.** The forest's western border begins just outside Bennington and stretches eastward to the town of Wilmington, a good 20 miles away. This part of the forest is one of the largest, most uninterrupted tracts in the state, and its untamed look proves it. The roadside signs with moose silhouettes are not there to look quaint but as a warning to drivers, especially at night and around dawn and twilight hours.

On the right is **Greenwood Lodge,** an American Youth Hostel facility that is rustic, yet homey and welcoming. Many people stay here for its remoteness and for its access to Prospect Mountain and the Long Trail; the location provides opportunities for short hikes and walks as well as serving as a jumping-off point for hiking the entire Long Trail end to end. Swimming, fishing, boating, and biking are available—and True's General Store is right across Route 9.

Greenwood Lodge consists of two dormitories and five private rooms, sleeping a total of fifty people; forty wooded campsites are also scattered throughout the hostel's 120 acres. The lodge is open mid-May through late October. For information and reservations, write to Greenwood Lodge, Route 9 East, Bennington, 05201, or call (802) 442–2547.

Woodford, by the way, is the highest town in Vermont, at an elevation of 2,215 feet. But with just 314 people, it ranks among towns having the smallest populations.

After its steep ascent, Route 9 drops into Wilmington, with an array of shops, eateries, and lodgings. From the center of Wilmington, head south on Route 100 for 8 miles into Jacksonville and Route 112. In the southern end of the village is the *North River Winery,* located in an 1850 farmhouse.

Apples grown at Dwight Miller's Orchards north in Dummerston are hand-pressed, and the juice is made into unique wines.

North River's offerings run from a tangy, crisp Green Mountain Apple to Vermont Pear, which resembles a slightly sweet pinot grigio. The Vermont Harvest Apple, flavored with cinnamon and a touch of maple syrup, can be served hot or cold.

ANNUAL EVENTS IN SOUTHWEST VERMONT

Last Weekend in March: Reggae Festival, Mount Snow Ski Area, West Dover, "pond skimming" (ski down the hill and across the pond); Duct Tape Derby (cardboard sled race pitting guests against employees); all accompanied by live reggae music; (802) 464–3333.

Mid-June: Ethan Allen Days, Arlington, with a reenactment of Revolutionary War skirmishes; Father's Day; (802) 375–6144.

August: Southern Vermont Craft Fair, Hildene Meadows, Manchester Village, with 250 juried artists and craftspeople; first Sundays of August, and October; (802) 362–2100.

Late August: Bondville Fair, Bondville, is the oldest continuously held fair in Vermont.

Late December: Candlelight tours, Robert Todd Lincoln's Hildene, Route 7A, Manchester Village, with two nights of entertainment, including bell ringers; (802) 362–1788.

Late December: Torchlight parade and fireworks display, Mount Snow/Haystack, held one evening between Christmas and New Year's; also Thanksgiving, Martin Luther King's birthday, and Presidents' Day; (802) 464–3333.

South Central MOOver

Wilmington is Vermont's definition of the beaten path, so we have not discussed it here. But the area around it is not as crowded and is worth exploring, which you can do by bus. Area towns have formed the Deerfield Valley Transit Association, which serves the area, including Wardsboro, Readsboro, Dover, Whitingham, and Wilmington, with buses painted in patterns of black-and-white cow spots that would make Gateway jealous. Call (802) 464–8487 for schedules or visit their Web site at www .moover.com.

The winery is open daily from 10:00 a.m. until 5:00 p.m. Tours of the winery and tastings are free. Write to the North River Winery, Route 112, Jacksonville, 05342, or call (802) 368–7557.

From Jacksonville, Route 100 swings west, paralleling (if a line so wiggly could be said to parallel anything) the Massachusetts border through Whittingham and Readsboro, before swinging north to join Route 8, which leads back to Route 9, a few miles west of Wilmington. It's a rolling, scenic loop, and on Route 8 you have a dramatic view of a windmill farm.

The eleven huge white towers of the ***Searsburg Wind Power Facility*** stand in a row along the mountain ridge, and interpretive signs at a roadside pullout explain how they work. One of the largest wind-power facilities in the eastern United States, this one was completed in 1997 as a research project, and its turbines generate enough power to run 2,000 homes. While they look smaller from the road below, each blade is 64 feet long and made of black fiberglass to prevent ice buildup in the winter. It takes only a 10-mile-an-hour wind to turn the blades, and at their elevation of 2,800 feet, the wind blows so steadily that the turbines can operate 95 percent of the time.

Although Lake Champlain is probably the best-known body of water in the state, locals and visitors know that one of the most dramatic is the ***Harriman Reservoir,*** west of Wilmington. And you can do more than just gaze at it, because the ***Green Mountain Flagship Company*** conducts narrated excursions in the form of ninety-minute cruises several times each day from May 1 until late October. Captain Richard Joyce welcomes visitors aboard the ***M/V* Mt. Mills,** a pontoon boat. Part of the fascination of the trip are his stories of the village of Mountain Mills, which was destroyed in the creation of the lake. He uses music and sound effects to spice up the narration, which centers on the history of the reservoir and the surrounding mountains, where logging was once the premier occupation.

Green Mountain also rents canoes, kayaks, and boats if you want to paddle yourself around the lake. For more information, call Green Mountain Flagship Company at (802) 464–2975; www.greenmountainflagship.com.

Not far from the top of Hogback Mountain, about 4 miles east of Wilmington, is the motel-style **Horizon Inn**. Its contemporary rooms are attractive and well kept, and the staff couldn't be more accommodating. All rooms have coffeemakers, and the rates are from $80 to $130. The Horizon Inn is at P.O. Box 817, Wilmington, 05363; (802) 464–2131; www.horizon.com.

If you follow the curiously named Screw Augur Road north from Route 9 in Marlboro, you'll come to South Newfane, a tiny village greatly overshadowed by the grand buildings of better-known Newfane. But it's an address well known to gardeners. Over the past decade, day lilies have become an important part of home landscaping, and much of this increased popularity, at least in New England, is due to **Olallie Day Lily Gardens**. The display plantings show an amazing variety of lilies in a riot of shades. There's also a shop with books, gifts, and tools for the gardener. To get to South Newfane from Brattleboro, take Route 30 north about 8.5 miles along the West River, then take a marked road left about 3.5 miles to Williamsville and South Newfane. Olallie Day Lily Gardens (129 Augur Hole Road, South Newfane; 802–348–6614; www.daylilygarden.com) is open 10:00 a.m. to 5:00 p.m. Wednesday to Monday from Memorial Day through mid-September.

Heading north from busy Wilmington, Route 100 quickly becomes a rural byway again, winding along a valley bordered by rolling hills, its meadows dotted with farmhouses. Although most are no longer the hub of a working farm, one family has kept its farming traditions alive.

Adams Farm is easy to spot from Route 100 by the huge quilt design that decorates one side of the barn. Six generations of the family have farmed the scenic hillside, and they now share the farm experience with the public. Activities change, following the rhythms of the seasons, with winter sleigh rides, Halloween hayrides, tractor rides, feeding farm animals, and watching maple sap boil into syrup. The accent is on family activities, and young children will always find plenty to do here. Fresh vegetables are for sale in the summer, pumpkins in the fall, and locally made quilts, knitwear, and hand weaving all year in their Fiber Arts Loft. The farm is on Higley Hill Road, Wilmington; (802) 464–3762, www.adamsfamilyfarm.com.

Just off Route 100 in West Dover is the **Inn at Sawmill Farm**, a gracious and sophisticated country inn with a highly praised restaurant. A vintage barn has been skillfully transformed into sitting rooms, with a balcony room overlooking from the former hay loft. Despite the elegant furnishings, fine art, and soaring ceilings, the inn's atmosphere is invitingly warm and informal.

Guest rooms are divided between the inn itself and a dozen in adjoining outside buildings, some of which are separate cottages. All of these outside rooms have working wood-burning fireplaces. Guests leave the outside world behind here, as the inn has no in-room telephones or television. In the summer two trout ponds on the property are well stocked, with a fly-fishing school located conveniently on the premises. Rates, which are in the $325 range, include a full breakfast and a five-course dinner. Dinner is served to nonguests by prior reservation, with a la carte entrees beginning at about $35. The inn is on Crosstown Road in West Dover; (802) 464–8131, www.theinn atsawmillfarm.com.

Although most people know about **Mount Snow** and its ski slopes, a less crowded time to visit is in summer. Many ski areas in Vermont open up their lifts for scenic gondola rides in the warm weather, but Mount Snow goes one better: Bicycles are available for guided runs down the trails. Call (802) 464–4040; or see www.mountsnow.com/summer for more information.

An addition to the ski area is the free **Snowseum** (802–464–4279), located at the base of Mount Snow. It has an interactive display on the history of skiing in the United States starting in the 1880s and covering the sport through the present day.

The town of Stratton, which is not to be confused with Stratton Mountain the ski area, is to the west of Route 100. You can reach Stratton the town by making a left in the town of West Wardsboro and driving about 4 miles into a tiny village. **Stratton Mountain** ski area is accessed by continuing north on Route 100, then heading west on Route 30 into the village of Bondville.

buttheydidn't buildcondos

Wardsboro, north of Stratton, holds the distinction of being the last town in Vermont that New Hampshire governor Benning Wentworth chartered, in 1764. The Vermont government officially granted the town's charter in 1780, when Vermont was its own republic, to a resident of nearby Newfane, Vermont—William Ward—along with sixty-two others. Although few chose to live and settle on their land grants, many people throughout southern New England wanted their own piece of Vermont even back then.

As you drive through the town of Stratton from West Wardsboro, continue on for 3 more miles until you reach the **Grout Pond Recreation Area,** a splendid, almost-unknown, 1,600-acre reserve with camping, boating, and swimming on seventy-nine-acre Grout Pond.

It's a peaceful, unspoiled area that contrasts sharply with the developed ski area in the northeast corner of the town. The concurrent Long Trail and Appalachian Trail pass nearby, and there are miles of hiking trails on old logging roads within the boundaries of the area. You might even see a few old cellar holes on the trails. For more information, call (802) 362–2307, or log on to www.fsfed.us/r9/forests/greemountain/index/htm.

In Wardsboro, as Route 100 curves through the village center and crosses the river, be sure to notice the roof of the general store, where the shingles form a giant American flag. Just before Route 100 merges with Route 30 in Jamaica, it crosses West River on an old-fashioned green metal bridge so narrow that it has a traffic light to signal one-way traffic.

At *Jamaica Coffee House,* you might think you'd stepped back into the 1960s, when Vermont had more back-to-the-landers than SUVs. From the mismatched chairs and tables on the long front porch to the deep sofas that share a back room with vintage clothing, records, and used paperbacks, this is a piece of another era. The tea is organic, the coffee is fair-trade, and the women who pour it for you are smiling, soft-spoken, and take time to chat. The PB&J sandwiches are slathered with locally made strawberry jam. If you long for the days before Vermont's general stores sold latte and wraps, mellow out here on Main Street. Open from 7:00 a.m. to 5:00 p.m. daily (except Wednesday in the winter); (802) 874–4643.

Green Mountains North

Route 100 weaves back and forth among the mountains as it makes its way north, connecting so many of Vermont's ski areas—from Mount Snow to Stowe and even Jay Peak—that it's known as the Skier's Highway.

In addition to the famed skiing, there are two other outdoor activities near Stratton Mountain. *Zoar Outdoor* runs a few white-water rafting trips on the Class III and IV rapids of the West River. The trip starts with a strenuous walk down a rockbound trail to the river, just below the Ball Mountain Dam, and goes all the way south to the takeout at Townsend Dam. Along the way there is a picnic and swim opportunity along the river, and the trip finishes with a chicken barbecue. There are only a few trip dates each year, usually in April and September, so arrangements should be made early. The cost is about $90, and a package with lodging and breakfast is available. Why go all the way to the Grand Canyon? Zoar Outdoor, P.O. Box 245, Charlemont, MA 01339, (800) 532–7483; www.zoaroutdoor.com.

Close by, at *Sun Bowl Ranch* on Stratton Mountain, you can explore the mountain trails on horseback or enjoy the countryside on a wagon ride. From mid-June to mid-October there are one- and two-hour horse rides for $30 and $55, respectively. For $60 you can saddle up for a ninety-minute ride, with a picnic lunch. Rides run from 9:00 a.m. to 5:00 p.m., traveling over backwoods roads and ski trails. An overnight package ($150) includes a three-hour ride, dinner, lodging, and breakfast. Reservations are strongly recommended. Write the ranch, Stratton Mountain, VT 05155, or call (802) 297–9210; (800) 787–2886; www.sunbowlranch.com.

Weston lies in a little valley, gathered around a large village green, and its best-known attraction is **Vermont Country Store,** a step-back-in-time general store that offers goods in cracker barrels and penny candy amid the aura of an antique, wood-burning potbellied stove. Although you'll find a lot of moose T-shirts and cow-spotted socks designed for tourists, the overriding mission here is to provide those useful things you might have thought weren't made anymore. You'll also find good warm, sensible clothing and quality kitchen utensils. A sister store flourishes on Route 103 in Rockingham.

talkabout unorganized!

Glastenbury was once a thriving township with a population peak of fifty in 1834. The charcoal kilns in the town were located near the Bennington and Glastenbury Railroad, which was built after the Civil War ended. A hotel, houses, and a trolley line soon followed, but the bust came as quickly as the boom. Today you can find cellar holes that run along the Appalachian Trail in an area that has become a ghost town. The town was officially unorganized back in 1937 after one member of the only family remaining served in every town office, from supervisor and fire warden to town representative in the state legislature.

The Vermont Country Stores are open seven days year-round (except Thanksgiving and Christmas) from 9:00 a.m. to 5:30 p.m.; Manchester Center: P.O. Box 3000, Manchester; (802) 362–8440. Weston store: (802) 824–3184. Rockingham store: (802) 463–2224. Visit www .vermontcountrystore.com.

The **Farrar-Mansur House,** a colonial tavern facing the attractive village green, is Weston's historical museum, showing furnishings, clothing, household implements, and firearms from the town's past. What distinguishes this from other historic-house museums in the state is its large collection of eighteenth-century household items brought to Vermont by a pioneer family (remember, this was out west in the 1700s). The later generations who lived in the house added items from their own eras, making the museum a reflection of more than two centuries of Weston life. The house is located on the green and is open 1:00 to 4:00 p.m. Wednesday through Sunday in July and August, weekends only in the fall.

Next door, and part of the same complex, are the Old Mill Museums, in an old sawmill building that was later converted to a gristmill. Today it houses collections representing both those functions, plus a tin shop, water-powered woodworking shop, and a variety of early farm and dairy tools. The mill is open from Wednesday through Sunday, Memorial Day through Columbus Day. Call ahead to accommodate larger groups; Peter Rosengarten, former president of the Vermont Historical Society, will be glad to help: (802) 824–8190.

Weston is hardly undiscovered, but even in "tourist season" it maintains its rural village air and is a very pleasant base for exploring this part of Vermont. Right in the village, within an easy walk of everything, is the ***Inn at Weston,*** with twelve guest rooms divided between two well-restored mid-1800s houses. Each room is different in decor and furnishings. Those in the main house have antiques, handmade quilts, sitting areas, whirlpool tubs, and fireplaces, while the neighboring Colman house has comfortable air-conditioned rooms at somewhat lower rates. A large library of books invites guests to curl up in a comfortable chair indoors or find a bench in the gardens. Rooms have VCRs and CD players, and the library is well stocked with tapes and CDs.

A talented young chef, Jennifer Cayer, runs the kitchen. Jen grew up on a small family farm in Barnard, Vermont, and learned to cook at about the same time she learned to read. She is a small-scale farmer herself, deeply rooted in sustainable agriculture. Her eclectic mix of styles includes down-home soul-warming soups, slow-cooked French-inspired cuisine, and creative interpretations of American classics. Dinner is served to the public, but a reservation is wise, since inn guests seldom eat elsewhere. Rooms begin at $185 and entrees in the restaurant begin at about $26. In the winter, packages include lift tickets at your choice of nearby ski areas. The inn is on Route 100, Weston; (802) 824–6789; www.innweston.com.

Music lovers will want to investigate the inn's semi-annual Piano Dinners, when a concert pianist plays following the first three courses of dinner. Dessert is served during intermission, then the concert continues. These programs, which feature a mix of classical, Broadway, and contemporary music, are in mid-December and on Memorial Day weekend, and they sell out every time.

Owner/innkeeper Bob Aldrich developed an interest in orchids when he took biology in college, and one of the first things he did upon buying the inn was build a 670-square-foot ***orchid greenhouse*** for his collection, which now numbers 375 different species and hybrids. Bob is happy to show guests and visitors his collection, and a tour with him is a short course on these fascinating plants. You will learn, for example, that their highly specialized roots are coated with a spongy layer that absorbs and holds rainwater, and that some orchids have bulbous bases that act as water tanks during dry spells. The blooms, which range from tiny white blossoms to giant, showy, bright-purple flowers, are beautiful, and the atmosphere—a humid rain-forest environment of 80 degrees—is a very welcome respite on a cold winter day. As you might expect, the inn's outdoor gardens are beautiful the rest of the year as well.

As you head north out of the town of Weston, where Route 100 and Route 155 meet, is a beautiful place called the **Weston Priory.** This monastery of Benedictine monks welcomes the public to its services every day. The gift shop carries books and crafts, many of which are made overseas and in northern New England.

A variety of Nativity scenes are on display from September through Christmas. One scene, from Spain, is made from terra-cotta and lacquered cloth; another is made of hand-carved wood from a Mexican monastery; still another has soapstone sheep from Kenya. Colorful hand-painted and-carved wooden ornaments and Christmas decorations from El Salvador cover a wall of the shop, which is a serene place, in keeping with the overall tone of the priory's grounds.

The Weston monks are well known for their liturgical choral music, which is available on tape and CD at the shop. The art gallery downstairs displays the work of both Weston monks and brothers from around the world. Prayer services are open to the public four times a day in one of two chapels, depending on the season. Walking paths invite strolling throughout the grounds.

For more information write to the Weston Priory, Route 155, Weston, 05161, or call (802) 824–5409; www.westonpriory.org. You are welcome to attend services, but the times of the liturgies vary with the season, so call ahead.

Just south of Weston, where Route 100 crosses Route 11, is Londonderry. Almost hidden in a little shopping center there is a restaurant opened not long ago by the former chef at the Inn at Weston, Max Turner. At the **New American Grill** comfort food meets New American in a happy marriage of two culinary worlds. Dinner entrees might include seared sushi-grade ahi tuna with a tamarind-soy glaze, wasabi, and pickled ginger, on the menu next to turkey pot pie or a homey lamb stew. Open for three meals a day, New American Grill can start your day with buttermilk biscuits and sausage gravy or a breakfast burrito—or a bowl of granola or old-fashioned grits. There's a kids' menu of six selections, and the entire menu is at family-friendly prices, with most dinner entrees from $8:00 to $22.00. The grill is open daily, from 11:00 a.m. until 9:00 p.m. on weekdays, and 7:00 a.m. until 9:00 p.m. on weekends, at Mountain Marketplace, Route 100, Londonderry; (802) 824–9844.

If you're in the area in late September, be sure to visit the **Peru Fair,** a wonderful example of a traditional country fair held during the peak of foliage season. Many residents plan all year for the event, much to the benefit of locals and visitors. The weekend-long fair has music, lots of food, arts and crafts, games, and an old-fashioned pig roast.

Before the mega-resorts hit the Green Mountains, **Magic Mountain** was known as a skier's mountain, one of those special places where people kept returning because of the variety and challenge of the runs. Then, in 1991, the last ticket was sold and trees began to grow on the slopes. No one expected to ski its trails again, but astute skiers who tired of long lines and snow bunnies helped the resort come back to life.

The fifty trails have been cleared, and 87 percent of the mountain has snowmaking coverage. Vertical drop at Magic is 1,600 feet, and the longest run is Wizard, an intermediate-to-expert slope (read that high-intermediate, with sections of heart-stopping expert), a bit over a mile and a half long. In fact, every trail, from beginner to expert, has at least one section that will challenge the skills of that level skier. Some of the double diamonds verge on extreme. Magic tends to be less crowded than other places, and during the week you practically have it to yourself.

The terrain here is fun, and it is a great family mountain; it has none of the high-pressure glitz of the bigger name brands, but all the services you need. In 2006 Magic Mountain opened an inn called Ski and Stay, which adds lodging and the option of inclusive packages. Daily rates are $39 for adults, $35 for teens, and $25 for juniors (holiday rates are higher). The lodge defines teens as thirteen to seventeen and juniors as seven to twelve. youngsters ages six and under ski free. A combined lift and tubing ticket (on Saturdays and holidays only) is $71 for adults, $66 for teens, and $54 for juniors. You'll also find a tube park with plenty of lanes, an all-terrain park, and a half tube for boarders. Magic

atownby anyname

Peru is the town where the movie *Baby Boom,* starring Diane Keaton, was filmed. For filming of the movie, the WELCOME TO PERU signs were changed to WELCOME TO HADLEYVILLE, the name of the fictional town in the movie. But back in 1761, the signs would have read WELCOME TO BROMLEY, the original name of the town. Residents changed the name to Peru in 1804, because they felt it was more affluent-sounding. Apparently, the name Bromley conveyed the attitude of a slumlord and thus slowed economic growth. After the name was changed to Peru, the fortunes of the town began to look up—a situation that continues today in this quiet town of about 300 people.

Mountain is on Route 11, Londonderry; (802) 824–5645; fax (802) 824–5199. www.magicmtn.com.

Viking Nordic Center has been around since 1970, long enough to learn how to take care of the trails so that they are skiable even when the snow levels are low. Nordic's 35 km of trails are all machine-groomed and tracked, on terrain that ranges from gently rolling to treks through forests. Instructions and rentals are available, and they have night skiing. Rates are adults $19.00, seniors $16.00, and juniors $12.00, with group lessons at $18.00 for one hour. A four-bedroom guesthouse right on the edge of the trails is available for rent (winter $850 for a non-holiday weekend, summer $950 a week). In summer the trails are used for hiking and bicycling. The center is at 615 Little Pond Road, Londonderry; (802) 824–3933; www.vikingnordic.com.

Another place for cross-country skiing is *Wild Wings Ski Touring Center* in Peru, off Route 11 toward Bromley Mountain Ski Area (from Peru village take the road opposite the Hapgood General Store, following signs about 2.5 miles). Wild Wings' 25 km of trails, through woods and along brooks, are groomed with a Sno-Cat for track skiing with no skate skiing. Rates are adult $18.00, junior $10.00, and rentals are $18.00 and $10.00, respectively. Lessons are also offered. Wild Wings is off North Road, Peru; (802) 824–6793; www .wildwingsski.com. The proprietors welcome you to hot chocolate and/or soup in the warming room.

Another well-equipped but down-to-earth ski area is a few miles farther down Route 11 at *Bromley Mountain,* only 6 miles from Manchester. Bromley was one of the earliest Vermont ski areas, founded in the late 1930s by Fred Pabst, who started the brewery. It was always a pioneering area: In 1947 Pabst was the first to contour the slopes, and he pioneered grooming by being the first in the state to roll snow to keep it packed. Bromley was also one of the first to install snowmaking machinery and its snowmaking covers nearly all its trails. Of the thirty-nine trails, 36 percent are rated beginner, 35 percent intermediate, and the balance expert. For the skier of average to low-expert ability there is plenty of challenging terrain. Bromley is one of the few areas where trails of a given skill level tend to be located together. From the Alpine lift beginners have mountain, not just base lodge, access to several novice trails. From the Sun lift intermediate skiers have access to a number of intermediate trails. The vertical drop is 1,334 feet, and the longest trail, suitable for an advanced beginner or intermediate, is about 2½ miles long. The variety of ability levels makes this a nice area for families, and even during holiday periods lift lines are rarely more than a five- or ten-minute wait.

At the rental shop you can try out demo parabolics during the first and last hours of the day. If you don't like the conditions during the first hour after you buy your ticket, you'll be given a pass for another day. The midweek rates are $39 for all ages, with weekend rates $63 for adults, $55 for teens (thirteen to seventeen), and $39 for juniors (six to twelve). Summers at Bromley also offer thrills on the mountain on the ⅔-mile **Alpine Slide,** the longest alpine ride in the United States. Bromley Mountain, Box 1130, Manchester Center, 05255; (802) 824–5522.

The Batten Kill Valley

As you travel up the Batten Kill Valley, you'll see the Taconics on the west and the Green Mountains on the east, divided by a valley that grows wider and flatter as you go north. These are fertile farmlands with rich alluvial soil, and in the north you will see large farms along the valley floor. Route 7 is a limited-access highway in some places, but the quieter Routes 7A and 30 provide an alternative.

The town of Arlington is best known for its famous citizen Norman Rockwell, who painted things as he saw them right here in Arlington. There's a museum devoted to Rockwell's art.

Another fascinating look at Vermont's people can be found in the **Dr. George A. Russell Collection of Vermontiana,** near the schools on East Arlington Road. Doc Russell was one of the subjects Rockwell painted, specifically for his Country Doctor portrait. The collection is considered one of the largest anywhere devoted to Vermont history and ephemera; the doctor collected the materials his entire life. When he died, he left the entire collection to the town of Arlington. The collection, which is really a library, not a museum of artifacts, is open on Tuesdays and by appointment if a volunteer is available; call (802) 375–6153 for more information.

There is no better way to see the Batten Kill Valley than from the river itself, which you can do with **Battenkill Canoe, Ltd.** The river rises on the west side of the Green Mountains and flows down through Arlington before leaving Vermont, finally emptying into the Hudson River in New York. It offers some of the nicest, most scenic water travel experiences in the state. The stream is nonthreatening and passes through fields and forests, under covered bridges, and through tiny settlements. Battenkill Canoe offers equipment rentals or whole packages, including drop-off and pickup. Ask about the "On the Batten Kill" day trip or the two- to five-day "Canoe Inn to Inn" packages. (The five-day package, including the exploration of five rivers, is available from $1500. Make arrangements with Battenkill Canoe at 6328 Vermont Route 7A, Arlington; (802) 362–2800 or (800) 421–5268; www.battenkill.com.

Friends Forever

In 1946, when an eleven-year-old classmate died of cancer, a group of Burlington girls raised $48 to buy a painting from Norman Rockwell to hang in the school as a memorial to her. Rockwell donated the painting *The Babysitter,* and the girls spent the money on a brass plaque to put on it. Class after class graduated, and the painting was, at some point, removed and stored in the boiler room. When the painting was found recently and appraised at $300,000, the school board decided to sell it and put the money toward the school budget.

But old friendships die hard in Vermont, and the classmates once again assembled and vowed to raise the money to buy the painting back from the school. They then donated it to the art gallery at the University of Vermont, this time as a permanent memorial.

If Arlington's Norman Rockwell connection fascinates you, reserve a room in his former home there, now the *Inn on Covered Bridge Green.* Rooms in the main house are nicely decorated, all with private baths, and some overlook the village green and church. Each is different in size, shape, and decor, but all have queen- or king-size beds, often four-poster. Two separate buildings are now guest cottages; one, formerly Rockwell's studio, has housekeeping facilities. Rates vary but run between $160 and $250 a night. The inn is on River Road at Covered Bridge Road, West Arlington; (802) 375–9489 or (800) 726–9480; www.coveredbridgegreen.com.

You may recall, with a bit of nostalgia, the cheese stores that appeared along New England's most traveled highways during the 1960s and 1970s. They were yellow and shaped liked huge wheels of cheese with a chunk taken out and were called *The Cheese House.* After a decade or so they all closed, or so we thought until we traveled down Route 7A in Arlington. There by the roadside stands a round building with a wedge taken out of it—and it's called *The Cheese House.* This is the original store and the prototype of the whole chain. Of course, they sell cheese, especially Vermont cheddar and their own two-year-old "Truck Driver Cheddar," but they also carry many other Vermont-made products, including maple syrup, maple candy, jams, and jellies. This slice of New England commercial history is on Route 7A, Arlington; (802) 375–9033.

Mount Equinox, a long mountain that lies almost parallel to Route 7A, rises to more than 3,800 feet. It is the highest peak in the Taconic Range, which is, admittedly, not known for its high elevations. But Equinox has some splendid views from the top, which you can reach by car via *Mount Equinox Skyline*

Drive. During foliage season the views are breathtaking—even native Vermonters make the trip this time of year. The road continues up the mountain for 5.2 miles, and your car will thank you for keeping an even speed of about 25 miles per hour on the ascent. Even with automatic transmission, you should descend in low gear.

This toll road is accessed from Route 7A between Arlington and Manchester Village and is open from May through foliage season and on into November, as long as the weather permits. Early snow or ice storms will end the season. A fee of $10.00 is charged per motorcycle, $12.00 per car and driver, plus $2.00 for each passenger. Mount Equinox Skyline Drive, Route 7A, Manchester; (802) 362–1114; www.equinoxmountain.com.

Manchester has a deeply split personality: Manchester Village and Manchester Center. The former is a gracious village with marble sidewalks and beautifully maintained homes—many of which are closer to mansions—lining the main square. Just a short way north, Manchester Center is a series of factory-outlet malls—albeit in nicely designed buildings for the most part—where you can buy everything from designer clothes to kitchenware.

"Hildene," the country mansion of Robert Todd Lincoln, son of the president and himself president of the Pullman railcar company, sits just off historic Route 7A. Built in the opening years of the twentieth century, this sumptuous building is a fine example of a period country home of a wealthy business magnate. Many of the furnishings came from Mrs. Lincoln's family, and there are personal items of the president, such as his famous stovepipe hat. On the landing of the grand staircase, a thousand-pipe 1908 Aeolian organ works again after a 1980 restoration. The elegant Queen Anne–furnished dining room and the wood-paneled parlor face each other across a broad carpeted hallway. Outside, stunning formal gardens overlooking the valley have been restored, re-creating many of the original plantings, and an ongoing project is restoring the kitchen gardens.

In the winter Hildene's grounds are traversed by twenty-one groomed cross-country trails, with facilities for all levels, a warming hut, a ski rental shop, and refreshments in a carriage barn. Annually after Christmas the house has Candlelight Tours with horse-drawn wagons or sleighs to bring guests through the snow to the front door. Approaching the house aglow in the snow-covered landscape is a magical sight. The schedule of events is worth checking at any time of year, since there are many treats, from pops concerts to garden parties, antiques shows to fairs. (802) 362–1788; www.hildene.org.

Although Manchester was chartered in 1761, the town didn't earn its bustling, upper-crust reputation until the mid-1800s, when it was promoted as a mineral springs vacation destination. The geology of Vermont consists of bedrock made up of granite and sedimentary rocks such as limestone, shale, and sandstone. This means that the groundwater contains a higher level of minerals than water where the rock is less porous.

During the second half of the nineteenth century, many urbanites were drawn to small Vermont towns for "spa vacations"—back then the phrase had a meaning very different from today's version. Somewhere along the line in the mid-nineteenth century, physicians and other health promoters claimed that regular partaking of this water would restore health to pasty-faced city people and even prolong life. Germany was then in the forefront of this "taking of the waters," and the practice spread to the United States.

Thus tourism in Vermont was born. Some Vermonters—most of whom never drank this mineral water, which was usually full of sulfuric deposits and smelled like rotten eggs—began to push the waters to out-of-staters. The popular belief was that the worse it smelled and tasted, the better it was for you. Some enterprising Vermonters even bottled the water and shipped it to Boston and New York for sale. Of course, proximity to a railroad line—rails were also being aggressively laid at the time—didn't hurt sales.

This influx of wealthy summer visitors inspired the expansion of the **Marsh Tavern,** which had stood in the middle of town since 1769, into a hotel, where guests could, for an extra fee, improve their health with Equinox Sparkling Water. Soon the hotel's columned facade was the centerpiece of the village.

In 1883 Charles Orvis, founder of the fly-fishing business, bought a "cottage" next to his brother's hotel, **The Equinox,** which had been in the Orvis family since mid-century. He opened C.F. Orvis Company in the brick bank building next door, where he manufactured split-bamboo fishing rods and artificial flies.

His home, which stands facing the classic white-spired church in Manchester Village, is now the **Charles Orvis Inn,** and his legacy of fly fishing lives on in the inn's restrained fisherman's-club decor. Old photographs of fishing camps share wall space in the public and guest rooms with beautifully framed fishing lures. The suites in this very upscale lodging include full-size kitchens, gas fireplaces, phones, televisions, and a blend of custom-built furniture and antiques. Guests enjoy all the services of The Equinox, plus their own concierge, a continental breakfast, and a complimentary bar adjoining the billiard room downstairs. Rates for these suites are much higher than rooms in the Equinox's main building. Historic Route 7A, P.O. Box 46, Manchester Village, 05254 (3567 Main Street); (800) 362–4747; http://equinox.rockresorts .com/accommodations/orvis.

Although The Equinox is far better known than its smaller neighbor, it has some unique and little-known experiences in store for its guests. It is also located at 3567 Main Street, Manchester Village; (800) 362–4700; www.equinox resort.com.

Devotees of fishing can complete the pilgrimage by visiting the *American Museum of Fly Fishing* next door to the Orvis Inn, open Monday through Friday from 10:00 a.m. until 4:00 p.m. 4104 Main Street, Manchester, VT 05254; (802) 362–3300, www.amff.com.

Unique in New England (and rare in the United States) is the *British School of Falconry* at The Equinox. While you may have seen raptors and read about them at the Raptor Center in Woodstock, here you get to see them up close and actually work with them, under the close observation of a falconry expert, of course. The school is the first of its kind in the United States and was started in 1995 by Steve and Emma Ford, Scots who started teaching falconry in 1982.

While a lesson here will not make you into a certified falconer, you will learn about raptors and how they hunt. You also get a chance to see an African tawny eagle, a Lanner hawk, and Harris hawks, all used for hunting. Once, each level of royalty had its own assigned species. Bob Waite, our certified falconer and instructor, explained the uses for different species and explained that the Harris is the best for most purposes because it is the calmest. We also learned that those funny little helmets they put on the birds are to keep them calm in transit; when they can't see, they don't worry.

All equipment, including warm jackets and boots, if necessary, is provided, and participants in the short lesson learn how to hold a falcon on their gauntleted hand, how to "cast" or release the bird into flight, and how to signal for the bird's return. It is a great thrill to see these magnificent birds in flight, but to see them do so at close quarters and to have them alight on your hand is a rare experience.

The school has a number of programs available. The "winter" introductory lesson, which lasts about forty-five minutes, costs $70. But there are also Hawk Walks ($180), during which you get the full lesson and also have the pleasure of seeing a free-flying hawk following behind you, landing in the branches of trees, and coming when you call. This program is an hour long. In the school's hunting program, guests actually hunt with the birds and specially trained hunting dogs and see how, for more than 4,000 years, man and bird have worked together. At press time, School of Falconry officials were considering major changes in the hunting program. Call for definitive information. The school is at 1550 River Road, Manchester Village; (802) 362–4780, fax (802) 362–4817; e-mail: falconry@equinoxresort.com.

Opposite The Equinox, in a building that once housed its staff, are several shops emphasizing fine arts and crafts.

Mount Equinox rises steeply behind the Equinox Resort in Manchester Village, and the land along this western slope is part of the Equinox Preservation Trust, which works with a consortium of other conservation and environmental organizations to protect and preserve the fragile lands on the mountain. While preserving the land, they also operate and maintain a large series of trails used for hiking, skiing, and horseback riding. Trails lead to ponds and the upper slopes of the mountain. One series of trails will take you across the lower slopes of the mountain to the Southern Vermont Arts Center.

The terrain of the mountain is quite varied and contains many rare species of plants. Among these is the very rare yellow lady slipper, a member of the orchid family. The rare protected environments of Table Rock and Deer Knoll are accessible only on tours led by naturalists from the Vermont Institute of Natural Science (VINS), which maintains an office at the Equinox Resort in Manchester. Call for a schedule of their programs, (802) 362–4374. Their programs focus on learning about the mountain's rare habitats.

There are two trailheads giving access to several trails, most of which are short. Although individual trails can be as short as a half mile, they do link together to create longer hiking opportunities. The Pond Road trailhead is at the end of Pond Road, the street south of the Equinox Resort. From here, a nice, easy trail rounds Equinox Pond to Bower Spring and the Mountain Bluff Trail ($\frac{9}{10}$ mile). To get to the Red Gate trailhead, take Seminary Road on the north side of the Equinox Resort to West Union Street, following it to the trailhead. The longest trail is the Blue Trail ($2\frac{8}{10}$ miles), which starts at the Red Gate and climbs upward along an old roadway, leading to a narrow, steep trail to the summit and lookout rock. From this ledge are sweeping views of New York, New Hampshire, and Vermont.

Free, But Valuable

As you travel through the state, look for the *Vermont Country Sampler,* a small newspaper that you can pick up free in tourist information centers, restaurants, and many other places. It features articles on historical subjects, along with features on local places you might not otherwise find. Seasonal activities and events are well covered, too, both in articles and in a calendar of events in each issue. In planning your trip, send for a free sample copy by mail, Vermont Country Sampler, P.O. Box 226, Danby, VT 05739. Call (802) 293.5752.

Look for a map of the preserve and its trails in a brochure entitled Equinox Preservation Trust, which you will find at the Tourist Information Office, at the Equinox Resort, and in brochure racks in most of the businesses in Manchester Village and Manchester Center. Equinox Preservation Trust, (802) 362–4700; VINS, (802) 362–4374.

Manchester Depot is a tiny corner of Manchester Center, only a block off a short stretch of highway shared by routes 11 and 30, but almost completely hidden. Locals know it for its charming architecture and for a clutch of shops that face Elm Street. At the intersection of Elm Street and Highland Avenue is a collection of wonderful old nineteenth-century storefronts that have not been defiled by modernization and are well worth the visit.

Al Ducci's Italian Pantry is at that intersection and itself is worth the side trip. Once inside, it's like being transported to Boston's North End, with the same tangy smells, friendly service with a touch of wise guy, and products you didn't think could be found this far from a city. In the cold cases you'll find a nice selection of salads, links of their own premises-made sausages, and chunks of their own mozzarella, made daily. They have really good made-to-order sandwiches that run about $5.00 and a list of their own special sandwiches such as a veggie combo (roasted eggplant, roasted peppers, fresh mozzarella, tomato, and basil), a prosciutto sandwich (with fresh mozzarella, roasted peppers, and fresh basil), and chicken cutlet with roasted peppers, fresh mozzarella, and fresh basil. These are served on your choice of white Italian, sourdough, semolina, focaccia, or multigrain breads (we suggest the focaccia). Get your sandwiches to take out or to eat in the dining room next door, a bright little room with a molded tin ceiling and red checkered cloths on the tables. Al Ducci's is at 133 Elm Street at Highland Avenue, Manchester Center; (802) 362–4449; fax (802) 362–0640; www.alduccis.com.

Next door to Al Ducci's, in another old-fashioned storefront, is **Maiden Lane at Le Depot.** Maiden Lane features a line of custom pillows made from specialty fabrics and trims, all originated by Shirley Maiden. It also offers antiques and period jewelry. Carol Lattuga brings a lifetime love of dressmaking to her decorative sewing and unique designs. The shop is a pleasure to browse through. You can find it at 145 Elm Street; (802) 362–2004.

Manchester has an abundance of places to eat, from bakeries, cafes, and pubs to elegant dining rooms. **Marsh Tavern** is our favorite, with a varied and seasonally changing menu that ranges from New England crab cakes and chicken pot pie to hazelnut-crusted trout and charbroiled filet mignon. Ingredients are impeccably fresh, with a preponderance coming from local farms and suppliers. The chef works closely with the Vermont Fresh Network to assure the finest locally grown ingredients. A sample item on the tavern's lunch menu is a croissant is served with sliced sirloin, Major Farm's Shepherd cheese, and sautéed mushrooms. Flavors and textures seem to play with each other on the plate, as in the New England bouillabaisse, a blend of lobster, shrimp, scallops, and clams served in a delectable lobster broth with fennel and fresh tomato. The single-malt mousse cake is an unexpected specialty on the dessert list. Dinner entrees are mostly between $16 and $23. The tavern is at the Equinox, Route 7A in Manchester Village; (802) 362–4700 or (800) 362–4747.

In a former tollhouse perched between the winding road and a rushing little brook in a ravine is *Mistral's*, where classic French flavors and techniques are skillfully updated. For openers there is a tapenade of black olives, capers, and a touch of anchovy served with thin crisps of bread. Their pâté maison is a triumph of flavor and texture, moist and lean with a tenderness that is almost crumbly, and a serving that is large enough to share. Entrees, which include bread, Salad Mistral (a mesclun of tender young greens), and vegetables, range from fish and seafood to chicken, duck, sweetbreads and beef, and specials. The signature dish of this chef-owned restaurant is the Norwegian salmon cannelloni, a pair of rolled salmon fillets, stuffed cannelloni-style with a mixture of lobster and finely diced shallots and vegetables, in a light pink beurre blanc. The service is exceptional, always there when needed but almost invisible. Among their enticing desserts is the signature Coup Mistral: coffee ice cream rolled in toasted hazelnuts with hot fudge and Fra Angelica.

The restaurant takes full advantage of its setting, with more than half of the tables along the wall of windows overlooking the dancing brook. The ravine is flood-lit at night, and although it is lovely at any time of year, we like it best in winter, when the brilliant white of snow and ice contrast with the transparent darkness of rushing water and deep greens of the overhanging conifers. Although they do virtually no advertising, Mistral is a top choice among knowledgeable locals, so a reservation is advisable even on weeknights. Entrees run $22 to $32. They are open Thursday through Tuesday for dinner from 6:00 p.m. Take Routes 11/30 east from Manchester, look for a sign on the left (north) side of the road; 10 Toll Gate Road, Manchester Center; (802) 362–1779.

Also highly thought of for the excellence of its dining is *Bistro Henry,* outside of town on Route 11. The appetizer menu tempts with offerings such as grilled shrimp with mango lime sauce or Alsatian onion tart. Entrees might include chicken breast stuffed with walnuts, herbs, and Boursin cheese or sweetbreads with bacon and shallot sauce. Lamb shanks, not commonly found on menus, are braised in merlot. Entrees include a salad, bread, and vegetables.

Henry's welcomes families and has a separate children's menu. Another good thing is that **Dina's Vermont Baking Company** is also on the premises, offering pastries, cakes, and other temptations such as Grand Marnier brûlée, pear and blueberry crisp, tangerine cheesecake, and sorbets. The team that owns the two enterprises is Henry and Dina Bronson, and they don't allow baseball caps or cell phones in the dining room—both rules we applaud. They are open 5:00 to 9:00 p.m. Tuesday through Saturday, and Sunday June through October. They close for about a month in May. 1178 Routes 11/30, Manchester Center; (802) 362–4982; www.bistrohenry.com.

The **Southern Vermont Arts Center** on West Road in Manchester is a respite from the bustle down below in the town. The art starts from the second you enter the grounds and continues all the way up the beautiful, gradually ascending drive to the main estate, the Yester House. The grounds at the top of the hill are nicely landscaped and highlighted by more sculptures. The **Boswell Botany Trail** leads from the 1917 mansion into the woods, where you will find more than one hundred varieties of native wildflowers and ferns. Many of these are rare species, such as the showy orchids and yellow lady's slipper. The woodland flowers are at their best bloom in the spring.

Inside space is used for constantly changing exhibits of art and for performances that may include chamber music, dance, or vocal music. Recent renovations have expanded the exhibit space and added a sparkling little cafe that serves luncheons and desserts. Admission is charged to the galleries, but the grounds are free. The center is open year-round Tuesday through Saturday 10:00 a.m. to 5:00 p.m. and on Sunday from noon until 5:00 p.m.

For a schedule of seasonal events, contact the Southern Vermont Arts Center, West Road, Manchester Village, 05254, or call (802) 362–1405; www .svac.org. Admission is charged.

Anyone rushing along Route 7 north of Manchester will probably miss the small sign that points travelers to **Danby,** a beautiful little town that once was the prosperous center of an active marble-quarrying industry. It sits on a hillside a quarter mile off the main road. Author Pearl S. Buck, who spent much of her life in China and wrote *The Good Earth*, spent her last years here, devoting much of her renowned energy trying to breathe life back into the town as the marble industry collapsed. Its nineteenth-century beauty has been saved, without the embellishments of more modern times, probably because no one had the money to modernize it.

The energetic new owners of the **Silas Griffith Inn** have modernized it where it matters, while preserving and restoring all the mansion's wealth of architectural and decorative detail. Each of the ten rooms in the Victorian main house and its carriage shed has a gas fireplace and private bath, as well as new beds, most of which are queen-size. The first thing you will notice as you enter the house from its wide veranda are the floors: They not only sparkle in their refinished glory, but the wood is rare red birch, curly red birch in the dining room. Intricately embossed tin ceilings, original fireplaces faced in brass, bronze, and copper, crown moldings, and a stunning oval pocket door are among the details you'll admire here. Outdoors there's a heated swimming pool and a six-person heated whirlpool tub built into the elegant gazebo. Summer/winter rates begin at $149; rates higher during foliage season and holidays. The inn serves dinner to guests by reservation on holiday and some summer weekends. The Silas Griffith Inn is on Main Street, Danby; (802) 293–5567, or (888) 569–4660; www.silasgriffith.com.

Mountain View Ranch is run by horse-lovers Letitia and John Sisters. From mid-October through mid-June, you can take horseback rides for just about any length of time you choose, through the woods and fields of this mountainous rural countryside. The two-and-a-half-hour ride is a tour of local farms and costs about $55. A one-hour ride is $35 for a group ride and $50 for a private ride. A one and one-half hour picnic ride is $65 per person, including lunch and a carrot treat for your horse. Hand-led pony rides for children are $5.00. In the autumn and spring, the ranch is open just about every day, but for winter riding the hours are 9:00 a.m. to 4:00 p.m. Monday through Thursday. Get the directions when you reserve; Mountain View Ranch, 502 Easy Street, Danby; (802) 293–5837; www.sunbowlranch.com/mtnview.htm. Rides are also offered at Sun Bowl Ranch, Stratton Mountain.

The Mettawee Valley

If you choose to drive north out of Manchester on Route 30, you'll soon come into the town of *Dorset.* So many artists, woodworkers, quilters, and other craftsworkers have set up shops in their homes along Route 30 that you could spend an entire day visiting them all.

Like Manchester, Dorset is genteel country, and you pass fenced-off estates lining both sides of Route 30. Dorset's population numbers half that of Manchester, with many more summer residents. In fact, the first summerhouse in Dorset was built in 1868, setting the tone for the future.

The *Dorset Playhouse* features performances by professional actors-in-residence in the summer and showcases community theater in the winter. There's also a local writer's colony in town that draws authors from all over the world June through September. For more information, contact American

Theatre Works, Inc., P.O. Box 510, Dorset, 05251; (802) 867–2223; www .dorsetplayers.org.

Some of the houses in the village were rescued from Massachusetts when whole towns were flooded to create the Quabbin Reservoir. They were taken apart and brought to Dorset for reconstruction, a project financed by a local philanthropist not only to save the fine old homes but also to provide work for local men during the Depression.

Mount Aeolus, which rises directly behind the village, was the site of Vermont's first commercial marble quarry and provided the stone for the columns and facing of the New York Public Library. About twenty-five quarries once employed hundreds in extracting, cutting, and shipping the marble, and you can still see one of them beside Route 30, just north of its intersection with West Road.

North of Dorset the towns of Rupert and Pawlet are on the Mettawee River, which follows Route 30. Follow Route 315 West off Route 30 once you cross over the border of Rupert from Dorset. Look for the historical marker that designates the site of *Vermont's first and only mint.* Back when Vermont was an independent republic, resident Reuben Harmon received government permission to operate the Green Mountain State's only mint, where he worked with copper coins.

Continue on Route 315 West until you come upon the *Merck Forest and Farmland Center,* a massive, 2,700-acre land preserve where a family can spend the entire day outdoors enjoying nature and farm life. There are hiking trails ranging from an easy walk to some that are more strenuous. A visitor center and a barn filled with horses, chickens, and other farm animals are also interesting learning experiences. You can watch and learn about a variety of farm chores, from boiling down maple syrup to breaking in horses. Camping is available in cabins on the land at prices ranging from $45 to $75 per night. Cabins have woodstoves, bunks, and outhouses. Lean-to shelters and tent sites are available for $25 per night. The center serves as an active community resource, with a summer day camp for children and a series of nature and farming workshops for adults. The center is open daily from dawn to dusk.

For a schedule of events, write to the Merck Forest and Farmland Center, 3270 Route 315, Rupert, 05768, or call (802) 394–7836; www.merckforest.org.

From the village of Rupert, west of the Merck Center, you can make a quick foray to West Rupert, on the New York border. Continue straight ahead at the village center, where Route 315 ends, following Route 153. On your left is a fine, if derelict, country-store building. In West Rupert is a stone church with good stained-glass windows, and Mountain Valley Maple Farm. You can always buy syrup there, but if you visit in late winter, you should stop in to meet Michael Lourie and see his new sugar house. He uses the modern reverse osmosis system to begin the transformation of sap to syrup, then boils it in a big baffled copper evaporator pan. Sweet steam permeates the air, and you can watch the syrup boil and taste a sample of syrup that was inside a tree less than forty-eight hours before; (802) 394–2928.

Back in Rupert, Route 153 heads north into West Pawlet. Contrary to current appearances, West Pawlet was a bustling outpost back in 1850; it was, in fact, considered one of the ten most populous employment centers in the state. You will see why as you leave the village heading north and cross the slate quarry and its slag piles. That explains the slate roofs on so many of the town's buildings.

Pawlet, on Lilly Road, is home to the ***Pawlet Potter,*** aka Marion Waldo McChesney. McChesney favors frog and seascape subjects, with oceanic color schemes brought out in her gently shaped pots and vessels. Look at the aqua plate that has frogs molded onto it; they're swimming and chasing flies and look like they're about to leap off the plate. She calls this style "Road Kill Impressionism." Her work these days includes more sculpture than she has produced previously.

The Pawlet Potter is at 746 Lilly Hill Road, P.O. Box 155, Pawlet, VT 05761; call (802) 325–3100; www.vtweb.com/waldo/. The shop is usually open Monday through Saturday 10:00 a.m. to 5:00 p.m. McChesney, however, is not always there. "By chance or appointment," says Marion.

Down the road is ***Valley Woodworking,*** run by Jim Boyd. Boyd moved up to Vermont in the late 1980s from Rhode Island, specifically to Rupert because there are a lot of craftspeople in this part of the state, and he wanted support from his peers. Jim does a lot of custom work, as well as refinishing, repair, and reproductions. He says he's been doing this kind of work "forever." He graduated from the Rhode Island School of Design.

Jim sells a unique piece of furniture made from solid oak that serves as an ironing board, a chair, and a step stool. It is based on a colonial antique. Jim has a few on hand—ask him to demonstrate one for you. A massive, true-reproduction china cabinet is a creation he built entirely with hand tools, using mortises and pegs; the cabinet is complete with plate and spoon racks built into the shelves. Along with detailed reproductions, Jim builds custom kitchen cabinets and vanities.

He welcomes visitors and spends most days working in the barn workshop, so you'll probably catch him in. Write to Valley Woodworking, Route 30, North Rupert, VT 05761; (802) 325–3910.

More Places to Stay in Southwest Vermont

(All area codes 802)

ARLINGTON

Arlington Inn
Route 7A
375–6532 or
(800) 443–9442
www.arlingtoninn.com
An elegant Greek Revival mansion with antiques and an excellent dining room. Rates are $99 to $259.

DORSET

Barrows House
Main Street
867–4455 or
(800) 639–1620
www.barrowshouse.com
Rooms in nine buildings spread over its extensive property, making it a favorite for families. Rates are $145 to $245, B&B rates.

Inn at West View Farm
2928 Route 30
867–5715 or
(800) 769–4903
www.innatwestviewfarm.com
Comfortable rooms with a relaxed country atmosphere.
Rates $110 to $200.

SANDGATE

Green River Inn
3402 Sandgate Road
(888) 648–2212 or
375–2272
www.greenriverinn.com
An attractive fourteen-room inn close to Manchester and Arlington, on a quiet dead-end road. Some rooms have whirlpool tubs, and some have fireplaces. Breakfast included and prix-fixe dinner (about $25) is available by reservation. Rates $119 to $243.

WESTON

Colonial House Inn and Motel
Route 100
824–6286 or
(800) 639–5033
www.cohoinn.com
Combines a homey B&B with motel units. Serves home-style meals. Rates $85–$175.

WILMINGTON

Nutmeg Inn
Route 9
P.O. Box 1899, 05363
(800) 277–5402
www.nutmeginn.com
A cozy New England classic, with wood-burning fireplaces. A full country breakfast is offered. Rates $99 to $189.

TO LEARN MORE IN SOUTHWEST VERMONT

Bennington Chamber of Commerce, (802) 447–3311 or (800) 229–0252; www.bennington.com.

Manchester Area Information, P.O. Box 569, Manchester Center, 05255; (802) 362–2100 or (800) 362–4144; www.manchestervermont.com, where you can learn about events, see the views, and vie for prizes.

Mount Snow Valley Regional Chamber of Commerce, P.O. Box 3, Page House, Main Street, Wilmington, 05363; (802) 464–8092 or (877) 887–6884; www.visitvermont.com.

More Places to Eat in Southwest Vermont

(All area codes 802)

MANCHESTER CENTER

Candeleros
5103 Main Street
362–0836
www.candeleros.net
The most popular Tex-Mex restaurant in the region, with a good selection of Hispanic dishes and New England regional foods at lunch and dinner.

PAWLET

Mach's Brick Oven Bakery
School Street
325–6113
Serves lunch, snacks, pizza, and sells fresh-baked breads and pastries. Thursday through Sunday.

WESTON

Village Sandwich Shop
Route 103, opposite the Country Store
824–5477
Open daily Memorial Day to Columbus Day from 10:00 a.m. to 4:00 p.m., serving sandwiches and pastries.

MIDDLE WEST VERMONT

Within an area that stretches from the northern segment of the Green Mountain National Forest to the lower Champlain Valley and the New York border is almost everything that's considered typically Vermont. Here are snow-covered ski trails, the Long Trail for hiking, wide flat valleys painted green by farmland and dotted with red barns, dirt roads winding through woods and over mountains, country inns, lakes, small tidy brick downtowns, and white-clapboarded villages set around the tall spires of their meetinghouses.

But there is more than the postcard image to this part of the state, and you don't even have to leave its main roads to find it. Although some of the state's best-known slopes bring skiers pouring in during the winter, and the year-round resorts that cluster at their bases are filled in the summer, much of this part of Vermont remains—or at least seems—largely untouched, the legacy of the national forest lands that form its eastern third.

To the west are the lower but often still rolling lands that stretch to Lake Champlain, as it narrows and finally seems more like a very wide river. Wetlands here provide migration and nesting grounds for a wide range of bird life,

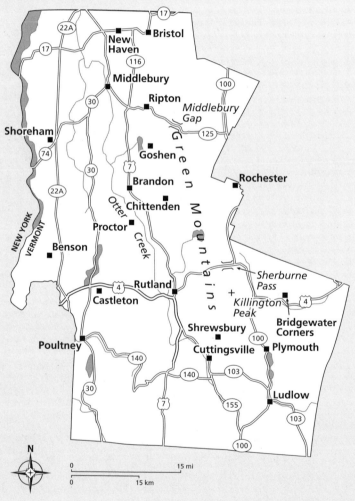

and smaller lakes provide swimming and boating, without being overrun by tourists.

Ludlow and Points North

Ludlow is a sizable town whose population doubles in winter. Ludlow is in Vermont's heavy snow zone—100 to 120 inches a year is not unusual. Standing tall behind the town, *Okemo Mountain* became a part of its economic life in 1955 when a group of local businessmen decided that the town should have a ski area. Starting small, it grew until it overcame a financial hurdle in the late 1970s. With new owners in 1982, rejuvenation began that has never ended. Since then it has become one of the top resorts in Vermont with keen client loyalty—and it has become a year-round resort.

Today it is boasts trails on two mountains and complete resort facilities, which make it popular with families year-round. At its highest point it has a vertical drop of 2,200 feet, and snowmaking covers more than 95 percent of its 117 trails. Eighteen lifts provide flexible access to trails with a good range of skiing for all skill levels. The newer Jackson Gore section added more challenging terrain. Okemo attracts boarders with six terrain parks, including the largest superpipe in the east. From its rebirth in 1982 the emphasis at Okemo has been service; on the slopes, this translates to the best snowmaking and grooming in the east. Conditions here are always good, and often great. An outstanding ski school, well-maintained rental equipment, and large, bright base lodges add to the package.

Service is also the keyword at the resort's lodgings, dining, and off-slope recreational facilities. Hotel and condo lodgings at the base and slopeside are in a number of price ranges (lodging 800–786–5366). Dining options range from casual snack bars and informal restaurants to romantic haute cuisine dinners in a wine cellar.

Specials include a Sunday-afternoon rate for skiers from Vermont and New Hampshire. If you buy a three-day or longer ticket you can use it at Stratton

AUTHOR'S TOP HIGHLIGHTS

President Calvin Coolidge State Historic Site

Texas Falls

Mount Independence

M/V *Carillon*

Chimney Point State Historic Site

Mountain for one day during your stay. Okemo's "Try Before You Buy" policy allows you to try the conditions free, from lift opening at 8:00 a.m. until ticket sales begin at 9:00 on weekends, and from 9:00 to 10:00 a.m. on weekdays. This is a good family area, with good variety and tremendous lift capacity on fast-moving chairs. At night there is a special nightclub for teens. In the non-ski season the focus turns to the first-class golf facilities at two eighteen-hole courses nearby. One, a 6,400-yard, par 70 course, is a Heathland-style course with an eighteen-acre golf-learning center. The Tater Hill Golf Club, 22 miles away, has another eighteen-hole course noted for its challenge and for its views. As of 2006, Okemo is completing a mammoth recreation facility in the Jackson Gore section, with a pool, handball court, and other sports. Okemo is just off Route 103, 77 Okemo Ridge Road, Ludlow; (802) 228–4041; snow line (802) 228–1782; e-mail: okemo@ludl.tds.net; www.okemo.com.

The **Fletcher Farm School** is located on Route 103 near the Cavendish-Ludlow town line to the south. Numerous outbuildings—barns, cabins, and motel rooms—serve as accommodations for visitors and guests who want to spend two weeks painting, weaving, folk dancing, and engaging in other arts-and-crafts activities. The school is owned by the Society of Vermont Craftsmen, which also runs a small arts-and-crafts store on the premises during summer, selling items made by guests at the farm. A single reasonable price includes lodging, three family-style meals a day, lessons, and studio and practice space.

The Fletcher Farm School offers classes from June through October. For the current year's schedule, write to Fletcher Farm School, R.R. 1, Box 1041, Ludlow, 05149, or call (802) 228–8770; www.fletcherfarm.com.

From Route 103 in Ludlow, turn onto Buttermilk Falls Road at the VFW building and go to the end of the road to see **Buttermilk Falls.**

The water rushes hard even in a dry autumn, and it completely drowns out the sound of heavy traffic on nearby Route 103. A couple of big flat rocks

Try This at Home

In case you grow fond of such traditional Vermont ingredients as maple syrup and cheddar cheese while traveling, or if you enjoy the flavors of updated New England cooking styles you encounter, look to the new omnibus of New England cuisine, *The New England Cookbook,* by Brooke Dojny (The Harvard Common Press, $16.95 paper, $29.95 hardcover). In its more than 350 recipes, you'll find very traditional dishes in their original forms and as interpreted by the throng of chefs trained in such bastions of creative cuisine as Vermont's own New England Culinary Institute.

ANNUAL EVENTS IN MIDDLE WEST VERMONT

Early July: Independence Day Celebration, Brandon, with Vermont's largest parade, on the Saturday nearest July 4; (802) 247–6401.

Mid-July: Summer Festival on the Green, Middlebury, a week of performing arts; (802) 388–0216.

Early September: Vermont State Fair, Fairgrounds, Rutland; (802) 775–5200.

Early December: Christmas in Middlebury, with artisan open houses, a festival of wreaths, and music; (802) 388–4126.

in the river are perfect for sunning and picnicking. And along the road are other footpaths leading down to the river. There are two good spots, one at the very end of the road and the other a few tenths of a mile before the end. A path leads to the falls from Buttermilk Falls Road, about 1.3 miles from its intersection with Route 103 in town.

In the town of Ludlow, the ***Black River Academy Historical Museum*** sits in a stately old brick building perched above the main road on High Street. Each room has a different theme: the President's Room, the Rotary Room, the Grange Room, and the Coolidge Room—this last being named for Calvin Coolidge, who graduated from the academy when it was a renowned private school in 1890. The building itself was constructed in 1889 and today sits next to a former schoolhouse, the old District School No. 1, which now serves as Ludlow's senior center and community center.

The museum—a truly fascinating place—is open Tuesday through Saturday from noon to 4:00 p.m. from Memorial Day through Columbus Day weekend and by appointment during winter months. Write to the Black River Academy Historical Museum, High Street, Ludlow, VT 05149, or call (802) 228–5050 for more information. Admission by donation.

The ***Crowley Cheese Factory*** is the antithesis of the mammoth Cabot Cheese Factory located in the town bearing its name, just north of Montpelier. Just past the Crowley Cheese Store on Route 103 is a sign reading HEALDVILLE ROAD. Two miles down is an old, weather-beaten house where several hundred pounds of cheese is made every day, by hand.

The store on Route 103 sells the cheese, as well as maple syrup and gift items. If you want to see this unique Colby cheese being made, though, go the extra 2 miles (year-round, except for November and December). The factory is open from 8:00 a.m. to 4:00 p.m. on weekdays, while the gift shop on Route 103 is open from 10:00 a.m. to 5:30 p.m. Monday through Saturday, Sunday

11:00 a.m. to 5:30 p.m. For information, write to the Crowley Cheese Factory, Healdville Road, Healdville, 05147; (802) 259–2340 or (800) 683–2606; www .crowleycheese-vermont.com.

As you head back to Route 103, you'll see that this is a good foliage road; Sawyer Rocks, a huge outcropping, is straight ahead, dotted with trees that in autumn are brilliant in their color.

On Route 100 north of Ludlow is *Echo Lake.* This is a summer camp area consisting of the three major lakes running alongside the road: Lake Rescue, Echo Lake, and Amherst Lake.

Echo Lake Inn, an imposing structure with a long, rocker-studded porch, is one of only five inns in Vermont from the 1800s that were built as inns. The new owner completed a thorough modernization of its facilities, including safety features, but at the same time feels strongly about keeping the building's character. He has retained rooms of varying sizes and prices, an individually chosen mix of antiques and newer furnishings in the guest rooms, and the general ambience of a venerable inn. Those who prefer a bit more privacy can choose the detached condo units, with fully equipped kitchens, TVs, cable, stereos, and microwave ovens.

The inn also has a fine dining room with such entrees as shrimp-and-broccoli-rabe ravioli with a lemon-red pepper sauce, a Rhodesian-spice-rubbed Angus steak, or medallions of venison in a currant-and-port sauce. Prices range from $17 to $24, most $20 or under.

thesoundof silentcal

Stories, many of them apocryphal, abound illustrating the taciturn nature of the Vermonter known as Silent Cal. One of them involved a society matron who was introduced to President Coolidge at a particularly tedious garden party in Washington. "Oh, Mr. President," she said, "I have a bet with a friend that I can make you say more than two words!"

"You lose," he replied.

Winter room rates range from $119 to $279, and summer from $99 to $209, including breakfast. Expect higher rates on holiday weekends, and ask about special packages and off-season discounts. All inn guests have access to a swimming pool, lighted tennis courts, and a private lake dock with canoes. Contact the Echo Lake Inn, P.O. Box 154, Ludlow, 05149; (802) 228–8612 or (800) 356–6844; www .echolakeinn.com.

From Route 100A in Plymouth to Route 103 in Ludlow, Route 100 is known as the Calvin Coolidge Memorial Highway. Coolidge was one of two American presidents born in Vermont.

WORTH SEEING

Vermont State Craft Center,
Frog Hollow, 1 Mill Street, Middlebury;
(802) 388–3177; www.froghollow.org.

UVM Morgan Horse Farm,
2.5 miles from downtown Middlebury,
at 74 Battell Drive (Route 23), Weybridge;
(802) 388–2011; www.uvm.edu/morgan.

Vermont Marble Museum,
52 Main Street, Proctor;
(800) 427–1396.

New England Maple Museum,
Route 7, Pittsford; (802) 483–9414.

Coolidge was born in Plymouth Notch on July 4, 1872. His position as governor of Massachusetts led him to a spot on the ballot as running mate to Warren G. Harding in the presidential race of 1920. On August 3, 1923, while Coolidge was in Plymouth helping his father get in the hay, President Harding died in California. The presidential oath of office was administered to Calvin by lamplight over the family kitchen table at 2:47 a.m. When John Coolidge, the father of the new president, was later asked why he thought he was authorized to administer the presidential oath, his reply was characteristically Coolidge: "I didn't know I couldn't," he said.

Today the hillside farm is the ***President Calvin Coolidge State Historic Site,*** with the homestead where he grew up furnished exactly as it was in 1923 (the president's son gave the house to the state). The farm's cheese factory still produces cheese, and its original equipment is shown, along with other farm implements and horse-drawn vehicles, in the Wilder Barn. The Wilder House, once a tavern and the childhood home of Calvin's mother, Victoria, is now a small restaurant where you can have traditional dishes such as chowder and chicken pot pie.

The site is open from 9:30 a.m. to 5:00 p.m. every day from Memorial Day through Columbus Day. Admission is $7.50 for adults; children under six get in free. Coolidge State Historic Site, P.O. Box 247 (not coincidentally the hour of his presidential oath), Plymouth Notch, VT 05056; (802) 672–3773; www.historicvermont.org/coolidge.

Past Lake Rescue and just before you reach Echo Lake as you're heading north on Route 100, take a right. About a mile up the steep, winding road is the ***Plymouth Kingdom Cemetery,*** where several Revolutionary War soldiers are buried. In the cemetery old slate markers stand in back of VFW markers and flags. The cemetery is surrounded by a split-rail fence, and stone steps lead up to the cemetery. Kingdom Brook rushes by on the other side of the road.

Back on this pastoral road is a pleasant drive, with rolling land, estates, and ponds. A mile up from the cemetery, there's a boat access area to Colby Pond.

To experience Vermont's out-of-doors without sacrificing luxury, consider a stay at *Hawk Inn & Mountain Resort,* right on Route 100 in the Black River Valley. The low-to-the-land buildings are contemporary, with large, comfortable rooms and public spaces built to please upscale young families. It is open all year and has a wealth of recreational facilities including an indoor pool, sauna, hiking trails, ice-skating, sledding, snowshoeing, and cross-country skiing. They also can arrange horseback riding or boating on Lake Amherst, and in the winter they offer sleigh rides. The dining room, which is open to the public, is stylish and cozy, with views onto the well-landscaped grounds. The menu is New American, and dishes are well prepared; appetizers are often ample enough for an entree. As you might expect in a place catering to this clientele, the wine list is quite good. Reservations are wise, especially in ski season. Hawk Inn & Mountain Resort, 75 Billings Road, Route 100, Plymouth; (802) 672–3811 or (800) 685–HAWK; www.hawkresort.com.

A short distance farther north on Route 100 is *Bear Creek Mountain Club,* a unique concept for skiers. This private ski club sits on its own mountain, with a 1,300-foot vertical drop and fifteen trails covering fifty-one acres. Plans are afoot to expand the number of lifts and trails. Nonmembers can ski ($75 a day, $30 half day from 1:30 p.m.), but only 450 people can ski per day. Members, of course, have priority. The difference in skiing here is the sense that you have the whole mountain to yourself. The clubhouse at the base has an excellent dining room, which is open to the public. Bear Creek Mountain Club, Route 100, Plymouth; (802) 672–4242; www.bear creekclub.com.

Route 4 leaves Route 100 in West Bridgewater, heading through Bridgewater Corners and on east to Woodstock. A short distance from the intersection, on Route 4, you'll come to *Blanche and Bill's Pancake House,* which serves country-style, lumberjack-size breakfasts. The blueberry pancakes come heaped with blueberries, while the French toast arrives with cinnamon sugar liberally sprinkled over the fat slices of bread. Eggs and waffles are also on the breakfast menu, with burgers and grilled sandwiches the mainstay of lunch. Blanche and Bill's Pancake House is open Thursday through Sunday from 7:00 a.m. to 5:00 p.m., and Tuesday and Wednesday from 7:00 a.m. to 2:00 p.m. It is closed Monday. 586 US Route 4, Bridgewater Corners; (802) 422–3816.

If it's lunchtime, or if you've a mind to sample some Vermont brew, keep going until you reach the three grain silos that mark the *Long Trail Brewing*

Company. We like the philosophy of its founder and owner: Since beer is 95 percent water, it shouldn't have to be imported. Everything at the brewery is made in Vermont, from the brewing equipment to the woodstove and heavy wooden tables in the beer hall/pub. A sampler of six different ales costs about $6.00, and you can savor and compare them at the bar, at a table inside, or on a deck overlooking the river. Through a glass wall you can see the giant gleaming vats and the business part of the brewery. Good, sturdy, goes-great-with-beer food is served, too—bratwurst steamed in Long Trail Ale, chili, ale and cheddar soup, or soft pretzels, made on the premises with Long Trail beer. The visitor center is open daily from 10:00 a.m. to 7:00 p.m., with food served from 11:00 a.m. to 6:00 p.m. It's on Route 4, east of Route 100, in Bridgewater Corners; (802) 672–5011; www.longtrail.com.

Just past the brewing company is the Bridgewater Mill, a large clapboard woolen mill that now houses an eclectic collection of shops and studios. Anchoring one end is the combined showroom of *Charles Shackleton Furniture* and *Miranda Thomas Pottery.* The furniture workshop is visible through glass windows, and Miranda's pottery studio is in a small building—where visitors are welcome—next door to the mill. The furniture is nothing short of spectacular—a Queen Anne–inspired sleigh bed, upholstered chairs that are at once art deco and classical, delicate candle stands. The pottery is a match for it, much of the work in a distinctive carved style that seems to turn damask into solid forms. The gallery is open daily; (802) 672–5175; www.shackletonthomas.com.

Several other crafts studios are in the mill, including a jeweler, an art gallery, a thrift shop, a potter, a glass workshop, and an oriental rug dealer.

You can take Route 100A here, then cut back southwest through Plymouth (passing the Coolidge homestead) and come out on Route 100, making a tidy little loop—a nice afternoon's excursion from the Echo Lake Inn or from the Lincoln Inn on Route 4 west of Woodstock (see the Woodstock section of the Connecticut River Valley chapter).

A Step Forward to the Past

Just in time for the twenty-first century, one Vermont town returned to the name that it abandoned at the turn of the nineteenth century. Like Constantinople, you can't go back to Sherburne, Vermont, anymore. In April 1999 its citizens voted to return the name of the town to Killington, to match the mountain that dominates the area and the ski slopes and resorts that give it its fame. This won't confuse very many people, since nearly everyone has been calling it Killington all along.

As you're heading back to Route 100, Killington Mountain looms so large that at times it looks like you're going to drive right into it. Killington, the second-highest peak in the state, is where Vermont purportedly received its name. A minister from Connecticut was traveling on horseback through the area in 1763, and when he reached the top of Killington—all 4,241 feet of it— the Reverend Sam Peters was said to have called the land verd mont, French for "green mountain." (The French actually would have called it mont verd. Slavishly following this dictum, though, would have led to a decidedly less euphonious state name.)

Under the shoulder of the mountain, on the west side of Routes 4/100, is a modest-looking restaurant with a lot to brag about. *Hemingway's* has been praised by just about every food publication in the country, and its chefs have been awarded, lauded, and invited to cook at the James Beard Foundation in New York. But despite all this attention, they continue to serve uncompromisingly good dinners to a full house almost every night. Each dinner is complete with three courses, hors d'oeuvres, and coffee. The first course might be seared scallops with truffle potato and an entree of snapper fillet with crispy sushi rice, lobster, and snowpeas. Four- and five-course wine tasting dinners range from $85 to $100 per person. A la carte entrees run from $24 to $38. Hemingway's is open Wednesday through Sunday, and occasional other days as well, for dinner only, from 6:00 p.m. Route 100, Killington; (802) 422–3886. You can browse the current menu at www.hemingwaysrestaurant.com.

From the many restaurants to the ski facilities and other activities around Killington, it's easy to get the feeling that the theme is on indulgence. There is one place you can go in the area, though, where the focus is on fitness and self-preservation. *Jimmy LeSage's New Life Fitness Vacations* is located at the Inn of the Six Mountains, and although the participants at Jimmy's spa may be surrounded by people who are hell-bent on cramming as much as possible into their time at Killington, the New Lifers find it doesn't matter: They're having a great time anyway.

From May through October Jimmy offers a variety of fitness weeks and weekends that combine just the right amount of healthfulness and pampering, from low-calorie meals that are nonetheless satisfying to a good dose of massages and leisurely walks, on which you can appreciate the activity for its sensual pleasures and not for the exact number of calories you've just burned. That's not Jimmy's focus.

For more information, write to Jimmy LeSage, New Life Fitness Vacations, P.O. Box 395, Killington, 05751, or call (802) 422–4302 or (866) 298–5433.

If the overwhelming size and masses of fashionably outfitted skiers at the other ski area in town are too much for you, give *Pico Mountain Resort* a try. Although under the same ownership, this area has retained its identity as a family-friendly, big-mountain venue for skiers.

The ski slopes run from the top of Pico Peak, which has an altitude of over 3,100 feet, tumbling down over the side of the mountain and three of its shoulders almost 2,000 feet to the base lodge. Four lifts from the base provide access to thirty trails covering 12 miles, with some nice long intermediate and expert trails from the top of Pico Mountain and a good choice of novice and intermediate runs from the three lifts that serve the three shoulder areas. Boarders will find a small terrain park. Pico has townhouse and condo lodging available as well; also a sports center.

If you plan to be there more than two and a half days, the Pico Card ($20) is a bargain, saving skiers of all age levels $10 every day they use it. Without the Pico Card, adults and young adults ski for $52 a day and juniors and seniors for $39. Pico Mountain is on U.S. Route 5, Killington; (802) 422–6200; (866) 667–7426 (PICO); snow line (802) 422–1200; (866) 667–7426 (reservations); www.picomountain.com.

For Nordic enthusiasts, ***Mountain Meadows XC Ski Area*** offers 57 km of machine-groomed and tracked trails, with snowmaking on one 3-km trail. Trails are for all levels of experience, and ski instruction is always available. The trails wind through fields and hemlock and hardwood forests, and have views of Kent Lake from a trail around its perimeter. Mountain Meadows has offered cross-country here for thirty-six years and has the longest season (Thanksgiving to mid-April) in the state. Rates are adult $19.00 (age thirteen and older), $16.00 (senior), $8.00 (ages six to twelve). Look for them at 2263 Route 4, Killington; (802) 775–7077; (800) 775–0016; www.xcskiing.net.

In Stockbridge on Route 100, you'll see a sign that reads THE ROCK SHOP. And that's just what it is: a shop for rock fans—the hard kind, not the musical kind. Randy and Marilyn Gibson run the ***Riverknoll Rock Shop,*** where you can find cheap jewelry, rock-scavenging and mining knickknacks, books, crystals, and prospecting equipment, all in one room off the side of a house.

If you like, they can also teach you how to cut gems—or will do it for you—and how to restring beads and pearls. They can also tell you where the best places to pan for gold are in the area.

The shop is open most days and weekends but it is wise to call ahead. You have to walk through the Gibsons' kitchen to get to the shop. Riverknoll Rock Shop, Route 100, Stockbridge; (802) 746–8198.

North of Stockbridge on Route 100, the town of ***Rochester,*** which abuts the Green Mountain National Forest, has always seen a lot of activity, although the businesses have changed their stripes over the years. The White River

Valley Railroad once coursed through the town, logging and mining and dairy farming being the primary industries in former times.

Today Rochester has a tidy village green, a cafe, and several shops, including one that rents bicycles. It also has a working guest farm, **Liberty Hill Farm,** located just off Route 100. When you first step out of your car, you'll be greeted by the ubiquitous sign of a dairy farm: the smell of manure. When you step into the house, you'll find the welcoming aroma of fresh-baked something or other, and your stomach juices will gurgle in anticipation of what that night's dinner might be.

That "innkeeper" Beth Kennett prepares everything from scratch is indicative of the farm as a whole: Liberty Hill is a thriving, old-fashioned dairy farm, a rare chance to step into an increasingly rare way of life for a few days.

The farm is also a cacophony of sounds: roosters sub for alarm clocks, tractors putt-putt by the house, cows moo, Lassie barks. Chickens, ducks, turkeys, rabbits, assorted barn cats, and, of course the Holsteins, are never out of earshot. Stirred up into one stew, they provide a gentle humming all day long that lulls you to sleep at nightfall. Dinner is bountiful and served family-style.

The farm is open year-round, and guests come for skiing, fishing, hiking, canoeing, and to work in the barn. If you like to feed calves or pitch hay, you can keep busy all day and night.

A night's stay at Liberty Hill Farm costs $90 ($50 for children under twelve) and includes full breakfast and dinner. Liberty Hill Farm, 511 Liberty Hill Road, Rochester; (802) 767–3926; www.libertyhillfarm.com.

Five miles north of Liberty Hill, at the junction of Routes 100 and 125, stands the **Old Hancock Hotel,** which now houses a casual restaurant serving three meals a day. The building has graced this corner since 1788, when it served as a tavern. Between the tavern and the present restaurant, it's been everything from a speakeasy to a hippy crash pad.

The menu starts with breakfast dishes, served all day, of which a venison sausage breakfast is the most expensive at $7.49. At lunch, a hefty Reuben on pumpernickel is $6.99, and most dinner entrees are under $10.00—including sole stuffed with crabmeat and scallops, vegetable lasagna, and linguine pesto. Venison sausage, made right here, is almost always on the menu. It's an informal country store/bakery/lunchroom/restaurant with a tiny and appropriately named Unknown Obscure Little Bookshop, where you can get real bargains on some amazingly diverse new titles, including many published in Europe. Owners John and Diane also have three rooms for rent upstairs at $65 a night. Open from 7:00 a.m. to 8:00 p.m. Sunday through Thursday and until 9:00 p.m. on Friday and Saturday; Routes 100 and 125, Rochester; (802) 767–4976.

Route 100 continues north into Granville, past two artisans' shops and through one of Vermont's several gulfs. ***Vermont Wood Specialties*** makes lazy Susans, as well as other wooden ware, including salad bowls, shelves, cutting boards, and spoons. The shop isn't fancy, but the work is nice and reasonably priced. Open daily in the summer, Thursday through Sunday in the winter; (802) 767–4253. Just up the road is the glassblowing studio of Michael Egan, who creates some simply stunning art glass. Vivid colors swirl as though they were still molten, forming vases and other vessels of heirloom quality; (802) 767–4547; www.glassartists.org/MichaelEgan.

The valley through which Route 100 travels, narrows suddenly just beyond the studio, becoming Granville Gulf. Vermont has several of these narrow defiles, where the road climbs alongside a stream through a ravine barely wide enough to accommodate both. Watch for a small pullout and wooden walkway on the left. ***Moss Glenn Falls*** drops suddenly over a stack of ledges, right beside the road.

In and around Middlebury

If you follow Route 125, it takes you over the Green Mountains, at Middlebury Gap, one of its few low spots (well, lower than most of the summits) with a road that's open all winter. As you begin to climb, look for a sign to ***Texas Falls,*** an easily accessed and lovely gorge, where the river compresses to rush through a narrow passage in the rocks, dropping through a steep chute before plummeting through the gorge and into a pool. After a June shower, it's a raging, swirling froth. The path leads down to a log bridge that spans the gorge and gives great views without ruining this woodland setting. It's one of the most accessible falls in the state, and one of the prettiest. The road sinews up (and up and up) until it reaches the height of land and begins to drop, more gently, onto the western side of the Green Mountains.

You know you're at a real "skier's mountain" when you find a can of Bag Balm on the ticket counter at a ski area. You'll also find smiles, families, college students, and laid-back skiers of all ages at ***Middlebury Snow Bowl,*** on uncrowded trails that work with the mountain's natural terrain. Gentle trails from the top are good for beginner and intermediate skiers, so you don't have to worry about getting on the wrong lift and finding yourself with nothing but black-diamond trails to the bottom. Experts will get a workout on several trails, too. Although the official number of trails is seventeen, Middlebury doesn't inflate the number by giving each segment of a trail a different name, as most other resorts do.

Grooming is good, lift operators know the trails and can give you reliable advice on their conditions and challenge, and the chili in the lunchroom (which closes at 2:00 p.m.) is rich and meaty. What more is there to a day's skiing? Rentals, which feature up-to-date equipment, are fast and easy; lift tickets are well below the glitzy places, among the lowest in the state at $28 on weekdays and $42 on weekends. Seniors and students ski for somewhat less. For conditions or information, call (802) 388–4356. The address is Route 125, Ripton; www.middlebury.edu/~snowbowl.

The most unexpected feature is the library in the ski lodge, where you can seek quiet and a selection of books and magazines if you decide to leave the trails early or take a midday break. You'll find it well used during midterms, when Middlebury students hit the books and the slopes alternately.

Ripton is a tiny town that lies totally within the Green Mountain National Forest but is one of the largest towns area-wise in Vermont, at 32,704 acres. Its population, though, numbers in the low hundreds.

Even though Robert Frost spent a good deal of his life in New Hampshire and Massachusetts, Vermonters in this part of the state still like to think of him as one of their own, since he spent many of his last summers writing in his cabin in Ripton. In fact, you can visit the **Robert Frost Cabin,** nestled in the heart of the Green Mountains. When you see the environs in which Frost worked, you'll better understand his intense creativity.

To get to the cabin, turn off at the Robert Frost Wayside picnic area; take the unmarked dirt road to the immediate right of the area. Drive ½ mile up the road, and you'll see the Homer Noble Farm, a white farmhouse. Park in the small lot and walk up the trail 100 yards beyond the house. There's an opening to the left. The cabin is unmarked from the main road because locals believe only those visitors who want to see it badly enough are worthy of receiving directions. Middlebury College owns the cabin and most of the land on both sides of Route 125 in this mountainous area. Although you can go only onto the porch and not in the cabin, the interior remains the same as when Frost lived there from 1939 until his death in 1963. Late in 2007, though, the cabin was vandalized by a group of young people, a source of dismay to nearby residents and distant Frost-lovers alike. It has since been furbished and is as viewable as before.

Also in Ripton you'll pass the **Bread Loaf** campus, maize-colored buildings that are home to the annual Bread Loaf summer writers' programs founded by Frost and maintained by Middlebury College. The trails are scattered throughout the forest, many with trailheads on Route 125, are Middlebury College facilities—more specifically, the **Carroll and Jane Rikert Ski Touring Center,** which is open to the public. Just 12 miles east of Middlebury and one and one-half miles west of the Middlebury College Snowbowl, the touring center offers 42 km of prepared trails bordering the Green Mountain National Forest, providing a wonderful place to ski. The trails accommodate all levels of experience, and the facilities include rentals ($12.00 adults, $9.00 students, and $3.00 children under five); equipment sales, repairs, and waxing rooms as well as a warm-up room where you can curl up next to a wood stove. It is open 9:00 a.m. to 4:00 p.m. and the trail fees are $15.00 adults ($10.00 half day), $6.00 students and children. Bread Loaf Center, Route 125, Middlebury; (802) 443–2744. Two miles west of the Frost cabin on Route 125, pull into the parking lot of the **Chipman Inn.** The sign you'll see gives the rates of toll for the Center Turnpike, as Route 125 was previously called, the stagecoach road from Middlebury to Woodstock. The turnpike was chartered in 1800, and some of the tolls are as follows: man and horse, 8 cents; person on foot, 2 cents; and sleighs drawn by two oxen or horses, 12 cents, with each additional ox or horse costing 2 cents.

Sheep and swine could travel over the road for a half cent each if fewer than a dozen of them were traveling the road. More than twelve cost 3 cents a dozen. But no need to reach into your pocket; the road is now free, no matter how many sheep you have with you.

Guests enter the Chipman Inn through a unique front door with a fanlight and separate side windows, just one of the features of this well-restored 1828 building, whose trim and woodwork are noticeably similar to that of the Sheldon Museum in Middlebury. Guest rooms are simply and tastefully furnished, several with both double and single beds and all with private baths. Hearty breakfasts are included in the rates, which range from $75 to $185, and a five-course dinner can be reserved ahead. The menu might include Maryland crab cakes or chicken breast with apricots and currants. The Chipman Inn is on Route 125, Ripton; (802) 388–2390 or (800) 890–2390; www .chipmaninn.com.

From Ripton, Forest Road 32 provides access from the south into the Moosalamoo wilderness area.

Once you get to Middlebury proper, park your car and walk around the bustling village that serves an extended college campus. Middlebury was chartered early in the state's history, in 1761, and received its name because it was located halfway between the adjacent towns of Salisbury and New Haven.

The **Vermont Folklife Center** is just off the green. The center encourages the promotion and development of folk traditions in Vermont and in other countries. It conducts special events in collaboration with its exhibits, which frequently involve children's art projects, from both Vermont and other places.

The gallery at the center is open Tuesday through Saturday from 10:00 a.m. to 4:00 p.m. year-round. Admission is free. Write to the Vermont Folklife Center, 88 Main Street, Middlebury, 05753, or call (802) 388–4964; www.vermont folklifecenter.org.

One of two **Frog Hollow Vermont State Craft Center** galleries thrives in an old mill building, conveniently located on Mill Street and set dramatically against the rushing Otter Creek Falls. The displays inside feature the work of more than 250 juried Vermont artisans. The goal at Frog Hollow is to promote original works of lasting beauty and impeccable quality by bringing the work of artists and craftspeople from remote and rural venues to two central and more prominent state locations. The craft school in Middlebury offers an array of classes to the novice and the seasoned master alike. The center offers classes for tourists, groups, and organizations. The gallery is open Wednesday through Saturday from 10:00 a.m. to 5:30 p.m., Sundays from 12:00 p.m. to to 5:00 p.m.; closed Mondays and Tuesdays. 1 Mill Street; call (802) 388–3177. www.froghollow.org.

The **Henry Sheldon Museum,** in an 1829 marble-built merchant's home in the center of town, is the oldest community museum in the United States. Like the Fairbanks Museum, it was founded by a man who was a tireless collector, but his passion was for antiquities and local history. Ten rooms show one of the state's best collections of early furniture, decorative arts, paintings, and implements of daily living. The museum is open from 10:00 a.m. to 5:00 p.m. Monday through Saturday June through mid-October, and Tuesday through Saturday the rest of the year. It is at 1 Park Street, Middlebury; (802) 388–2117; www.henrysheldonmuseum.org.

Skiing is a way of life for students and faculty at Middlebury College, and the school lights a downtown cross-country trail until 10:00 p.m. for those who want to take a bracing glide under the stars without driving up the mountain. To tour the downtown campus, which has some fine examples of architecture, pick up a map from the admissions office in the Emma Willard House on South Main Street (Route 30), or join a tour there any weekday morning during the academic year (except during exams); (802) 443–3000.

Look for **Neil & Otto's Pizza,** begun by two friends from high school days. You can get a staggering variety of pizzas starting at $6.49 for a small cheese. They're open daily from 4 p.m. until 10:00 p.m. at 52 Merchant's Row; (802) 388–6774 or (802) 388–6776.

Outside of town, in the most unlikely of places, you will find three fascinating businesses to visit. Look for Exchange Street, which runs through the middle of an industrial park on the north end of town. From Route 7 North, turn west onto Elm Street, just north of the Methodist church. Exchange Street is the next street on the right.

You will come first to ***Vermont Soapworks,*** makers of fine-grade handmade soaps and identified by a small sign at the roadside. Here are some of the mildest soaps made anywhere, the same ones you will find in the best gift and bath shops in Vermont (at much higher prices). The factory store has first-quality soaps for sale, as well as seconds—those bars that were slightly unshapely when cut for wrapping. Herbs and flowers create the wonderful natural scents in the soaps. While there, notice the little "museum" of old soap packaging and advertising pieces, which you might miss; they are in a glass-topped case that doubles as the sales counter. Unfortunately, Vermont Soapworks is no longer able to give individual tours. It is in an industrial building on the east side of the street, open Tuesday through Friday 9:00 a.m. to 5:00 p.m., Saturday 10:00 a.m. to 4:00 p.m.; 616 Exchange Street, Middlebury; (802) 388–4302 or (866) 762–7482; www.vermontsoap.com.

A short distance from the soap factory, on the other side of the street, ***Otter Creek Brewing*** is one of the best small artisanal brewers in the state. Brews run from a light pale ale all the way to stouts, with many in between. Last time we were there, we found a very nice hickory-smoked ale (they smoked the malt, not the ale). They also produce Wolaver's, one of the few organic ales around. Organic hops, organic malt, Vermont water—how healthy can a brew be? Case specials are available; you never know what good deals they may have. The brewery is open Monday through Saturday 10:00 a.m. to 6:00 p.m., with tours at 1:00, 3:00, and 5:00 p.m., and they offer samples all day. It's at 783 Exchange Street, Middlebury; (800) 473–0727 or (802) 388–0727; www.ottercreekbrewing.com.

On the same side of the street, a few buildings farther along, is ***Maple Landmark Woodcraft,*** a real find if you have young kids in your life. This is a maker of high-quality small maple toys designed for toddlers. Little wooden engines with brightly colored cars run on grooved maple tracks that you can arrange into any configuration. Bright letters of the alphabet ride on flatcars, so you can personalize the train with the child's name. Other toys include wooden farm animals, wild animals, and old-fashioned cube-shaped blocks with deeply engraved alphabet letters. Look also for checkerboards, cribbage boards, domino sets, and other small cherry and maple gifts. Firsts and seconds are available, with seconds and discontinued items at half price. Call for their catalog or visit Monday through Saturday from 9:00 a.m. They close weekdays at 5:00 p.m., Saturday at 4:00 p.m. 1297 Exchange Street, Middlebury; (802) 388–0627 or (800) 421–4223; www.maplelandmark.com.

Also a few minutes north of Middlebury on Route 7, on the way to ***Vergennes,*** is a restaurant that draws people even from Burlington just to have dinner. And for good reason. ***Roland's Place*** is in a former home and tavern built while George Washington was president and Middlebury and Vergennes were battling it out to determine which of them would be the capital of Vermont. In 1796 they were the two biggest towns in the state, and a spot about halfway between them was a perfect place for a tavern. (No better reason for calling it the 1796 House.) Now they are two of the most attractive and historic towns in the state, and it's a perfect place for a fine restaurant owned by a French chef with a passion for fresh products grown and raised in Vermont and seafood from its New England neighbors.

Roland's menu, and his masterful presentation, should put his prices up there in the top range of Vermont restaurants, but we've never seen anything on the menu, except lobster, at more than $20; most entrees average around $18. Locally raised rabbit is served with tartiflette, a savory dish of Yukon gold potatoes with Canadian bacon, cheddar cheese, and cream; veal is sautéed with several varieties of wild mushrooms and served with wild rice and baby asparagus spears. Slices of tender pink duck breast are fanned vertically over mashed Yukon gold potatoes (which Roland was featuring on his menu long before these flavorsome tubers were available in grocery stores). Beside them a river of crisp-cooked snowpeas is bridged by half a ring of squash. Venison may be served with tender spaetzle, crisped just before serving. Each plate is garnished with fresh herbs that Roland and his wife, Lisa, grow in the garden behind the restaurant.

Don't even try to choose from among the appetizers—smoked Vermont emu, Roland's savory terrine, home-cured salmon with currant vinaigrette, grilled portobello mushrooms with goat cheese and colby polenta. Ask for a sampler plate to share, and try a little of each. When you see the size of it, you may rethink ordering an entree. In the winter, when Roland scales back his usual menu to eight or nine choices of appetizers, you may find a creamy sweet-potato soup, a rich puree perfumed with clove with finely shredded raw sweet potatoes stirred in. Delicately smoked trout (smoked here) is paired with grilled portobello in a swirl of light sour cream.

While the primary focus here is on the food, Roland's has three cozy guest rooms upstairs, which he does not advertise. But if you ask, you can stay there, particularly nice in the winter when you can just toddle upstairs after dinner instead of going outdoors. One room has a deep whirlpool bath in an alcove, and all have private baths. The next morning, breakfast is served in front of a glowing Franklin stove, and if you are lucky, Roland will start your day with a hearty wedge of quiche, each mouthful of which is infused with the flavor of smoked meat. The home fries are like none we have eaten elsewhere, subtly seasoned, soft inside, and crispy on the outside.

The best-quality dining bargain in Vermont may be the early-bird special for a full dinner between 5:00 and 6:00 p.m. Roland's is open daily year-round for dinner from 5:30 to 9:30 p.m. Sunday brunch is served from 9:00 a.m. to 2:00 p.m. Roland's Place is on Route 7, 3629 Ethan Allen Highway, New Haven; (802) 453–6309.

Route 116, a north-south road connecting East Middlebury with the town of Bristol, is a lovely road to drive, with mountain views and attractive farmland, and Bristol is a small but busy and attractive town. If you follow Route 116, which joins with Route 17 through town, until just shortly after the two separate again, you'll see a parking area for the **Bristol Memorial Forest Park.** One of Vermont's loveliest picnic sites, it has tables overlooking a gorge and paths along its brink with railings and bridges to give you the best and safest views of the entire gorge and its waterfalls.

If you follow Route 17, it will take you over the Appalachian Gap, with an elevation of 2,300 feet as it climbs over the sharp spine of the Green Mountains and drops into Waitsfield. An equally dramatic route over the mountains, on an unnumbered and less-used route, is across the **Lincoln Gap,** with a 2,400-foot elevation. Before Routes 116 and 17 diverge, take a road to the south marked lincoln, then follow signs to Warren. It is one of the state's most memorable drives, closed in winter because of the difficulties in keeping the road passable. When you see the pitch of the road, you'll know why the snowplows don't tackle it. As you leave Bristol, you can't miss seeing the **Lord's Prayer Rock,** a boulder on Route 17 on the eastern side of town that has the complete Lord's Prayer inscribed on it. A doctor from Buffalo who grew up in Bristol saw many loggers drag their loads and horses up the road, which back then was muddy most of the year. As a boy, he was offended by the laborers' language, so he paid a local stonecutter to chisel the complete Lord's Prayer into the rock.

Bristol's short Main Street is a thoroughly charming place to shop or browse. Two facing rows of well-kept brick and wood mercantile buildings contain small shops, artisans' studios, cafes, and friendly people who take the time to chat. Park anywhere (no parking meters to worry about) and admire the architecture as you stroll. Admire, too, the signs, some of which are works of art, especially the metal one that announces The Bobcat Café (see listing at the end of this chapter).

Almost next door is **Vermont Honey Lights,** where a chandler works only in pure local beeswax. If you can tear yourself away from the beautiful candles and the antiques in which they are displayed, visit the workshop in the back to watch candles being poured and finished. You will learn a lot about candle making and about why you owe it to your lungs—and the ecosystem—to burn only those made of beeswax. The stylish candles made here are in solid colors—the amber and soft pearl of natural wax and warm earthy tones of sage, lavender, and mellow rose—and in shapes that reflect the season or imitate shapes of objects from artichokes to tassels. Square tapers of beeswax will burn for twenty-four hours, larger candles much longer. The antiques are for sale, although they were often chosen for the shop as decorative holders or companions for the candles. The shop is open weekdays 10:00 a.m. until 5:00 p.m., Saturdays 10:00 a.m. to 4:00 p.m., at 9 Main Street; (800) 322–2660, (802) 453–3952; or www.vermonthoneylights.com.

Behind Deer Leap Books is *Art on Main,* a cooperative gallery of fine crafts and art, much of it by local artists and artisans. Pottery, soaps, silver jewelry, handmade books, glass photography, original prints, paintings, and hand weaving are only some of the variety represented here. The gallery is open January through April, Tuesday through Thursday noon to 5:00 p.m., Friday noon to 6:00 p.m., and Saturday from 10:00 a.m. to 6:00 p.m., May through December weekdays and Saturday 10:00 a.m. to 6:00 p.m., Sunday noon to 5:00 p.m. The address is 26C Main Street; (802) 453–4032; www.artonmain.net. Next door, The Bristol Shoppe carries a wide range of antiques.

From Memorial Day until Labor Day, Bristol's town band plays concerts in the bandstand at 7:00 p.m. on Wednesday evenings, just as they have since the Civil War.

If you're fascinated by tales of lost treasure, before you leave Bristol, ask directions to *Hell's Half Acre.* This was the site on a dirt road 2 miles south of town where, supposedly, a huge deposit of silver was buried. Many people have spent thousands of hours over the years trying to locate it, without luck. The story is a long one, involving foreign intrigue and revenge. Maybe you'll have more luck than the hordes before you.

West of Middlebury, also on Route 17 (which you can best reach from the center of town via Route 23), are the vast lowland marshes and waterways of the *Dead Creek Waterfowl Area.* This is birders' paradise, especially during spring and fall migrations, when thousands upon thousands of birds rest here during their journeys. Few sights in life can match that of a flock of snow geese filling the sky as they resume their trip. You can canoe here, except in the area south of Route 17 between the road and the dike, but be careful to stay well away from the shore between April and June, when birds are nesting.

At its southern end, Lake Champlain narrows to a small passage before broadening again even farther to the south. Originally settled by the French as a part of New France, the point became known as Chimney Point for the blackened chimneys rising from the cellar holes of homes burned by the settlers as they fled the advancing British during the French and Indian War.

The narrows made this spot a popular ferry crossing, and, of course, where there was a ferry, there was a tavern to house and comfort travelers. ***Chimney Point State Historic Site,*** at the Champlain Bridge crossing of Routes 17 and 125, has its visitor center and museum in the eighteenth-century tavern on the banks of the lake. It has exhibits on the original native peoples and on the French settlers who were driven from this land. The site is open from Memorial Day through Columbus Day from 9:30 a.m. to 5:00 p.m. Wednesday through Sunday. It is at 7305 Route 125, Addison; (802) 759–2412; www .historicvermont.org, use "Quick Links from Historic Sites."

The Brandon Area

A total of five routes, each with interconnecting side roads, lead from Middlebury to Brandon. The most direct is busy Route 7. More scenic are Route 30 to the west and Route 53 to the east around Lake Dunmore. Our favorites are the other two. Between Routes 30 and 7 is a sometimes-unpaved road through West Salisbury and Leicester Junction. And farthest to the east is the totally unpaved National Forest Road 32, which takes you through the thickly forested heart of ***Moosalamoo.***

You won't find Moosalamoo on any map. It's an area defined by a unique partnership of landholders and groups with a passion for keeping the wildlands wild but accessible. Public Service, the Green Mountain National Forest, Branbury State Park, Middlebury College, the Green Mountain Club, the Audubon Society, the Vermont Institute for Natural Sciences, an association of snowmobilers, and a few inns are among the partners. Their purpose is to protect the unique natural environment, maintain trails for year-round use, and provide interpretive signs and materials for the people who use the area. Look for the black brochure with a moose silhouette, which contains a good map and more information about the area. Moosalamoo has a lot of raw wilderness, but it also has three numbered highways, homes, businesses, a boys' camp, and two ski areas. That's the point of it—a coexistence that is to

whenallelse fails...

So suspicious of newly tilled gardens in remote areas were the narcotics agents in Vermont a few years ago, that when Judith first planted her extensive perennial beds, narc-squad helicopters repeatedly circled overhead as she worked. "So close, I could see the whites of their eyes," Judith recalls. "I got so tired of the pot cops snooping over my delphiniums that I went out in the driveway and shook my fist at them." Evidently that scared them off because they haven't been back since.

everyone's benefit, including the moose. For a schedule of free events, which may include guided hikes, garden tours, fishing lessons, or a falcon program, contact the Brandon Chamber of Commerce at their little white house on the green in Brandon; P.O. Box 267, Brandon, 05733; (802) 247–6401; www .brandon.org.

In the middle of the Moosalamoo wilderness area, surrounded by national forest, is *Blueberry Hill Inn,* a handsome inn on a hilltop at an altitude of 1,600 feet. Some of the rooms are in the nineteenth-century farmhouse; others in a carefully designed modern addition. This is the place for active outdoors lovers who want a pleasant place to relax at the end of the day.

The inn has beautiful gardens to explore, and 47 miles of trails lead through the nearby wilderness area, some connecting with the Catamount and Long Trails. The inn will provide shuttles for guests who want to walk segments of the Long Trail without doubling back. In winter it's a cross-country and snowshoe center, with equipment rentals and well-kept trails. As owner Tony describes it, "With 60 to 70 kilometers of different trail options available from the front door, there's no gerbil-cage skiing here."

After a hike, we especially like to grab a cookie (or two or three) from the jar in the large open kitchen and go out into the solarium to read a good book. The spacious and well-decorated guest rooms have private baths, and in each you will find a jar of the inn's own dreamy skin cream, made right here from extractions of calendula and chamomile petals and other herbs from the inn's gardens. Children are welcome at Blueberry Hill and are sure to enjoy the private garden of the owners' daughter.

Rates include breakfast, and Blueberry Hill Inn also serves dinner, carefully prepared and presented—but you must reserve a space. The chef uses only the freshest local produce in season, much of which comes from the inn's own extensive organic gardens or from neighboring farms. Dinner might

Take Your Pick

Places to pick wild blueberries are usually closely guarded secrets, like the location of the best fishing holes. But in Moosalamoo there's one everybody knows about, since there are signs pointing it out and a parking lot for your car. It's located on Forest Road 27, a short distance to the east of Road 32, both of which are north of Route 73, the road over the Brandon Gap. You are welcome to go there with your pail and pick away—or to just wander in for a handful or two eaten on the spot. They ripen in midsummer. You can tell if they are ready by the number of cars in the lot; if it's empty, there are probably no berries.

And Take Your Attitude with You!

While traveling on Cape Breton Island in Nova Scotia a few summers ago, we were eating breakfast at our B&B with a woman who told us she was from Brandon, Vermont. We said how much we've enjoyed going there, and she replied rudely: "That's what's wrong with Brandon: The tourists are ruining it."

Since we'd never noticed that Brandon had very many tourists, we were a bit taken aback by this, but even more astonished when she went on to say that she often worked in the town's visitor center. As we drove away later, we pondered this, thinking of all the friendly and hospitable people we'd met in Brandon—especially in the little white house on the green that serves as the information office. We decided that the other people who worked there had taken up a collection to send her to Canada for a vacation and get her out of town!

begin with a delicate salmon pâté or tangy chilled gazpacho and move on to a perfectly cooked and subtly herbed rack of lamb.

Accompaniments are given the same attention as the main event; last time we were there, the couscous was prepared with mascarpone. Blueberries will be on the menu during the season, perhaps in a blueberry Napoleon. The inn has no license, but you are welcome to bring your own wine. Blueberry Hill is just the other side of nowhere, on Goshen-Ripton Road, Goshen; (802) 247–6735; www.blueberryhillinn.com.

Route 73 leads east over Brandon Gap or west into the town of *Brandon.* This attractive town, filled with beautiful old homes, was first chartered in 1761 with the name Neshobe and is the birthplace of Stephen Douglas, Lincoln's adversary, and home to a whole slew of inventors, such as Quimby Backus, who invented one of the first electric heaters, and John Conant, who produced the first iron stoves in the state after bog iron was discovered in 1810.

This is only the beginning of Brandon's long and fascinating history, which includes its claim to a place in the Morgan-horse hall of fame, as well as the story of the early industry of Vermont and the Underground Railroad.

On the same street, in an elegant Arts and Crafts–period mansion, is the *Lilac Inn,* once the home of the Farr family, whose public and private benefactions are still appreciated by the people of Brandon. It was later owned by an architect, who made the house's transition from the home of a wealthy family to an inn so seamless that you wouldn't be surprised to find the formidable Mrs. Farr at the head of the breakfast table. Instead, you'll find breakfast served in a sunny room overlooking the landscaped grounds, or outdoors, in the summer.

The inn is well known for its oak-paneled dining room, where a New American menu displays the skillful use of fresh ingredients. You may find pomegranate-glazed scallops, loin of venison rubbed with coriander, or seared rabbit loin with sweet-corn flan. Entree prices range from $17 to $24. Rates for the bright, stylish rooms are from $125 to $320, including breakfast. The Lilac Inn sponsors frequent concerts, both outdoors on the terrace and in the salon, a perfect venue for chamber music. The inn is at 53 Park Street, Brandon; (802) 247–5463 or (800) 221–0720; www.lilacinn.com.

In Central Park, on Fridays from mid-June through mid-October, the Brandon Farmer's Market sells local produce, flowers, and herbs, as well as maple syrup, baked goods, jams, and jellies.

East of Brandon is Orwell and Lake Champlain, an area that played a significant role in the American Revolution. On the way you will pass through Sudbury, through which the earliest road was built. Its route is marked by the **Crown Point Military Road Monument,** located a short distance west of Route 30, where it is joined by Route 73 from Brandon. A part of this original road is still passable to the north of the monument, but to the south it is little more than a trail. The road was built to connect Lake Champlain to the Connecticut River. Modern roads have used the original route in many places.

The **Crown Point Road Association** is a group of dedicated enthusiasts whose purpose it is to research, locate, mark, and preserve the first major highway in the state. The road was built in 1759 by British general Jeffrey Amherst to supply his outpost at Crown Point during the French and Indian War. During the Revolution it was expanded as the need to protect Fort Ticonderoga and Mount Independence became imperative. From spring through fall, the group conducts hikes over the known sections of the road. You are invited to bring lunch (and mosquito repellent). Contact the association c/o James Moore, 51 Eden Street, Proctor, 05765; (802) 459–2837. www.crownpointroad.org.

Mount Independence, east of Orwell, is still in the active process of restoration, its historical significance having been largely ignored until the 1970s. Two hundred years earlier, Mount Independence was an important sister fort to Fort Ticonderoga, across the lake in New York, and the two were connected by a floating bridge. Garrisoned by about 2,500 soldiers, it had extensive earthworks. In July 1777 it was attacked, and the defending continental troops finally abandoned it, retreating to Hubbardton, where they managed to beat off an attacking troop of British soldiers, blunting General Burgoyne's drive to the south. These two battles were precursors to the crucial Battle of Bennington.

You can learn more about this conflict at the museum and visitor center. There are four trails around the 400-acre site, from ¼ mile to 2½ miles in length, and in winter the trails are available for cross-country skiing. Trail

Get Those Sheep off Grannie

The town of Orwell maintains two cemeteries, one on Chipman Point overlooking Lake Champlain and the other off Route 73 on the road to Shoreham. The maintenance of these two cemeteries created a bit of a town feud in 1991, when a flock of seventeen sheep was placed in the cemeteries to graze and trim the grass.

Some townspeople thought it was a great idea; the town would save on gasoline and manpower. The sheep also ate everything from poison ivy to wild grapevines—things regular lawn mowers usually miss—and their owner, Jean Beck, transported them back and forth between the two cemeteries for one month before protests began from townspeople who didn't like the idea of sheep manure covering their loved ones' graves.

A group of ten residents volunteered to mow the cemeteries in place of the sheep, but selectboard chairman Ronald Huntley warned that the volunteers would be closely monitored to make sure they were doing their jobs. "If they don't maintain the cemeteries, the sheep go back in," he said.

So when you're in Orwell, stop by to see if the sheep or the human beings won. We're all betting on the sheep, especially since Orwell for many years served as the top sheep-raising town in the Champlain Valley.

maps with historical notes and descriptions are usually available at either the trailhead or at the visitor center. The park remains an active archaeological site and has an ongoing program of investigation and restoration. The park is on Catfish Bay Road in Orwell, and can be reached summers at (802) 948–2000. It's open daily from Memorial Day through Columbus Day from 9:30 a.m. to 5:00 p.m. Admission fee is charged; www.historicvermont.org.

A great way to see Mount Independence and a lot of Lake Champlain is to take the **M/V Carillon,** which leaves from Teachout's Lakehouse Store and Wharf at Larrabee's Point, to the north in Shoreham. The 60-foot-long knife-bowed cruise boat was built in 1990 especially for this run. It is a replica of the sleek power yachts built for the wealthy from the 1920s through the 1950s, and, as was the custom, there's lots of shiny woodwork. The one-and-a-half-hour cruise leaves at 1:00 p.m. in July and August. The boat does a figure eight between Larrabee's Point, Fort Ticonderoga, and Mount Independence. Fares are in the $14 range for adults, and $10 for children 11 and under. Special all-day foliage cruises run in the fall. Call for reservations and information at (802) 897–5331. Shoreham is on Route 22A; follow Route 74 west to Larrabee's Point; www.carilloncruises.com.

Off Route 22A south of Orwell, a small road is signposted to **Benson.** A half mile off Route 22A, the road intersects with Benson's main street. Up the hill to the right is one of the finest examples of what the Main Street of a small Vermont town once looked like. Along both sides of the street are beautiful nineteenth-century buildings, mostly big, well-spaced homes but also including the Chauncy-Walker Store with its historic business front and the classic white United Church. You could almost imagine that you had stepped back into a different world.

At the intersection at the foot of the hill is **The Book Shed,** open Wednesday through Sunday 10:00 a.m. to 6:00 p.m., a used-book store where you are likely to find local people sitting on the floor reading; (802) 537 –2190. Across the street from the bookstore, the small building on the corner was built as a law office in the nineteenth century and is being restored to its original purpose. Beyond Benson, the road wanders through attractive countryside for 5.4 miles, over hills and around sharp corners until it reaches the narrow end of Lake Champlain. A boat launch provides the only place to put in canoes and kayaks for miles in either direction. It is also just a beautiful place to visit, with New York State a few hundred yards away across the water.

Before leaving Benson, follow Sage Road to **Snowflake Farms,** an alpaca farm that opened to the public in 2003. The wool of these animals makes a wonderfully soft, warm, and comfortable fabric. Snowflake Farms welcomes visitors to see these camel-like South American creatures in their Vermont home and visit their gift shop. The farm is at 5676 Stage Road, Benson; (802) 537– 2971; www.snowflake-farms.com.

Rutland and Its Environs

Situated as it is on a bed of marble, and close to the western border of the Vermont–New York line, the city of **Rutland** has at various times been known as Marble City and Gateway City. Today it is a thriving city that serves as a business and social magnet for the surrounding towns.

It was named for Rutland, Massachusetts; John Murray, of the Massachusetts Rutland, was the first grantee of the town, which was chartered in 1761. The first settler of Rutland was James Mead, of Manchester, Vermont, who came to town in 1770 with his wife and ten children. Mead built a log cabin and soon followed with a gristmill and a sawmill nearby, thereby cementing the active industry of Rutland that continues to this day.

Rutland's downtown has some interesting architecture—an Art Deco building on West Street just past the courthouse is not in good repair but is a fine example of an architectural period that's beginning to be more appreciated. Merchant's Row is lined with well-kept commercial buildings, and there is a neighborhood of excellent brick Victorian mansions and churches, along with the library, along Court and Center Streets, up the hill from the business district.

But on West Proctor Road is the city's most unusual building, **Wilson's Castle,** one of the few historic houses/museums open to the public where you can walk on rugs, sit on chairs, feel the texture of the old draperies, and take flash pictures. The admission fee, which includes a tour, is $6.00, but this is as close as you'll probably get to an American royal palace.

The estate consists of 150 acres and sixteen buildings. The castle was built in the mid-1800s, and its thirty-two rooms hold eighty-four stained-glass windows and thirteen fireplaces. The rooms contain everything from a Louis XVI crown jewel case to a Tiffany chandelier. The castle also boasts a library, a music room, a drawing room, an art gallery, and a veranda.

Wilson's Castle is open daily from 9:00 a.m. to 6:00 p.m. from late May through mid-October. Follow the signs from Route 3. For more information, write to Wilson's Castle, West Proctor Road, Rutland, 05701, or call (802) 773–3284.

Also on the north side of town, on busy Route 7, is **Seward's Family Restaurant,** a local dairy and restaurant with window and table service and a gourmet food shop that sells freshly brewed Green Mountain Coffee in thermoses that keep the coffee fresh and piping hot. Try the hazelnut cream coffee with a dollop of Seward's fresh milk—that is, if the thermos isn't empty.

The dairy is out back behind the restaurant, and you'll find the milk in most local supermarkets and general stores. The restaurant offers food as fresh as the dairy, along with sandwiches and soups, in a comfortable, homey atmosphere.

Seward's is open from 6:30 a.m. to 10:00 p.m. seven days a week. Seward's Family Restaurant is at 244 North Main Street, Rutland; call (802) 773–2738.

Just west of Rutland and Route 7 is Route 3, known as the Marble Valley Highway. Even if you are not fascinated by geology (as we admit we are), this area is interesting to visit because it is the heart of Vermont's marble industry. Each of the fifty states and some foreign countries have buildings made of Vermont marble. Two of the best known are the U.S. Supreme Court and the Jefferson Memorial, both in Washington, D.C. So versatile is this building stone that the Beinecke Rare Book and Manuscript Library at Yale University in New Haven, Connecticut, has even used thin luminescent slabs of this marble as "windows" to let light in.

The **Vermont Marble Museum,** headquartered in Proctor, not far from Wilson Castle, explores this stone in a comprehensive exhibit. A visit starts with an eleven-minute film about the company and about the immigrant workers who labored here. Displays include a miniature marble chapel with a carved Last Supper and the Hall of Presidents. The latter is a work in progress, and will contain bas-relief busts of all U.S. presidents. In the sculpting studio, visitors can watch the sculptor-in-residence at work.

The exhibit, displayed in seventeen rooms with a total of 27,000 square feet of space, looks at how marble was formed, explaining the evolution of the earth and the titanic energy of its crust as the plates move, collide, and create new continents. "Raymond" is an actual cast re-creation of the only articulated triceratops ever found. Plan on several hours to explore all the corners of this fascinating place.

Tickets for the exhibit are available at the site for $7.00 adults ($6.00 seniors, $54.00 ages thirteen to eighteen) or in advance at a $1.00 discount. The exhibit is open mid-May through the end of October 9:00 a.m. to 5:30 p.m. daily, at 52 Main Street, Proctor; (800) 427–1396 or (802) 459–2300; www .vermont-marble.com.

A nice loop drive out of Rutland takes you into countryside far removed from the city's streets. Leave town on Route 4 East, which leads over the mountains toward Pico Peak and Killington. You will come to Mendon, and an unusual monument that thousands of people pass by every day without even knowing it's there. Once you cross the border into Mendon from Rutland on Route 4 East, pull into the parking lot of the Sugar and Spice Restaurant. Park in the far lot and look for the biggest rock in the forest that rises from the lot. Most days there's a tiny American flag flying on top. This is Mendon's *Civil War Horse Monument.* The inscription on the concave section of the rock reads: The grave of General Edward Ripley's Old John—gallant war horse of the great Civil War 1861–1865.

Just past this monument, a road goes north to East Pittsford and Chittenden, toward the Chittenden Reservoir. You will pass the *Fox Creek Inn,* a quiet retreat in the woods beside a brook owned by Tim and Sandy Robertson. Rooms vary in size and decor, with stenciled walls, whirlpool tubs, and gas fireplaces. The inn is elegant but comfortable, and breakfast is included in the rates. A four-course candlelit dinner is available for $30. The wine list is excellent.

Rates are from $175–$285 per room, rising to a $215–$325 range in foliage

soapand pittsford

Pittsford was the home of Samuel Hopkins, who received the first patent in the United States, in 1790, signed by George Washington. It was for the making of pearl-ash, an ingredient for soap making upon which was founded Vermont's first main economic base.

season. Fox Creek Inn is at 49 Dam Road, Chittenden; (802) 483–6213 or (800) 707–0017; www.foxcreekinn.com.

Since this road dead-ends at the dam, you need to backtrack to the intersection and continue on to the settlement of Holden, where the road changes direction and follows Furnace Creek back to the south and into Pittsford. Here you should go north (right) on Route 7, but only briefly. The historical society museum in the center of town is open from 9:00 a.m. to 4:00 p.m. on Tuesday from March to December and the same hours on Saturday in July and August; (802) 483–6623.

Follow signs left to Florence, on Kendall Hill Road, where you will soon see the **Hammond Covered Bridge** on your right. It is one of four in Pittsford, a 139-foot Town lattice style built in 1842. In the infamous freshet of 1927, when much of Vermont was washed away, this bridge ended up in a field about a mile downstream from its abutments. The following winter they hauled it back to its original location, which is where you now see it. A new bridge has made it redundant, but you can still walk through it.

Any of several left turns along here will take you south and back to Rutland. One goes through Proctor, where you can see the marble works, or you can follow signs to Whipple Hollow Road, for a real back-road drive past farms tucked into little hollows, meadows dotted with horses nibbling grass, and dairy farms where herds of Holsteins pasture with a backdrop of valley and mountain scenery.

At Route 4 you can turn west instead of going back into Rutland, and head for Castleton and Castleton Corners, home of Castleton State College, Vermont's first college, having been chartered in 1787. The **Christine Price Gallery** at Castleton State College is located in the foyer of the Fine Arts Center on campus. The display area is huge, and the exhibiting artists range from Castleton students who have created their own masks, to community residents who have combined the avant-garde and traditional Vermont themes in line drawings and paintings, as well as more traditional Vermont pastoral landscape scenes. A showcase contains works in progress in sketchbooks, and the smell of freshly dried oil paint permeates the room. The gallery also has international art in its permanent collection, from Africa, New Guinea, and India.

The gallery and Fine Arts Center are open from 8:30 a.m. to 4:30 p.m. weekdays, year-round. Write to the Christine Price Gallery, Castleton Fine Arts Center, Castleton State College, Castleton, 05735, or call (802) 468–5611.

From Castleton Corners, the unnumbered East Hubbardton Road leads north about 7 miles to **Hubbardton Battlefield.** When American troops had to evacuate Mount Independence and Fort Ticonderoga on July 6, 1777, they withdrew to the east, planning to travel south again to join up with other colonists in Manchester. British advance troops, cocksure of themselves and holding the ragtag local militia in contempt, caught up with them on July 7. At East Hubbardton the rear guard of the colonial troops turned and stood their ground on a broad hillside, firing from covered positions and showing a determination to stop the British and protect the retreat of the main force. To the chagrin of General Burgoyne, the royal troops were defeated and forced to withdraw back to Mount Independence. This victory saved the colonial army from destruction, freeing them for the Battle of Bennington and the ultimate defeat of the British northern army at Saratoga later that same year.

An interpretive center is open 9:00 a.m. to 4:00 p.m. Wednesday through Sunday Memorial Day through Columbus Day. If it's open when you visit, look at the fiber-optic map of the battle, then go out onto the battlefield to the walking trail that leads visitors to key points in the battle. Signs tell the importance of each stop along the way. The battlefield itself is open all year. Write Division of Historic Preservation, State of Vermont, 135 State Street, Drawer 33, Montpelier, 05633-1201; (802) 828–3051; www.historicvermont.org.

West of Castleton is Fair Haven, an unusual town with one large brick commercial block facing a broad common, with two fine mansions built of marble. Down the hill behind one of them is *Fair Haven Inn,* where entrees range mostly from $15.00 to $25.00, with early-bird specials at $7.00 to $10.00 Monday through Saturday from 5:00 to 6:00 p.m. The menu is Grecian/Mediterranean, and the restaurant is open daily for lunch and dinner. It is at 5 Adams Street, Fair Haven; (802) 265–4907 or (800) 325–7074; www.fairhaveninn.com.

On the southern edge of town, shortly before Route 22A crosses the border into New York, is *Maplewood Inn.* The 1843 house is furnished in antiques and reproductions, as well as the owners' collection of antique farm and household implements. Hot drinks, with a good selection of teas, are available to guests at all times, along with complimentary cordials. Rooms are priced from $110 to $150, suites $140 and $250 all year, with a $20 increase for holidays and foliage season. The rate includes a hearty breakfast that begins with hot oatmeal. Maplewood Inn, 1108 South Main Street (Route 22A South), Fair Haven; (802) 265–8039 or (800) 253–7729; www.maplewoodinn.com.

South of Fair Haven and Castleton, and three miles south of Poultney, is the beautiful *Lake St. Catherine,* site of a state park with trails, beaches, and a campground with boat access to the lake. Campsites are spaced well, along the shore and in the woods, some with lean-to shelters. The park is open from Memorial Day weekend until Labor Day weekend. Lake St. Catherine State Park, 3034 Route 30, Poultney; (802) 287–9158 in season.

To the south, this region is bounded by Route 140, a very scenic drive through several interesting towns. Route 140 is not very long—only about 25 miles—but it's pretty at any time of year, whether the maple forests that line it are hung with sap buckets and tubing or ablaze in fall color. The terrain seems never to rest, and the driver certainly can't, as the narrow road is constantly climbing, dropping, or turning.

Route 140 begins in Poultney, on the New York border, almost literally in the front lawn of Green Mountain College. After its short stretch as Poultney's main street, it climbs into the countryside before passing through East Poultney, a charming cluster of buildings around a common. These include an imposing schoolhouse and a classic general-store building.

The road follows the course of the Poultney River, which is visible much of the way to *Middletown Springs.* While it may seem small, when fed by a sudden spring melt-off or thunderstorms, the river can become quite a torrent. In July of 1811, all but one of the mills along the river in Middletown were swept away, and the course of the river was changed. The one mill that survived became the factory for a talented inventor who made the New England farmer's life a lot easier (see sidebar).

Albert Gray was a man of vision, and his next project changed the town's name and identity. Another flood once again altered the course of the river near Albert's mill, and as he surveyed the damage, he noticed that a spring that had been covered up by the 1811 floods had appeared again. With his sons, he cleared out the area and began bottling the water. By then—this was in the 1870s—taking the cure at mineral springs was the latest health fad, so Albert

Albert Gray's Labor-Saving Machine

Albert W. Gray began work in the mill beside the Poultney River at the age of fifteen. Six years later he was in business for himself, in 1844 he patented a machine that made his name a household word on Vermont farms. His invention was a treadmill that was operated by a horse, and he began to manufacture them at the same mill where he had worked as a boy.

The first treadmill operated a thresher, replacing a job that had consumed many hours of back-breaking labor. It revolutionized the family farm, as farmers began renting treadmills by the day from threshers who carried the machines from farm to farm, mounted on wagons. Large farms bought their own, keeping as many as one hundred employees busy making them in Middletown. Expanding on the theme, Albert designed treadmills to save labor in other farm chores, such as cutting silage and sawing wood.

and his sons built a grand hotel, four-and-a-half stories tall and the biggest in Vermont. The Montvert Hotel offered a number of treatments, including "Turkish showers" and massage, and its dining-room staff was imported from New York to cater to the exacting clientele.

Middletown changed its name to Middletown Springs, and its economy became very healthy indeed. But the fad faded and the wealthy clientele moved on to more fashionable watering holes. The hotel was torn down, and the 1927 floods again covered up the spring and washed away the spring house. In 1970 it was uncovered, and a replica of the spring house was built, which is now the centerpiece of a pleasant little riverside park on Burdock Avenue, close to a historic marker that tells about the treadmill factory. You can see an example of the treadmill in the free *Middletown Springs Historical Society Museum,* next to the church on the green, open Sunday from 2:00 until 4:00 p.m. from late May through early October. The entire village center, which has several distinguished buildings, is a historic district listed on the National Register of Historic Places.

Route 140 turns at the common, then makes a right turn 2 miles past town. The road climbs through maple woods and makes an abrupt left in the village of Tinmouth before climbing over more hills, doglegging through a valley farm, and climbing over another ridge to descend into the Otter Creek Valley. The vertical mountainside of White Rocks is straight ahead.

After crossing Route 7 in Wallingford—a town worth stopping in to see its fine Victorian buildings—Route 140 climbs over the spine of the Green Mountains, through a narrow rocky defile that it shares with a rushing little brook. Before coming to the Long Trail, which crosses the brook on a wooden footbridge beside the road, you will come to the turn for *White Rocks National Recreation Area.* You can access these rocks on a strenuous hike of about 3 miles or you can admire them at a little more distance, from the picnic area below. Route 140 ends as abruply as it began, in East Wallingford, where it meets Route 103 and Route 155, either of which connects to Route 100, "The Skiers' Highway."

Not far north of East Wallingford on Route 103 is Cuttingsville. In the village of Cuttingsville is *Vermont Industries,* where they make hand-forged wrought-iron lighting fixtures and home accessories. The shop seems small when you first enter, but each room leads to another, taking you through a large building where you'll find candleholders, sconces, weathervanes, wall hangings, lamps, fireplace tools, garden furniture, hooks and racks, hinges, and decorative items. It's open daily from 10:00 a.m. to 5:30 p.m. year-round; Route 103, Cuttingsville; (802) 492–3451 or (800) 639–1715; www.vermont industries.net.

If you choose to travel northwest on Route 103, make a detour in Shrewsbury, following signs up into the scenic hill towns to find one of the most comfortable, welcoming, and relaxing places that we have found in Vermont: *Maple Crest Farm Bed & Breakfast,* in the tiny town of Shrewsbury. When it was built in 1808 by ancestors of the present owner, one side of the first floor was a coaching tavern and the other a general store and post office. Today these rooms are cozy places to curl up and read a book. Family antiques are used throughout the house, but you shouldn't get the idea that it's at all like a stuffy museum. Its comfy and casual atmosphere is popular with people hiking the nearby Long Trail. Rooms are $56 to $62 with shared or half baths, and two apartments rent at an astonishing $75 per night for two, with $10 per extra person. Two couples on a getaway weekend could have separate bedrooms, a living room, and a full-size, well-equipped kitchen for $75 per couple per night. Quilting weekends are held at the inn on four weekends during September and October each year. From Cuttingsville, head east from Route 103 toward Shrewsbury on Town Hill Road. The inn is on the right when you get to 2512 Lincoln Hill Road, in the center of the old village; (802) 492–3367; http://travel.to/maplecrestfarm.

TO LEARN MORE IN MIDDLE WEST VERMONT

Brandon Area Chamber of Commerce,
P.O. Box 267, Brandon, 05733; (802) 247–6401.

Middlebury Area Chamber of Commerce, (802) 388–7951; www.midvermont.com. The information center is in the tiny white building opposite the Civil War monument.

More Places to Stay in Middle West Vermont

(All area codes 802)

For other lodgings in the area, contact Historic Lake Champlain/Middlebury Region Lodging Association, P.O. Box 711, Middlebury, 05753; www.vermont-lodging.com.

More Places to Eat in Middle West Vermont

(All area codes 802)

BRISTOL

The Bobcat Cafe
5 Main Street
453–3311
Open daily from 4:00 p.m.

Mary's at Baldwin Creek
1868 N. Route 116
453–2432
Serves an innovative menu of dishes based on fresh local ingredients Wednesday through Sunday from 5:30 p.m.

MIDDLEBURY

Storm Cafe
Frog Hollow
388–1063
www.stormcafe.com.
Serves a great penne carbonara. Big portions, little restaurant.

Index

About the Author

Robert F. Wilson has worked as a promotion writer for *Reader's Digest;* and as an editor for McGraw-Hill, Houghton Mifflin, Macmillan, Scholastic, and the sadly swallowed Silver Burdett. He has written twelve books including *Vermont Curiosities* (Globe Pequot Press).